VANCOUVE

Book of Musts
of

The 101 Places Every Islander MUST See

Peter Grant

Second Edition

MacIntyre Purcell Publishing Inc.
Lunenburg, NS

MacIntyre Purcell Publishing Inc.
194 Hospital Rd.
Lunenburg, Nova Scotia
B0J 2C0
(902) 640-3350

www.macintyrepurcell.com
info@macintyrepurcell.com

Printed and bound in Canada by Marquis.

Design and layout: Alex Hickey and Channel Communications

Library and Archives Canada Cataloguing in Publication

Grant, Peter, 1948-, author
    Vancouver Island book of musts : the 101 places every islander must see / Peter Grant. – 2nd edition.

Includes bibliographical references.
Issued in print and electronic formats.
ISBN 978-1-77276-015-6 (paperback).--ISBN 978-1-77276-016-3 (pdf)

        1. Vancouver Island (B.C.)--Guidebooks. I. Title.

FC3844.2.G73 2017   917.11'2045   C2016-902627-2
                                                    C2016-902628-0

MacIntyre Purcell Publishing Inc. would like to acknowledge the financial support of the Government of Canada and the Nova Scotia Department of Tourism, Culture and Heritage.

TABLE OF CONTENTS

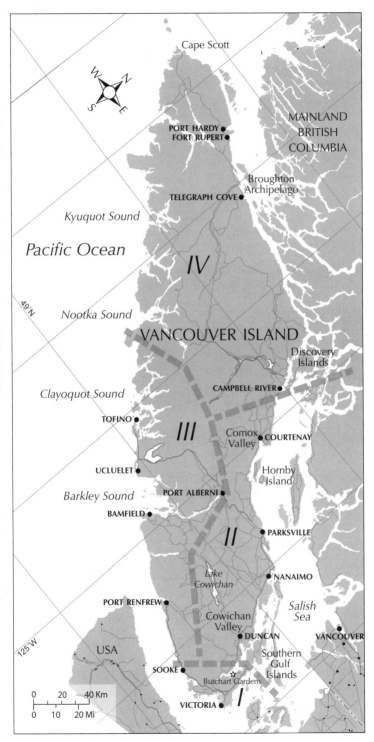

Cape Scott

MAINLAND BRITISH COLUMBIA

PORT HARDY
FORT RUPERT

Broughton Archipelago

TELEGRAPH COVE

Kyuquot Sound

Pacific Ocean

IV

Nootka Sound

VANCOUVER ISLAND

Discovery Islands

Clayoquot Sound

CAMPBELL RIVER

TOFINO

III

Comox Valley

COURTENAY

UCLUELET

Hornby Island

Barkley Sound

PORT ALBERNI

BAMFIELD

II

PARKSVILLE

Lake Cowichan

NANAIMO

Salish Sea

PORT RENFREW

Cowichan Valley

DUNCAN

VANCOUVER

USA

Southern Gulf Islands

SOOKE

Butchart Gardens

I

0   20   40 Km
0   10   20 Mi

VICTORIA

Weights & Measures, etc

This book provides measures in both British and US numbers, sparing our neighbours the bothersome task of converting metric values. The terms are always abbreviated without punctuation. Same with some locational terms, physical features, etc.

DISTANCE	
Foot/feet	ft
Metre(s)	m
Mile(s)	mi
Kilometre(s)	km

AREA	
Acre(s)	ac
Hectare(s)	ha
Square mile(s)	sq mi
Square kilometre(s)	sq km

VOLUME	
Cubic foot/feet	cu ft
Cubic metre(s)	cu m
Litre(s)	l
Gallon(s)	gal

WEIGHT	
Ounce(s)	oz
Gram(s)	g
Pound(s)	lb
Kilogram(s)	kg

TEMPERATURE	
Fahrenheit	F
Celsius	C

LOCATION	
Street	St
Road	Rd
Avenue	Ave
Drive	Dr
Point	Pt
Terrace	Terr

PHYSICAL FEATURES	
Mount	Mt
Lake	L
elevation	el

Introduction

Klahowya, welcome, to the second edition of the *Vancouver Island Book of Musts*, our 101 best places. The guide has been revised top to bottom, with twenty new articles and more Take 5s. The choices reflect the islands' superlative and unique and iconic places, a few popular favorites, and a few curiosities, like the market with goats grazing on the roof. Some places open a window on history, another locates a story of our tribe. Accessibility counts, whether in physical difficulty or cost.

Vancouver Island is a giant ridge, hugely under the influence of the North Pacific Ocean, stretching 454 km/282 mi from end to end and an average 80 km/50 mi wide, with a rugged mountain spine down the middle. More than 3,400 km/2,113 mi of coastline are washed by the Pacific or its inlets, mostly the Salish Sea. The exposed west side has true rainforest ecosystems, while on the more protected east side, it's milder and drier. Factor in the Gulf and Discovery islands, Broughton Archipelago and the islands to north and west, and this amazing stretch of Canada's west coast measures up at 33,650 sq km/12,992 sq mi.

Inhabited by First Nations for thousands of years, Vancouver Island was discovered by Europeans in the 18th century and, in the 19th, colonized, settled, governed and exploited by agents of the British Empire and its successors, the rulers of British Columbia and Canada. Our population in 2016 totaled 777,140. Ninety percent of us live in the southeast quarter. We are fortunate to share these islands with peoples who have a radically different take on nature, history, culture and society. This book celebrates the richness of First Nations culture, among the great achievements of these islands.

Vancouver Island is famous for the wilderness experience. Some of the best places involve challenging self-propelled travel. Anyone going into back country should be well-prepared and well-equipped, with a human guide if necessary. We treasure our islands' many beauties, love to share them, and hope that our visitors will be inspired to practice low-impact travel. If you bring it in, please take it out.

Sincere thanks are due to the many people who provided information and helped flesh out the details about these extraordinary places, especially the contributors of Take Fives, and in particular Steven Murray, who did original research for this book.

Special thanks to publisher John MacIntyre, whose crazy, wonderful idea this book is, for the freedom to write about matters dear to my heart, and to designer extraordinaire Alex Hickey. And to Paula, partner in my life and travels, *grazie mille* for the support and encouragement that makes this work possible.

The Islands' Top Attractions

These are the very best destinations that Vancouver Island and nearby islands have to offer. They were chosen for their character, for unique or superlative features, for their history, or their significance in the larger order of things, or yes, just for popularity, buzz, charisma. The top five were selected from a short list of 32. Both lists are in alphabetic order.

☆ ☆ ☆
The Butchart Gardens, Central Saanich (See #20.)
In this balmy zone on the North Pacific Coast, Gardens Are Us. The 22 ha/55 ac Butchart family's show gardens are a Vancouver Island icon, especially the signature Sunken Garden, once a limestone quarry (the Butchart fortune was built on cement). The quarry was spectacularly reclaimed, and four other gardens, now more than a century old, furnish hours of sensory delight, year round, with charming light displays evenings in winter months. This major attraction is replete with restaurants and shops and historical displays in the family home *Benvenuto*. There are musical performances on an outdoor stage every evening in the summer. On Saturday evenings, The Gardens light up with exquisite musical fireworks displays. Take a picnic or order one there, and blankets if need be, but don't miss the fireworks.

☆ ☆ ☆
The Gulf Islands (#s 39-44)
The bucolic Gulf Islands extend 163 km/101 mi between East Point, Saturna Island and Tree Island, north of Denman Island. Hundreds of tiny islands, rocks and nine or ten sparsely-populated larger islands, each with a distinct character, comprise this stupendous tiny archipelago. Accessible by BC Ferries, they invite exploration, whether in search of an art exhibition opening on Galiano or Salt Spring's annual apple festival. Gorgeous scenery abounds, from little shell beaches with arbutus trees overhanging to must-climb prominences — Mt Maxwell on Salt Spring (driveable), Mt Galiano on the eponymous isle, and Mt Warburton Pike on Saturna (driveable). Vistas unfold of ridges, little valleys, narrow marine passages and the surrounding straits. A web of marine campgrounds stretches across the southern Gulf Islands in national and provincial parks. Take your pick of routes; it's all pretty fine.

☆ ☆ ☆
Tofino/Ucluelet (#s 74-82)
Outrageously colorful twin villages at either end of 40 km/25 mi-long Esowista Peninsula, on Vancouver Island's wild west coast, Tofino and Ucluelet frame the magnificent Long Beach section of Pacific Rim

National Park Reserve. Tofino (2016 pop 1,932) is the year-round outdoor recreation centre and surf-boarding Mecca known as Tuff City. It is an urbane food-and-drink destination. Tofino has the islands' most luxurious lodgings. It is the jumping-off point for the endless pleasures of Clayoquot Sound, with its incomparably scenic inlets, islands, beaches and mountains, some of it profoundly wild. Tofino offers outstanding Indigenous tourism experiences. Tofino and Ucluelet are both peninsular, rocky, composed of docks and picturesque coves. Where Tuff City is sheltered from the open ocean, Ucluelet is not. Ukee, as it is commonly called, is Tofino's reclusive twin, and Ukee (pop 1,576) has become a destination in its own right: the best place on the island to walk on trails beside the wild open Pacific coast. The Wild Pacific Trail is punctuated by lookouts above beaches of rock, the headlands beyond and offshore reefs where the ocean swells crash and explode in spray that leaves a soft mist in the air all around you. Ukee is the place to stage a foray into the island wonderlands and wildlife habitats of Barkley Sound.

☆ ☆ ☆

Victoria waterfront scenery (#s 9, 10, 14-16)
The waterfront along the south and east coasts of Victoria is a 22-km/14-mi-long succession of bays, beaches, rocky headlands and hills that overlook charming waterfront neighbourhoods of quiet streets, some of them like country lanes, heritage houses and exquisite gardens, with many points of access to the shores (all of them public below the high tide line). Across Juan de Fuca Strait, on the city's southern shores, looms the ever-changing snow-capped wall of the Olympic Mountains. Victoria's east coast overlooks myriad islands and waterways, and the volcanic cones of mounts Baker and Rainier are sometimes visible beyond in the American Cascades. Waterfront highlights: Ogden Point breakwater (#9), Gonzales Hill lookout (#15), Willows Beach and Cattle Point (#16).

☆ ☆ ☆

Watching Orca whales in Broughton Archipelago (#s 95 and 96)
East, west, south and north, numerous centres on the islands host marine wildlife-watching tours that operate in season. Broughton Archipelago, off northeastern Vancouver Island, has the ecosystems accounted the best of many good places for observing *orcinus orca*, the endangered Orca whale, in its natural habitats. It's remote: the human population is sparse, and whale populations are relatively large and healthy. The unique Orca "rubbing beach" is there, protected as an ecological reserve. Broughton even has resident whale scientists and also the island's longest-operating whale-watching company, in Telegraph Creek, where the one street is a boardwalk and where the Whale Interpretive Centre complements a day on the water. Local waters also nurture Humpback and Gray whales in season.

THE ISLANDS' TOP ATTRACTIONS

☆ ☆

Bamfield and Barkley Sound (#70)
West Coast village poised at the edge of island-studded Barkley Sound and the beginning of the West Coast Trail. The main street is an inlet. Footpath and boardwalk meander along the western shore, approachable only by boat. Historic Coast Guard station (#71).

☆ ☆

British Columbia Parliament Buildings, Victoria (#2)
The imposing legislature, completed between 1897 and 1916, is a living museum of government in BC; tour, stay for lunch, watch the proceedings.

☆ ☆

Cathedral Grove in MacMillan Park (#57)
Best place to see an old-growth Douglas fir forest. With a few 800-year-old monsters, it's a religious experience for some. Highway 4 runs through it.

☆ ☆

Chemainus Murals (#46)
In the islands' original milltown, the ho-hum sides of buildings have been painted in vivid graphic tableaux to celebrate the riches of local history.

☆ ☆

Clayoquot Sound (#s 77 and 78, 80-83)
Scenic inlets, islands and beaches, ancient trees in temperate rainforest wilderness ecosystems, two protected intact watersheds and abundant wildlife in 3,500 sq km/1,351 sq mi of West Coast splendor.

☆ ☆

Comox Valley (#60)
Farms and suburbs on the lowlands between mountains and Strait of Georgia, with First Nations and agricultural roots. The foodie beat includes luscious seafood from Baynes Channel (see #59).

☆ ☆

Cowichan Bay (#33)
The one-street, many-docked village, among BC's most scenic, overlooks a broad estuary and distant Mt Tzouhalem (#30). It's a Slow Food centre.

☆ ☆

Craigdarroch Castle, Victoria (#11)
The Dunsmuir family's turreted 1880s Rockland mansion is now a splendid museum showcasing its many uses over time. The Dunsmuirs, coal magnates of Nanaimo, Cumberland and Ladysmith, proprietors of one-quarter of Vancouver Island, were pretty colourful — for a clan of frosty Scots.

☆ ☆

East Sooke Park (#23)
Much loved West Coast backcountry on a peninsula facing Juan de Fuca Strait between Becher Bay and Sooke Harbour. The park has beaches and a waterfront trail end to end, plus several trails to heights-of-land.

☆ ☆

Emily Carr (#s 10, 12 and 74)
The shrine of Canada's pre-eminent artist of the West Coast is Emily Carr House, the Carr family home in James Bay, built 1863. Carr's neighbourhood and Beacon Hill Park feature prominently in her accomplished memoirs of a lifetime spent there (1871-1945). Carr was a spiritualist and pantheist who was able "To see a World in a grain of sand, And a Heaven in a wild flower."

☆ ☆

Fairmont Empress Hotel, Victoria (#4)
The island's iconic original resort hotel has a stunning lobby and verandah. Ramble around, grab a bench on the spacious front lawn, stay for Afternoon Tea. You can also read a shocking story of jealous mayhem that had its beginnings here.

☆ ☆

Goldstream Provincial Park, Langford (#22)
A narrow defile near Victoria, where Route 1 parallels the Goldstream River, worth stopping for the walk to the Nature House overlooking a beautiful estuary. A Victoria highlight every autumn is the Chum salmon returning to their Goldstream birthplace to spawn.

☆ ☆

Government House grounds, Victoria (#13)
Nearly 15 ha/38 ac of sumptuous show gardens, trails lacing a rocky escarpment, and the best remaining Garry oak woodland in the city. It's close to downtown Victoria, open every day, dawn to dusk, and absolutely free. Light fare served at the tea room.

☆ ☆

Gulf Islands Protected Areas (#44)
National, provincial and regional parks that are destinations in their own right, providing a network of waterfront campgrounds, memorable scenery everywhere and protection of some pristine ecosystems. Forty-three percent of Saturna Id is protected, 30 percent of South Pender Island and 24 percent of Hornby Island.

☆ ☆

Hornby Island (#58)
The most beautiful Gulf Island, hot sandy beaches, the warmest water, wonderful rock formations, an upland park laced with trails popular with bicyclers, and a subtidal park famous among divers. It's an island full of delightful eccentricities, with an exciting music festival in August.

☆ ☆

Kinsol Trestle, near Shawnigan Lake (#28)
One of the largest remaining wooden railway trestles in the world, rebuilt in the age of bicycle touring to provide a vital link in the Trans-Canada Trail. A crossing pairs well with Shawnigan Lake (#27) and Deerholme Farm (#36).

THE ISLANDS' TOP ATTRACTIONS

☆ ☆

Long Beach, Pacific Rim National Park Reserve (#76)
Incredibly huge, 10 km/6 mi from end to end, Long Beach is the centerpiece of Vancouver Island's stupendous West Coast.

☆ ☆

Meares Island Tribal Park, Clayoquot Sound (#81)
The island with its twin peaks on Tofino's doorstep is BC's first tribal park. Meares is the best place to walk through an ancient rainforest of western red cedar. One of the island's great climbs, although difficult, is up Lone Cone to view the coast magnificent.

☆ ☆

Oceanside, Parksville-Qualicum (#51)
Between Nanaimo and Campbell River on the island's balmy southeast side, the coastal route, Highway 19A, takes you through beachy Parksville, resorty Qualicum Beach (#53) and a succession of delightful vistas across the Strait of Georgia.

☆ ☆

Port Renfrew and the San Juan Valley (#s 65 and 66)
A tiny west coast outport provides access to two of the islands' natural jewels: the remarkable tide pools of Botanical Beach and the big trees of the San Juan Valley, home of the famous Avatar Grove and the world's biggest Douglas fir tree.

☆ ☆

Royal British Columbia Museum, Victoria (#5)
This busy complex handy to Victoria's Inner Harbour has the best introduction to BC's natural history and the human record. The first Nations exhibit is stunning. With an Imax theatre and other kid-friendly attractions.

☆ ☆

Salt Spring Island Saturday Market, Ganges (#42)
From April to October, Saturday is market day on the waterfront in well-heeled Ganges, metropolis of the Gulf Islands, in gorgeous Ganges Harbour. The market features local fare, crafts and wearables, with buskers and other entertainments. Fishing boats sell their fresh catch on the docks.

☆ ☆

Sooke Potholes (#24)
This eroded rock riverbed in the foothills north of Sooke Harbour is a favorite swimming spot of generations of Victorians. The best pools are difficult to get to.

☆ ☆

Strathcona Park (#s 63, 88-90)
In the sea of mountains at the island's heart, multiple trails lead to alpine marvels. Fitness and perseverance are required: to get to the Marble Meadows, you have to boat to trailhead, then climb for five

to six hours. A more accessible approach is via Mt Washington to Forbidden Plateau (#63).

☆☆

West Coast Trail, Bamfield–Port Renfrew (#67)
This difficult five to seven day hike, amid heartmeltingly beautiful scenery, most notably the sandstone shelf that replaces beaches on the southern half, is part of Pacific Rim National Park Reserve. Difficult access aside, it's a top attraction.

☆☆

The Wickaninnish Inn, Tofino (#78)
World-class oceanside resort, in a spectacular setting, is a wonder of woodwork throughout. Its dining room is legendary. The place is locally-owned and -operated and a member of the prestigious Relais et Châteaux association.

☆☆

Yuquot (Friendly Cove), Nootka Island (#92)
Scenic stop on the route of the MV *Uchuck* is an ancient summer village of the Mowachaht/Muchalaht First Nation and the site of the first European landing on Vancouver Island, Captain James Cook, in 1778. Book a stay in the rustic cabin facing out. The whale-watching is great.

Statue of Queen Victoria in front of the BC Parliament Buildings, Victoria.
Photo by Benson Kua, Wikimedia.

I. Victoria and Southern Vancouver Island

Southern Vancouver Island occupies the more than 60 km/37 mi between Sidney and Sooke, with Victoria at its centre. The straits of Haro and Juan de Fuca are at its feet, the Sooke Hills and Highlands at its back. It's an area of great beauty and magnificent hilltop vistas, with a spectrum of climatic conditions, from Sooke's *wet coast* feel to the rain-shadow heat trap in Victoria and further north. The traditional homeland of Salish First Nations, Victoria was where the English colonial project started in 1843. It grew from a little Hudson's Bay Company trading depot to include three cities, two towns and eight municipal districts. Victoria has been a seat of government since 1849 and the capital of British Columbia since 1868. Esquimalt has had a naval base since the 1850s. Three institutions — company, government, navy — molded the character of the city and produced its wealth of cultural and heritage sites. The economic comfort reflected in the area's fine homes and gardens is matched by the many parks and natural areas within hailing distance of the 368,770 people who, as of 2016, call Victoria home.

Songhees Point — 1

Many visitors love the summer vibe of Victoria's crowded Inner Harbour Causeway and Government Street shopping area — the line-ups to get ice cream, to get on the Harbour Ferry, the buskers and clowns and mimes, the artists who deftly sketch your caricature.

To get a good look at Victoria Harbour and understand its role in the history of this whole island, it's well worth a short walk across the nearby bridge to Victoria West — bear left for Songhees Point. From a lookout perched on the rocks you get a 270° vista of the harbour. Old Town is due east across the water. Southeast lies the Inner Harbour complex. To the south is Victoria's original suburb, peninsular James Bay. Southwest, the harbour opens to the Strait of Juan de Fuca and the Salish Sea. It's the mouth of a tidal waterway that winds through the city 10 km/6 mi to its head at lakelike Portage Inlet.

The waterway buzzes with float planes, ferries to the USA, the little harbour ferries, catamarans, tugs and sailing ships and yachts and barges as well as an ever-increasing numbers of kayaks, stand-up paddleboards, rowing shells, dragon boats and so on. This waterway and the strait beyond loom large in the history of First Nations inhabitants and their European successors.

Near the point, a display beside the carved poles profiles the Lekwungen people. *Lekwungen* was the traditional name of the local Salish people. Their villages were located in protected waterfront areas along 50 km/31 mi of coast, between Metchosin and Saanich, and on the waterway above the harbour. In their society, a few families owned the local land and its resources. "They recognize no superior chief," a Spanish visitor of the 1790s wrote.

On a prominence is a bronze monument which represents a spindle and whorl, a traditional Salish wool-spinning technology and an icon of the Coast Salish people. The monument is one of seven **Signs of Lekwungen** installed around Victoria to mark sites of significance to First Peoples. This one is decorated with motifs of salmon, an essential part of coastal First Peoples' traditional diet. Coho salmon still spawn in the creeks that feed the waterway. An actual spindle whorl was commonly 20 cm/8 in across. In the traditional process of making thread for weaving or knitting, work that Salish women are past masters of, the spindle is rotated back and forth, often against a thigh, by hand, and the other hand feeds the loose wool thread. Spinning tightens the twist of its fibres and bonds them. The carving in the whorl was said to induce in the spinner a trance from watching it flash into focus at the end of each spin, forward and backward. The trance state was said to instill energy in the wool. A flat disk of polished stone is engraved with the traditional name of this place: *p'álac'əs* (pah'lu-tsuss), meaning "cradle-board." The brochure online (see below) says of that: "Traditionally, once infants had learned to walk, their cradles were placed at this sacred headland because of the spiritual power of the water here."

Into the Salish domain ventured the Hudson's Bay Company, an English fur-trading "company of adventurers," in 1843. In charge of the operation was James Douglas. He is considered the founder of both Victoria and British Columbia. Douglas chose to build Fort Victoria here because the harbour was protected from winds and deep enough to allow sailing ships to tie up alongside the rocks. At first, the few European residents of Fort Victoria dwelt among many hundreds of Indigenous people. After a period of hostility, First Nations gathered near Fort Victoria and settled on the west side of the harbour, the better to trade or job out their labour. *Songhees* was the Europeans' name for the residents. They took the name of one nation and made it the name of all. Songhees Village stood about where the Ocean Pointe Hotel now stands. Their territorial boundaries were described in the Fort Victoria Treaties of 1850. By that time, the English company's directors were "the true and absolute lords and proprietors" of the new colony of "Vancouver's Island." The head men of the Lekwungen sold their lands forever to the

Queen of England for blankets with a retail value of £107. They retained the right to use their traditional territories for hunting and fishing. In this, the Hudson's Bay Company was ruled by the 1763 Royal Proclamation, which acknowledged Aboriginal Title. The proprietors soon abandoned the practice of buying land and just moved in.

The island was settled first slowly, then quickly in the rush of the Fraser River gold fever of 1858. Gold made Victoria's fortune. Some of the commercial buildings in Old Town (#6) went up in the late 1850s. Vancouver Island's settler population included the Company's fur traders; Scottish coal miners and their families; farmers who were indentured servants of the Company; farmers willing to pay £1/- an acre; and so on. Industrial extraction was promoted by selling land off piecemeal or alienating it in wholesale giveaways.

Facing each other across the harbour for more than fifty years were the Songhees First Nations village, the city and the Parliament Buildings that imposed British government on the vast province of British Columbia. Although designated an Indian Reserve, the area around Songhees Village was used by industries and institutions. A solution to the encroachment was reached in 1912, whereby the nation sold their land (again) and resettled on Esquimalt Harbour.

Hard to believe, but a century ago the shores of Victoria Harbour were filled with smokestacks. Songhees Point was the site of Sidney Rubber Roofing's asphalt shingle plant. Four concrete footings are leftovers of the plant's water tower. An oil tank farm later occupied the hill to the north. Directly south, across the harbour at Laurel Point, was a paint factory. The Inner Harbour was crowded with steamship docks.

The **Westsong Walkway** park makes for a fine waterfront walk from the bridge 2.7 km/1.7 mi to West Bay, in Esquimalt, where the harbour ferry calls. For the intrepid, a walk further to **Macaulay Point**, about 2.5 km/1.5 mi, is rewarding. On Head St, you pass the former Work Point Barracks. The area became a military post during the naval rivalry of England and Russia in the 1870s. It housed a garrison of Canadian or British gunners who manned the heavy artillery at nearby Macaulay Point and elsewhere. A later, and much larger gun emplacement guards the entrance to Esquimalt Harbour (#17).

Details

- The west side of the harbour is accessible from downtown by the bridge at the foot of Johnson St; it's 1.1 km/.7 mi from the Visitor Information Centre to Songhees Pt; or by **harbour ferry** (seasonal) from well-marked docks along both sides of the harbour; maps, schedules, fares: victoriaharbourferry.com.
- Signs of Lekwungen self-guided tour: victoria.ca.
- Readings:
  Songhees (Victoria: Songhees Nation, 2013), an impressive exposition of

tribal history, culture, language and society.
Songhees Pictorial: A History of the Songhees People as seen by Outsiders 1790-1912 by Grant Keddie (Royal British Columbia Museum, 2003).

■ Map: Salish and Other First Nations Markers and Places in Victoria: google.com/maps.

■ Songhees Nation, operators of the impressive (and well worth visiting) Songhees Wellness Centre: songheesnation.ca.

■ Songhees Seafood and Steam food truck (often parked near the Victoria Clipper dock, on the James Bay side of the harbour): songheesseafood.com.

■ The Fort Victoria Treaties: royalbcmuseum.bc.ca.

■ Wilson Duff's definitive 1969 essay The Fort Victoria Treaties in *BC Studies* journal, downloadable: ojs.library.ubc.ca.

■ Esquimalt Township walking tour digital brochures: esquimalt.ca. Recommended: #2, with spectacular openings on the Strait of Juan de Fuca at Fleming Beach (parking), Macaulay Point and Saxe Point.

■ There are several watercraft rental concessions along the harbour.

■ About 3.8 km/2.4 mi along the scenic **Gorge Waterway** from the Inner Harbour is the tiny reversing falls at The Gorge. It can be forceful, with a challenging drop, or simply impassible. Check tide tables at waterlevels.gc.ca.

2 | The BC Parliament Buildings

The domed British Columbia Parliament Buildings are well worth a visit — to take a tour, get a bite to eat in the dining room and, when the legislature is in session, attend question period in the gallery of the awe-inspiring assembly hall. Many interesting corridors and meeting places are open to the public, and the building is full of memorabilia relating to the history of the province.

A four-line ditty called *Victoria* goes like this:

> *From East to West the circling word has passed,*
> *Till West is East beside our land-locked blue;*
> *From East to West the tested chain holds fast,*
> *The well-forged link rings true!*

Huh? Rudyard Kipling penned those lines in 1896, when the imposing Parliament Buildings were taking shape in limestone and sandstone, following the designs of British-immigrant architect Francis Rattenbury, who was then age 29.

Kipling, the British-Indian writer and to-be Nobel prize-winner, wrote a whole suite in praise of the British Empire. He called it *The Song of the*

Cities. Kipling's jingo-lingo was the versical equivalent of our Parliament Buildings. Both were conceived as propaganda for the British Empire. Actually, the legislature was principally there to anchor the provincial government in Victoria, rather than a mainland city.

The Empire ran in Kipling's veins, and he was a big fan of Victoria. He had already visited our city twice and would see the legislature building in 1907. In Kipling's mind, Victoria was a "well-forged link" in the "chain" of the Empire on which, it was said, "the sun never set." No wonder BC's flag depicts the rays of the sun, and our province's motto is *Splendor sine occasu*, "Splendor without setting."

The English Hudson's Bay Company established a toe-hold here in 1843. By 1849, Fort Victoria was capital of the colony of Vancouver Island. The British Government took over after the Fraser River Gold Rush which made the western colonies' fortunes. By 1862, Victoria was a city. In 1868, it became the capital of British Columbia, which in 1871, became the sixth province in the Canadian Confederation. Within 30 years, the frontier space was transformed into the tiny metropolis of a vast hinterland. British Columbia encloses 950,000 sq km/367,000 sq mi, an area larger than France and Italy combined. Today, BC's population approaches a respectable 4.7 million, while France and Italy together have 126 million. When the legislature was completed in 1898, fewer than 100,000 souls called BC home.

The British Empire disappeared long ago. Similarly, Victoria's massive, solid legislature, with its air of order and permanence, has not prevented the government from slipping away to where the money is: Vancouver. Much of the Province's workforce (totaling some 26,000 employees) is now located there because Vancouver is BC's financial and business capital. Most of the province's executive business is likewise conducted there.

The Province's centre of authority is the Premier's Office in the legislature. Like the USA, Canada is a federal state, so we have governments at two levels, national and provincial. Our Premier is like a US state governor, with an important difference. The premier has almost untrammeled authority to run BC's affairs. Unlike the Republic-type government of the US, we have British-style *Parliamentary* governments, where the *executive* body conducts the Province's business under the leadership of the Premier and his or her *ministers*, who are elected Members of the Legislative Assembly (MLAs), as is the premier.

The Premier leads the governing party not by a vote of the electorate but by party members province-wide. In a *majority* government, the premier's party controls more than half the votes in the Assembly. A *minority* government, on the other hand, controls more votes than any other party, but not enough to win 51 percent of the vote in a division. Minority governments have to make deals with members of opposition parties. A governing party can actually be turned out of office if a majority of MLAs vote *no confidence* at budget time. The proper name for our system is *parliamentary responsible government*. "Responsible" means that, in theory at least, our leaders are accountable to their peers as well as to the electorate.

The key point here is that in our system, the executive effectively controls the legislature. "We've not had democracy," said Bill Vander Zalm, BC's Premier 1986-91, in 2010. "I don't recall ever seeing democracy in this province, or any other province or the country. We always elect a dictator and for four years a dictator determined what was. I'll qualify that a little bit by saying, fortunately, for the most part we've elected benevolent dictators."

Our democratic rights have been abridged by electoral dictatorship? At least we still have the right of peaceful protest, based on hallowed principles of free assembly and free speech that are enshrined in the *Canadian Charter of Rights and Freedoms*. Right?

The steps of the legislature are where protesters gather to demonstrate — ordinary citizens joining voices against the executive steamroller. This has included gatherings of unemployed workers during the Great Depression, to the pro- and anti-logging demonstrations of the 1990s, First Nations groups, advocates for children with autism and health care workers concerned about budgetary cutbacks. They come from all over to confront the Province over a host of social welfare and labour issues, as well as unregulated fish farms, privatized tree farms, private deals for power projects, against pipelines, for First Nations, for wild salmon ... Democracy is alive on the steps of the legislature.

Details

- The **Legislative Assembly of BC** has a robust website related to its law-making mandate: leg.bc.ca.
- The executive branch maintains the British Columbia Government website: gov.bc.ca.
- When the Legislative Assembly is in session, the public may attend in the Gallery; best time is Question Period, about 2 pm Mon and Wed, 10:30 am Tues and Thurs; 3rd floor, Main Block.
- Guided tours of the Parliament Buildings, year round, from the Tour Office, left of the main entrance: leg.bc.ca.
- *Self-Directed Guide Book*: leg.bc.ca.
- The Legislative Dining Room is open to the public year round, 9 am-3 pm, Mon to Thurs, 9 am-2 pm Fri; reservations: 250-387-3959.
- The Legislative Library, with its eye-popping rotunda, is open to the public when the Assembly is *not* in session, i.e., most of the time. Best to call first: (250) 387-6510. Online catalogue: llbccat.leg.bc.ca.
- Rudyard Kipling's 1896 poem "The Song of the Cities": bartleby.com.

Steamship Terminal 3

Ferries are a fact of life for islanders. The huge BC Ferries fleet is our marine highway system. The latest models are decked out like cruise ships. But turn back the clock, and Victoria Harbour would be wreathed in the black smoke of tiny ocean liners. A steam whistle would announce an arrival or departure.

For more than sixty years, the Canadian Pacific Railway (CPR) ran an ever-changing fleet of handsome coastal steamers, the Princess ships. The larger ships, weighing 5,000-6,000 tons gross, offered comfortable, fast, frequent sailings to Vancouver and Seattle and, in the 1920s, summer cruises to Alaska. The Princesses *Maquinna* and *Norah* provided essential services to isolated Vancouver Island communities. The CPR's Victoria docks were beside the pillared Steamship Terminal on Belleville St. Built in 1924, replacing a 1905 wooden structure, it was Victoria's temple of transport.

Princess Ship Roll Call:— *Beatrice*! *Victoria*! *Charlotte*! *Adelaide*! *Mary*! *Alice*! *Patricia*! *Marguerite*! *Sophia*! *Maquinna*! *Irene*! *Margaret*! *Louise*! *Kathleen*! *Elaine*! *Norah*! *Elizabeth*! *Joan*! *Marguerite II*! *Patricia II*! — There were others that don't quite fit the mould of inter-city passenger boats.

Over time, the coal that powered most steamships was replaced by oil. Slowly, but surely, between the 1920s and 1950s, petroleum-powered motor vessels took over the CPR routes. Likewise, the ships' designs morphed into the modern. The names lost that quaint quality — the latest built were the *Princess of Nanaimo* (1951) and *Princess of Vancouver* (1955). End-loading ferries met changing public demand more efficiently, and the CPR dropped out of the business. The last gasp for CPR's marine operations came in 1998.

An early memory: being hoisted into the arms of an old man beside a stone wall. That was my grandfather. It's my only memory of him. My three other grandparents died before I was born. Grandfather was standing by the Inner Harbour causeway, I guess, about to catch the Night Boat to Vancouver. He made the long train trip from Owen Sound, Ontario to meet my two older siblings and me. We were his only grandchildren — my father's four siblings all died before my time, without issue.

I took the Night Boat once, with my family. You went aboard the *Princess Joan* in the evening and settled into your room. While you slept the boat slipped its moorings. In the early morning, you went on deck to find the boat already gliding under the Lion's Gate Bridge into Vancouver Harbour.

I sailed to Seattle on the *Princess Patricia II* to attend the 1962 World's Fair, an afternoon sailing that allowed me and my friend to stay aboard overnight. We had to clear out of our room early but could return in the evening. For 14-year-old boys, it didn't get any better.

I sailed on the *Princess Marguerite II* when she was 40 years old and in a sorry state. Sheer nostalgia kept her on the Seattle-Victoria tourist run until 1989. The *Princess of Vancouver* survived until 1991.

We loved the Princess ships. We'll never see their likes again.

The Steamship Terminal is now the home of the **Robert Bateman Centre**, a conservation-themed exhibition of the popular Salt Spring Island artist's work. On the main floor is the **Steamship Grill and Bar**.

Details

- Steamship Terminal building: 470 Belleville Street (west of Government), Victoria; info at steamshipterminal.com.
- Reading: *The Pacific Princesses: An Illustrated History of the Canadian Pacific Railway's Princess Fleet on the Northwest Coast* by Robert D. Turner (Victoria: Sono Nis Press, 1977, many reprints).
- BC Ferries: bcferries.com; nearest terminal is Swartz Bay, 35 km/20 mi north of downtown Victoria, with frequent daily service to Tsawwassen, south of Vancouver, and the southern Gulf Islands.
- Victoria Clipper high-speed, passenger-only catamaran service Victoria-Seattle, daily, year-round: clippervacations.com.
- MV Coho, Victoria-Port Angeles vehicle ferry, daily service year-round: cohoferry.com.

 4 Fairmont Empress Hotel

The gigantic Fairmont Empress Hotel is the very icon of Victoria. Built on reclaimed mudflats by the Canadian Pacific Railway Company (CPR), the Empress opened in 1908, joining such CPR railway hotels as the Banff Springs and Château Frontenac. Francis Rattenbury, the architect of the Empress, was already famous for having designed the BC Parliament Buildings (#2). The CPR soon engaged Rattenbury to add symmetrical wings to the back of the hotel. In the 1920s, the CPR added the Crystal Garden, with a salt-water swimming pool under a glass roof, on Douglas St, and the pillared CPR Steamship Terminal (#3) on Belleville St. Rattenbury had a hand in both. (The Empress's outsized north wing was undertaken in the late 1920s, after Rattenbury's time. The reception area and tower date from the 1980s.) Reflecting on the architect's achievement, Anthony Barrett, co-author of *Francis Rattenbury and British Columbia*, wrote that "In a sense he created not just buildings, but a cityscape, Victoria's Inner Harbour, arguably the most beautiful urban ensemble in Canada, and for a century or so, his legacy has been a focal point for residents and visitors alike."

For decades, the Empress was a summer spa for rich visitors. The dining room, lounge and crystal ballroom were among the city's favorite gathering places. Fast forward to 1999 when Canadian Pacific Hotels bought the upscale Fairmont hotel chain. Present owners of the Empress are Vancouver developer Mr. and Mrs. Nat Bosa, who initiated a $40 million restoration in 2016. Fairmont continues to manage the hotel.

Visitors are welcome to stroll around the Empress's heritage lobby, with its quaint carpeting and grandfather clock, and browse in the upscale shops. There's an entrance under the porte cochère near the corner of Government and Belleville Sts.

The Lobby Lounge is famous for the Empress's sumptuous **Afternoon Tea**. The tale of a fateful encounter begins there. It comes with an advisory: sensitive readers may be disturbed by these details of illicit romance gone horribly wrong.

Our story begins in 1923. It is the Saturday evening after Christmas. The Empress is decked out in festive greens. In the Lounge, a hotel guest is visiting with a local friend. She will describe, in a letter that surfaces 12 years later in the London *Daily Express*, "the sounds of revelry and singing." There's a big dinner party in the nearby Crystal Ballroom. Victoria's businessmen are singing a rousing "For He's a Jolly Good Fellow."

They peek into the ballroom. The friend discovers that "the honoured guest, the man who had inspired this outburst, was an acquaintance." The banquet breaks up. Some of the diners move to the Lounge. "K introduced me to his acquaintance," the visitor would write.

The acquaintance is Francis Rattenbury. The noted architect, now 55 year old, is introduced to a young woman named Alma Pakenham. She is a classical concert pianist with a knack for writing and selling popular songs. She grew up in Kamloops, BC, but is a woman of the world. Her first husband, an officer in the British Army, died in battle in the Great War. Alma became a stretcher-bearer with the French Red Cross on the battlefield in Salonika, Greece. The French decorated her with the Croix de Guerre. She and her young son recently deserted her violent second husband and fled New York. Now a single parent, she gives piano lessons in Vancouver. She came to Victoria to give a classical piano recital.

When Rattenbury, known familiarly as Frank, happens to meet her at a private party a few days later, she says, "You have almost the kindest face I ever saw." Frank's 25-year marriage is unhappy. Husband and wife live apart in their Oak Bay waterfront paradise. They communicate with each other through their daughter.

Soon Alma and her son have moved to Victoria. Frank and Alma conduct an affair, with little regard for the scandal that erupts. A divorce ensues. Frank and Alma marry and have a child, John. Victoria society shuns them. Frank cannot get work. His debts pile up.

They flee with the two children, eventually settling in Bournemouth, on England's southwest coast. Besides the children, Alma has a live-in *woman companion*. Beginning in September 1934, the Rattenburys engage a 17-year-old *chauffeur/handyman* named Robert Stoner. Frank, now in his late 60s, drinks heavily and is depressed. He often threatens suicide. "Well, get on with it," Alma teases him. She loves him dearly, the companion will testify. The thing is, there's no longer any romance. They have an Arrangement.

In November, Stoner having turned 18, he moves in. He is seduced by Alma, and they become lovers. They run away to London, where Alma lavishes gifts on him in what the Crown will call *an orgy*. A doctor will testify that she has flare-ups of tuberculosis, which can induce *nymphomania*. Two days after their return from London, Alma makes plans to take the ailing Frank to see a doctor in a nearby town. Stoner becomes inflamed with jealousy. That very evening, he borrows a mallet from his grandfather and bludgeons Frank in his easy chair. Francis Rattenbury died four days later.

Driven mad with grief, yet desperate to protect her lover, Alma lies. She confesses to the crime. Alma and Stoner are tried together for murder. The four-day trial electrifies the country — think O J Simpson, but much quicker. Stoner is found guilty and sentenced to hang. Alma is acquitted but soon takes her own life, having lost husband, lover, reputation, all. (Some believe her only crime was to feel too much.)

The British public is moved to pity for the young Stoner. A petition to have his sentence commuted circulates, and more than 300,000 sign it. Alma Rattenbury is seen as having used sex to dominate a mere boy. The slain architect is himself an object of contempt for winking at his wife's affairs. Stoner's sentence is commuted and he is out of prison within seven years. A modern tragedy. It all started here. Enjoy your tea!

Details

- The Fairmont Empress Hotel, 721 Government St, Victoria: fairmont.com/empress-victoria; 1-866-540-4429. If one wishes to stay in one of the hotel's 450+ rooms, the Fairmont Gold program offers enhanced service and top-drawer rooms; rooms above the Lobby Lounge, overlooking the harbour and the Sooke Hills beyond, are among the nicest in the city.
- Tea at the Empress: fairmont.com/empress-victoria. In summer, reservations (250-389-2727) are recommended; cost $75CDN per person; dress code.
- Q at the Empress restaurant: qattheempress.com; reservations 250-389-2727; first-come service on the Verandah in season.
- Readings: Terry Reksten, *Rattenbury* (1978) and *The Fairmont Empress: The First Hundred Years* (2008).
- John Rattenbury, Alma and Francis's child, b. 1928, is a famous architect closely associated with an icon of the profession, as suggested by the titles of his coffee-table books, *A Living Architecture: Frank Lloyd Wright and Taliesin Architects* (2000) and *A House for Life: Bringing the Style of*

Frank Lloyd Wright into Your Home (2006).

■ In 2007 Victoria resident John Motherwell had a memorial stone put
on Francis Rattenbury's grave, unmarked for 73 years, in Bournemouth.
On the marble is a picture of the BC Parliament Buildings with the
text: "In remembrance of Francis Mawson Rattenbury, 11 October
1867–28 March 1935. A British Columbia Architect." (That was how the
25-year-old Rattenbury signed his entry in the competition to design
the new Parliament Buildings.)

Royal BC Museum   5

The Royal British Columbia Museum (RBCM) is one of the best regional museums on the continent. A recent surf reveals that, according
to TripAdvisor, it's the Number 1 of 172 Things To Do In Victoria. The
museum, on Belleville St, kitty-corner to the Harbour, has permanent
exhibitions that give the visitor a sense of British Columbia's vast geography, natural history and human history, and it mounts special exhibitions
from time to time, including boffo travelling shows like *Titanic: The
Artifact Exhibition* (2008). Even the entrance is impressive: just inside is
an imposing suite of Aboriginal carved and painted monumental figures
from up and down BC's Pacific coast. The museum is a bustling place that
brims with enthusiasm. Leave plenty of time.

In the exhibits hall, the **First Peoples Galleries** on the third floor is
endlessly interesting — simply the most accessible way I know to begin
understanding BC's indigenous heritage. The section on the disastrous
effects of European contact is guaranteed to give one pause. The displays were created in the 1970s with the collaboration of dozens of First
Nations people. Detailed woodwork down to the handrails was honed by
the artistic Hunt family of the Fort Rupert Kwakiutl First Nation. There is
a scaled-down walk-in model of a big-house built by Henry Hunt and his
sons Tony and Richard.

Other permanent exhibits include the Modern History and Natural
History galleries. Kids like the walk-in of the HMS *Discovery*, Captain
Vancouver's ship. The train station is fun too.

Since 1886, the museum's mission is "to preserve specimens of the
natural products and Indian antiquities and manufactures of the Province
and to classify and exhibit the same for the information of the public."
The Provincial Museum long inhabited the East Block of the Parliament
Buildings. I attended Dr. Clifford Carl's Saturday morning talks on science
there, between a glassed-in ant colony and a stuffed mountain goat. The
present complex took shape in the 1960s, and it's way more immersive
than the old-style of cases and drawers.

The heart of the Museum is arguably the little-seen **tower**, where the majority of the museum's employees collect, study and curate the collections. Among the Museum's men and women of science are such legendary field workers as Charles Newcombe, Frank Kermode, and Wilson Duff. There's way more to the collections than what's on display, as the RBCM website's fascinating *100 Objects of Interest* attests.

The museum complex has other notable parts. The **BC Archives**, by the sunken courtyard, is an indispensable resource for historians and genealogists. The reference room is one of the most useful public spaces in the city. In the lobby, meaningful artifacts in the Archives are displayed.

On the Belleville St side of the exhibit building are glassed displays of original **carved monumental art** from coastal villages. Of the weathered masterworks, a bearded, human-sized Cowichan house figure of the 19th century stands out for its iconic simplicity. It's an image that has been reproduced many times.

To me, the most fascinating part of the whole complex is the painted bighouse in **Thunderbird Park**, at the corner of Belleville and Douglas Sts. It's the centerpiece of a huge presence of Kwakiutl artists in Victoria that continues to this day. The builder of the house was paterfamilias and principal exponent. **Mungo Martin** (c1881-1962) trained in carving and painting, dancing, singing and storytelling in his native Fort Rupert (see #s 98 and 99). He collected a museum's-worth of artifacts and folkways. His people's remoteness protected their Kwakwaka'wakw traditions from the fate of many other First Nations. Their traditions survived more or less intact.

Mungo had several chiefly titles, some inherited and some acquired. One was *Nakapankam*, Ten Times a Chief. After a life in commercial fishing, Mungo took a post at the University of British Columbia to carve poles and teach the arts. He moved to Victoria in 1952 to be carver-in-residence at the Museum and settled here. Martin replicated many of the poles in Thunderbird Park. Originally a repository of monumental art removed from house and village, the park was in bad shape. The old poles were deteriorating, as they do when serving their purpose on site. Wood decays. Museums are dedicated to preserving. The replicas carved and painted by Mungo and his son-in-law Henry Hunt comprise much of the collection in the park today. Mungo Martin House, built in 1953, is a scaled-down version of a Fort Rupert big house. Its four interior houseposts are elaborately carved with the owner's heraldic crests. The RBCM website has an account of the big house and the park.

Martin, a modest fisherman in blue-jean overalls, was really this cultural dynamo whose stature as an artist is difficult to overstate. Among those whom he influenced were Bill Reid and Doug Cranmer. His protégé, Tony Hunt and Tony's brother Richard Hunt are artists of standing who made Victoria their homes. The next generation is well-established. Their work known worldwide. When I reflect on the contribution of the Kwakiutl First Nation, with their living connection to ancient north island cultures, it seems to me one of our strongest legacies. Did I say *our*? Whether it's ours or theirs, it's alive and kicking in Victoria.

Two historically important structures comprise Heritage Court, behind Thunderbird Park. **Helmcken House** was built in stages beginning in 1852 on the site it occupies today. Dr John Sebastian Helmcken married Cecilia, the daughter of Governor and Mrs James Douglas, later Sir and Lady, whose "mansion" stood where the exhibits hall is. Beside Helmcken House is **St Ann's Schoolhouse**, built about 1844 by the Hudson's Bay Company and acquired by the Sisters of St Anne in 1858. It was the Quebec-based missionary teaching order's first convent, school, hospital and orphanage. The log building was moved to its present location in the 1970s.

The Belleville St side of the RBCM has a host of plantings that are representative of different ecological zones in BC. Oh, yes, and dinosaur tracks.

Details

- Royal British Columbia Museum, 675 Belleville St, Victoria; 1-888-447-7977; royalbcmuseum.bc.ca; has a full-size IMAX Theatre, café and shop; much to explore on the website.
- BC Archives, 655 Belleville St; bcarchives.bc.ca. The online visual records database is an outstanding historical research tool. Register in person to use the reference room; there are restrictions.
- Mungo Martin House (*Wawadit'la*): royalbcmuseum.bc.ca.
- That ringing in your ears may be coming from the **Netherlands Centennial Carillon**, corner Belleville and Government Sts, the 1967 gift of BC's Dutch community in gratitude for Canada's significant role in liberating Netherlands from the Nazis. Sometimes real ringers work the 62 bells.

 Munro's Books

A veritable temple of culture in the heart of Victoria's Old Town, Munro's Books may be the most beautiful bookstore in Canada, or the world. In the National Geographic Society's 2016 guidebook, *Destinations of a Lifetime*, Munro's ranks third on the list of Top 10 Bookstores anywhere. It's partly a matter of the setting, a refurbished 1910 bank building designed to resemble a Greek or Roman temple. Outside, lofty granite pillars frame an elegant recessed portico. Inside, the former banking hall soars to a ceiling of ornate plasterwork enclosing an oval window (originally of art glass), and the walls are graced with modernist tapestries of heroic size, depicting the seasons.

Munro's is a bookstore that dares to stock a huge inventory of interesting literature, and its knowledgeable staff are ever ready to special-order books they don't have on hand. The fiction section covers a whole side wall. Three shelves are devoted to new hardbacks, which I inevitably browse when looking for a gift book.

Another section I always browse is social commentary, which brims with provocative titles. Same with the science and technology section. The local interest section is the amplest I know of anywhere. The children's section rates a separate room in the back and is very kid-friendly. Even the gift card racks are notable, the best in town, with many limited edition art cards on display.

The story of Munro's Books has an aura of national significance. Its founders were Jim and Alice Munro — yes, that Alice Munro, 2013 Nobel Prize winner for Literature. When Jim opened the little bookstore on Yates Street in 1963, it was among the first to carry contemporary Canadian literature. (I remember Alice working the till. I was 15 and hooked on Signet Classics at the time.) When Jim bought and restored the old Royal Bank

TAKE 5 *Interesting Shops*

Local, independent, enduring, diverse; all in downtown Victoria; alphabetic.

1. Aurea Gems & Essential Luxuries
614 Johnson St; 250-381-6260; aureagems.com.
Canadian designer women's clothing — all so wearable, says my wife Paula — but, after 38 years, not so much the gems; on the LoJo (Lower Johnson) shopping area, along with many interesting locally-owned specialty shops.

2. Cook Culture
1317 Blanshard St; 250-590-8161; cookculture.com.
Durable cookware, informed by the owner's commitment to sustainable food; cooking workshops; in the happening Atrium, a short worthwhile hike from the Old Town.

3. Hughes Clothing
564 Yates St, Victoria, 866-483-4405; hughesclothing.com.
Urbane women's and men's clothing; shoes, accessories; all chosen by the owner; a fixture for 30 years in the funky brick-walled former Majestic Theatre in the trendy Lower Yates area.

4. Lore General Store
1322 Government St; loregeneralstore.com.
Locally/regionally sourced prepared foods, soaps, pottery, woolens, plants, kitchenware, gifts; intensive crafting workshops; in a pleasant space; eclectically Victorian.

5. Robinsons Outdoor Store
1307 Broad St, Victoria, 1-888-317-0033; robinsonsoutdoors.com.
A family-run Victoria institution since 1929, on two floors, with a huge inventory of quality clothing, footwear, camping gear, fishing gear, adventure travel gear and incidentals.

building on Government St in 1984, it married his interests in heritage, community and literature. And when he retired in 2014, Jim Munro gave the store — yes, gave it — to four long-term employees, who cherish the tradition of service he nurtured. Jim Munro passed on in 2016, having enriched the city immeasurably.

Details

- Munro's Books, 1108 Government St, Victoria; 1-888-243-2464; munrobooks.com.
- Top Ten Bookstores: nationalgeographic.com.
- Royal Bank Building: historicplaces.ca.
- Reading: *Government Street: Victoria's Heritage Mile* by Danda Humphreys (Heritage House, 2012).
- Notable neighbours of Munro's Books include **Out of Ireland Irish Importers**, 1000 Government, which stocks handsome knitwear and other Old Country goods in an 1860s heritage building with splendid show windows; the **Bard and Banker Public House**, at the corner of Government and Fort Sts, in the 1880s Bank of British Columbia building, workplace and (next door) residence of Robert Service, who later struck gold with his poems about the Klondike Gold Rush ("A bunch of the boys were whooping it up in the Malamute Saloon" — The Shooting of Dan McGrew, 1907); the **Irish Times Pub** at Government and Bastion Square, in the former Bank of Montreal building designed by Francis Rattenbury (see #4) and built 1896; **W & J Wilson Clothiers**, which has been at 1221 Government, corner of **Trounce Alley**, since 1862.

Brasserie L'École   7

A brasserie is "an informal, usually French, restaurant serving simple hearty food" (Merriam-Webster). Brasserie L'École, a 38-table dinner spot *cum* beer and wine bar in Victoria's Chinatown (#8), is just such a place. It occupies the high-ceilinged ground floor of the restored 1905 Chinese Empire Reform Association headquarters building. Next to the brasserie is a Chinese fruit and veggie shop whose wares occupy much of the sidewalk. It's a busy spot. In the high season, a line forms on the sidewalk about 4:30, an hour before it opens. You may see someone in a folding chair, reading while they wait. The restaurant fills by about 5:31. Get there early or you'll be killing a couple of hours. They don't take reservations.

The menu has not changed much since Brasserie L'École was opened in 2001 "by two guys with credit cards," to use the words of chef Sean Brennan. Actually, the menu changes every day, five days a week, and is posted on the website. "The brasserie staples," Brennan says, "the things you need to have if you want to call yourself a brasserie — French onion soup, steak *frites*, mussels and *frites*, chicken liver mousse, endive salad" — have always been on the menu. "From there, the rest of the menu opened up to what we have here locally. We only serve local fish, no farmed fish … Well, we do get our trout from Sooke, that's been on since day one, getting wild trout just doesn't happen. It has to be grown in a small pond. Awesome product." But the numbers on the beef, OMG! — "Last year just under 9,000 steaks alone, not counting other dishes."

When you're doing the math, consider the restaurant is closed almost one-third of the year, including every Sunday and Monday. As an example of the search for additions to the menu, Sean relates how in a Paris restaurant he discovered beef *paleron*, a shoulder cut braised to tenderness yet agreeably crunchy outside. "It was stunning." He figured out how to make it: "Basically, it's seared, then braised, then kept in the braising liquid, then sliced into 2-inch strips and seared again." Paleron became a fixture on the Brasserie's menu.

I will attest to the divinity of the 16 oz/454 g ribeye steak ($50) — more than enough for two — finished with Roquefort butter. The frites are long thin fries dressed with Parmesan cheese, garlic, parsley and truffle oil, $10 if ordered separately, among the very best I've ever had. I could eat a dozen *gougères*, little pastry puffs filled with cheese ($5). The burger ($19) is also a contender for Best I Ever Tasted, with bacon, Gruyère cheese, watercress and mustard aioli. Dessert? The server brings an incongruously large chalkboard around with today's creations in huge letters. A dozen of those little lemon-filled pastries would not suffice.

Brasserie L'École logged 17 years on *Vancouver Magazine*'s best Victoria restaurants list. Its mystique is in the ambience that radiates from the staff, beginning with courtly maître d'-sommelier Marc Morrison, the Brasserie's co-owner. The conspiratorial smile is letting you in on a wonderful secret: the place is special, and you are special. Sean talks about the breaks that came first with an early review by Amy Rosen in the *National Post*. Then in 2002, *EnRoute Magazine* voted it the third best new restaurant in Canada. Soon *Gourmet*, *Bon Appetit!* and *Martha Stewart* were knocking on the door.

"I've always liked French cooking, the more rustic style," Sean says. "I like Spanish cooking, too. I like Italian cooking for its simplicity and rustickness, and its big flavours. Here we stick to French. We might swing a little bit towards Spain or Morocco, that sort of thing, as opposed to the other side of the Mediterranean."

Details

- Brasserie L'École, 1715 Government St, Victoria: 250-475-6260, daily menu posted on website: lecole.ca; open 5:30 to 11 pm, Tues-Sat; no reservations, "first-come, first-serve," wait-list.

8 Victoria's Chinatown

Chinatown is centred on the lower blocks of Pandora, Fisgard and Herald Sts, and the connecting blocks of Government St. The heart of it is the 500-block of Fisgard, with its portal Gate of Harmonious Interest, grocery produce on sidewalk display, and evenings awash of neon restaurant signs. There's an old-fashioned Chinese butcher, side by side with art galleries, niche shops and curious passageways that invite exploration. Chinatown has an urban vibe you don't experience anywhere else in the city or, for that matter, on the island.

Chinatown's vibrant street life is matched by its cultural and historical significance as the oldest, and once the largest, Chinatown in Canada. The district was first settled in the 1850s, when Chinese men from Guandong Province began to immigrate from California to join the Fraser River gold rush.

In the wake of Canadian Pacific Railway construction in the 1880s, a Chinatown of sturdy brick and masonry buildings grew up in Victoria. "In its prime," writes David Chuenyan Lai in *The Forbidden City within Victoria*, "Chinatown boasted more than 150 firms, two theatres, a hospital, three Chinese schools, two churches, more than five temples or shrines, over ten opium factories, and many gambling dens and brothels." The whole area was honeycombed with secret passageways — the Forbidden City, a shadowy place where lookouts would alert the largely male population of police raids, which were frequent. **Fan Tan Alley**, the narrow passage between Fisgard and Pandora Ave, hints at that architecture. Reputedly the narrowest public thoroughfare in Canada, Fan Tan Alley is lined with little shops. My favorite is **The Turntable**, a music store with bins of well-sorted vintage LPs. (Their prizes are displayed on the walls.)

A distinctive element of Chinatown design is the door on the street that leads to multiple apartments with open-air commons. One such complex is **Dragon Alley**, 532 Fisgard. It has been renovated into an interesting mix of residential, commercial and retail uses. The passage leads to lower **Herald St**, an emerging retail zone.

Most recently, lower Fisgard St and Pandora Ave have benefitted hugely by filling what used to be a huge parking lot with a mixed-use building. Hard to believe that Chinatown suffered decades of population loss and decay before David Lai, an immigrant professor from Hong Kong, spearheaded a revival that has taken its place among Victoria's civic success stories.

There are plenty of restaurants in the vicinity. For a light meal, the **Grindstone Café**, 504 Herald. **Jam Café**, 542 Herald, is tops for breakfast. For fine dining, check out **Brasserie L'École**, 1715 Government (#7) and **Olo**, 509 Fisgard. **Canoe Brewpub**, 450 Swift St, has an attractive patio

TAKE **5** *Best Victoria Restaurants*

1. Agrius by Fol Epi

732 Yates St; 778-265-6312; agriusrestaurant.com.

Agrius is an evolution of Fol Epi bakery, to which it is annexed.

2017 *Vancouver Magazine* Best Restaurants in Victoria: #1.

"The lamb tartare at Agrius by Fol Epi is, hands down, the brightest, tastiest, singular most impressive dish I have eaten in years. Beyond being jaw-droppingly delicious, the tartare captures this stellar new restaurant's slow-food ethos and unwavering – almost unreasonable – commitment to the highest standards." That was how Alexandra Gill, Vancouver restaurant critic for *The Globe and Mail*, began her first-ever four-star review, on February 12, 2016.

2016 *EnRoute* Magazine (enroute.aircanada.com) Best New Restaurants in Canada: #4. From the review: "Rice for that perfectly tender shrimp risotto – bakers have a thing for texture – is grown in Abbotsford, and the sea asparagus and sea plantain garnish is from Sombrio Beach."

2017 Canada's Best Restaurants (canadas100best.com): #48. From the review: "Deploys the Slow Food ethos with exemplary French technique: roasted black trumpets and Savoy cabbage are sautéed in a satiny sauerkraut butter sauce; non-traditional soupe de poissons is made extra-grainy with smoked trout bones; and meltingly tender duck confit is crisped in golden skin. Metchosin-raised lamb tartare mixed with preserved Meyer lemon and tossed with sourdough croutons sautéed in rendered lamb fat is a must-try when available. Paired with Cowichan Valley wines and superb B.C. craft cocktails, it's all surprisingly sophisticated and delightfully wholesome."

2. Brasserie l'Ecole

1715 Government St, near Fisgard; 250-475-6260; lecole.ca.

2016 *Vancouver Magazine* Best Restaurants in Victoria: #2. From the 2015 citation: "French country cooking with local ingredients and reliable service excel at this hopping yet cozy brasserie, where tables are first come, first served. Chef and owner Sean Brennan provides the standbys: moules, steak frites, endive salad with lardons, rich onion soup, but the plats du jour really show off his chops. Beer lovers can navigate through an array of French, Belgian, and local suds."

2015 Exceptional Eats! Award (eatmagazine.ca): Best Restaurant of the Year. "Always delivers — in service, selection, atmosphere and execution."

3. Stage Wine Bar

1307 Gladstone Ave; 250-388-4222; stagewinebar.com.

In the Fernwood neighbourhood, 2.8 km/1.7 mi from the Empress.

2017 *Vancouver Magazine* Best Restaurants in Victoria: #1. 2016 *Vancouver Magazine* Best Restaurants in Victoria: #1. From the 2015 citation: "A tremendous cocktail selection (half a dozen different Manhattans!) … small plates—most under $15 … a salad in which grilled halloumi mingles with Israeli couscous, cucumber, radish, and greens … rounded out by artisan cheeses and house charcuterie."

4. Pizzeria Prima Strada

2960 Bridge St, 250-590-4380; 230 Cook St, 250-590-8595; 1990 Fort St, 250-590-8599; pizzeriaprimastrada.com.

2016 *Vancouver Magazine* Best Restaurants in Victoria: Honorable Mention. From the 2015 review: "Brick and clay ovens ... seasoned B.C. birch ... local, artisanal ingredients ... blistered crust ... the right char ... a classic *Margherita* with Fairburn Farm buffalo mozzarella and fresh basil ... *Funghi* with porcini cream, roasted mushrooms and onions, thyme, pecorino, and mozzarella ... craft brews, ciders ... ever-changing wine list."

5. Sooke Harbour House

1528 Whiffen Spit Rd, Sooke; 250-642-3421; sookeharbourhouse.com.

2016 *Vancouver Magazine* Best Restaurants on Vancouver Island: Honorable Mention.

A temple of Slow Food on Vancouver Island since the 1980s, still going strong despite a recent ownership shake-up.

Also making buzz (alphabetical):

10 Acres Bistro/Commons/Kitchen

611 Courtney St, 250-220-8008; 620 Humboldt St, 250-940-0735;
614 Humboldt, 250-385-4512; 10acres.ca.

Café Brio

944 Fort St; 250-383-0009; cafe-brio.com.

2015 *Vancouver Magazine* Best Victoria Restaurants: Honorable Mention. From the review: "A charcuterie-curing room built by chef Laurie Munn has added depth to Brio's Italian-sponsored menu. From coppa to braesola to pâté to the daily sausage, Munn shows abundant talent. The menu changes weekly (even daily) to reflect what's fresh and available. Hosts Greg Hays and Silvia Marcolini warmly work the room."

2013 Exceptional Eats! award for Victoria Restaurant of the Year: #3.

North 48 Restaurant

1005 Langley St; 250-381-2428; northfortyeight.com.

2016 BC finalist for Gold Medal Plates ((goldmedalplates.com).

Nourish Kitchen & Café

225 Quebec St; 250-590-3426; nourishkitchen.ca.

2016 BC finalist for Gold Medal Plates ((goldmedalplates.com).

Part and Parcel

2656 Quadra St; 778-406-0888; partandparcel.ca.

2016 *Vancouver Magazine* Best Victoria Restaurants: Honorable Mention.

Q at the Empress

721 Government St; 250-389-2727; qattheempress.com.

2016 BC finalist for Gold Medal Plates (goldmedalplates.com).

Zambri's

820 Yates St; 250-360-1171; zambris.ca.

Venerated Italian trattoria.

and deck overlooking the working harbour. Funky **Bean Around the World**, 533 Fisgard, serves impeccable coffees and teas.

Store St has interesting shops. **Ocean River Sports**, 1630 Store, is Victoria's premier retailer of kayaks, paddleboards and gear. **Chintz & Company**, 1720 Store, is a roomy, eclectic furnishings and adornment shop; fun to explore. **Value Village**, 1810 Store, is a sort of upscale thrift store, visited by serious shoppers for donated threads and probably the city's best-supplied knick-knack shelves. **Capital Iron**, 1900 Store, is the city's most interesting hardware/department store, in an 1860s heritage building.

Approaching Chinatown from the Inner Harbour district means a walk through Victoria's **Old Town**. It has many attractions for walkers. Besides 200+ heritage buildings, Old Town has a number of intriguing passageways, one-of-a-kind shops, and a goodly array of restaurants, watering holes and coffee houses. There are many points of access to the waterfront and the beginnings of a 5-km/3-mi-long walk known as the David Foster Harbour Pathway. (Victoria is the music producer's home town.)

Old Town, (including Chinatown) is "an historic place of profound importance in Canadian history," to quote a City planning document:

> It is the largest single historic area in British Columbia. Within Old Town are three areas of distinct character: the commercial district, Chinatown, and the waterfront. Old Town includes six National Historic Sites including Victoria's Chinatown, the oldest surviving Chinatown in Canada, and a further 200 municipally-recognized historic places. The role of the commercial district, as western Canada's principal port up to 1900, is recognized by its designation as a National Historic Event.

Details

- Victoria's Chinatown, a BC Archives photo essay: bcarchives.gov.bc.ca.
- "Victoria's Chinatown: A Gateway to the Past and Present of Chinese Canadians": chinatown.library.uvic.ca.
- The Turntable, 107 – 3 Fan Tan Alley; turntablerecordsbc.ca.
- Interactive map of Victoria's more than 900 heritage buildings, with links to informative material on each: arcgis.com.
- City of Victoria downloadable maps and guides to four themed Old Town tours: victoria.ca.
- Discover the Past walking tours: discoverthepast.com.
- Come See Victoria walking tours: comeseevictoria.com.
- David Foster Harbour Pathway at victoria.ca.

Ogden Point Breakwater 9

The Ogden Point Breakwater is a delightful 762 m/2,500 ft walk at the entrance of Victoria Harbour. It puts you in the middle of the marine environment, especially the often blowy weather on the Strait of Juan de Fuca, and provides wonderful vistas across the strait to the Olympic Mountains.

In these parts, you will hear references to the Salish Sea (see #41). **Juan de Fuca Strait** is a major inlet of the inland sea. The strait is 153 km/95 mi long, more or less east-west. To the west, where it meets the Pacific Ocean, it's about 22 km/14 miles wide. The strait widens to about 36 km/23 mi east of Christopher Point, visible 16 km/10 mi southwest of the breakwater. The eastern strait is spacious and its weather ever-changing. The strait's saltwater surface area (4,400 sq km/1,700 sq mi) totals nearly one-quarter of the Salish Sea. It has long been a major international merchant and naval shipping waterway. It provides access to the major ports around Seattle, Washington and Vancouver, BC and many smaller ports on a protected coast with a population of about nine million.

Victoria is the major centre on Juan de Fuca Strait. Its location, some 105 km/65 mi from the open ocean (as the wind blows), gives Victoria a distinctly maritime flavor. You can just about set your clock by the offshore breeze that springs up late on a summer afternoon. Near the open Pacific, yet shielded, how nice is that?

The breakwater was recently made accessible for persons with disabilities with the addition of railings. Below, on the outside, you might see scuba divers resting on the massive granodiorite blocks while diving in the protected marine site. A dive shop is nearby. The breakwater is also popular with fishers who cast their lines from the blocks and pull in the big ones. Recently, a 14.5 kg/32 lb ling cod made the paper.

For walkers, an excursion from the harbour to the breakwater totals about 7 km/4.5 mi. En route is one of the city's most charming places. **Fisherman's Wharf** does a bustling business amid a colorful floathouse community, with fishing boats docked nearby. **Barb's Fish and Chips** does a roaring trade on a summer day. There are ice cream vendors and kayak rentals, a bang-up marine adventure operator, **Eagle Wing Whale Watching Tours**, and fresh-off-the-boat seafood sales.

The Canadian Coast Guard regional base occupies the once busy deep-sea moorage of the Outer Wharf. The CPR Empress ships berthed here. The No. 6 streetcar — they were called *trams* — turned around here. An immigration centre stood across the street. (If you were Chinese, it was a detention centre.) The Coast Guard's Pacific Region coordinates search and rescue and other vital functions in the Victoria area and serves the needs of the agency's bases along British Columbia's 27,000 km/16,777 mi of coastline.

Further south along the harbour are wide open spaces that were formerly the shipyards of Victoria Machinery Depot (VMD). Founded in 1862, VMD flourished during World War II and into the 1960s, building the first ferryboat for BC Ferries and ten more in years to come. The company folded its tent in 1994. The **Helijet** port is on the site now.

In the shelter of the Ogden Point Breakwater are **cruise ship docks** that are scheduled to handle 240 vessels in 2017, making it the busiest in Canada. The Canadian Pilotage base is nearby. Anytime a passing ship enters Canadian waters, the pilots zip out into the strait in their 1,800-horsepower boats to board and do the paperwork.

The inner façade of the breakwater is animated by the ever-growing **Unity Wall mural**, a project of artists Darlene Gait of the Esquimalt First Nation, and Butch Dick of the Songhees First Nation, with the participation of First Nations youth and support from the Greater Victoria Harbour Authority. The mural can best be seen from the little park near the pilotage dock.

Breakwater Café and Bistro, 199 Dallas Rd, is the only waterfront eatery on the city's south coast. Service is cafeteria style with a liquor license.

East of Ogden Point, via Dallas Road, trails lace the waterfront parks, especially near **Holland Point**. Several flights of steps link the bluffs to interesting beaches; lightness of foot required there.

James Bay has many side streets worth exploring. There are charming blocks of Victorian houses on Oswego, Battery and Toronto streets. Check out the self-guided walking tour online. **James Bay village**, centred on the five-point intersection of Menzies, Simcoe and Toronto streets, has a goodly array of shops and restaurants.

Ogden Point marks the terminus of Victoria's amazing shoreline, 22 km/14 mi of the south and east shores, described in #s 10 Beacon Hill, 14 Ross Bay Cemetery, 15 Gonzales Hill and 16 Oak Bay Waterfront.

Details

- From the Empress Hotel area to Fisherman's Wharf: proceed west along Belleville Street; the road zigs and zags, and directional street signs are posted. Angle right to the walkway beginning west of the Victoria Clipper dock and follow the shore around Laurel Point. Or, catch a harbour ferry from the Causeway Marina dock; access is opposite the Empress Hotel.
- Eagle Wing Whale Watching Tours, Fisherman's Wharf, Victoria; 800-708-9488/250-384-8008; eaglewingtours.com.
- James Bay Heritage Walking Tour in the Victorian neighbourhood around Government St, south of the Parliamentary precinct; map and text at victoriaheritagefoundation.ca.
- Canadian Coast Guard Western Region: ccg-gcc.gc.ca.
- Ogden Point Terminal: gvha.ca.
- Cruise ship schedule: victoriacruise.ca.

10   Emily of Beacon Hill

Beacon Hill is the gentle, southerly prominence in **Beacon Hill Park**, Victoria's 82-ha/203-ac civic pleasure grounds, a short walk southeast of the Inner Harbour. The hill faces the Strait of Juan de Fuca and the Olympic Mountains on the American side. A joke about Victoria's ever-changing weather goes, "If you don't like the weather, wait 15 minutes." That's especially true about the Olympics — they can disappear behind a veil of cloud, only to reappear. On clear days, the mountains are arrayed in splendor and wreathed with clouds lighted from within or shot through with god-rays. They are in a sense "our" mountains, Victoria's ever-familiar, often snowy backdrop.

Remnants of First Nations burial tumuli are visible on Beacon Hill's south slope. The traditional name of the place was *míqan* (MEE can), "warmed by the sun." A Sign of Lekwungen (see #1) stands at the drive-in lookout, and the tumuli, now just piles of rocks, are nearby. A palisaded village stood for hundreds of years on Finlayson Point, directly south of the lookout. Early visitors remarked on a matrix of poles strung with netting, used to catch birds. In spring, the wilder bits of the park are awash with the five-starred indigo blue camas lily.

The name Beacon Hill is a remnant of the early days of European settlement. Beacons were lit in a certain alignment visible from afar to warn ships away from the shallows of Brochie Ledge.

The lines of the mile-long racetrack that used to circle Beacon Hill — a popular gathering place in the early days — are visible in the roadways, Douglas St, Dallas Rd, Camas Circle, Circle Dr, that ring it today.

Outside the ring is the 39-m/128-ft-long pole Mungo Martin (see #5) put up in 1956. The **world's tallest totem pole** — but it's not any more — is well loved. It was taken down in 2000, restored, recarved, repainted and remounted.

Beacon Hill is of wider significance on the cultural plane as part of the home range of the artist and writer **Emily Carr** (1871-1945). Carr's family home was half a kilometre west of here. She was born and lived 18 years on a 4-ha/10-ac property between James Bay and the Dallas Road cliffs. She recounted her more-English-than-the-English early life in *The Book of Small*. Carr was tied to her home turf by temperament and fortune. She would leave only to return.

Carr painted from an early age. Her watercolours of First Nations villages date from her thirties. They did not catch on, at first. Carr grew discouraged and all but gave up art. She built an apartment house on a lot carved out of the family property and, at age 41, settled in there for 23 years to run a rooming house. She called it Hill House, but it has become known as House of All Sorts after the collection of memoirs she published with that name recounting her adventures as a landlady. Carr legendarily painted a thunderbird on an upstairs wall. She put her kitchen chairs on pulleys and would let them down only if you were judged worth a visit.

When she was 56 and had been a rooming-house operator for 15 years, a door opened. She found new motivation, a new style and a new theme for painting. She painted forests. She painted logged-off clearcuts, too — for the sky, the light, the energy, the power.

At length, she moved a few blocks away and, three years later, re-located to the house her sister Alice built where the family's vegetable garden used to be. Her last abode was St Mary's Priory — now the James Bay Inn — a block from the family home.

We can glimpse this small world in the journals Carr kept from 1927 to 1941, edited and published posthumously as *Hundreds and Thousands*. In her later years, Carr often visited Beacon Hill Park to sketch and paint the cliffs, the sea, the Olympic Mountains and the sky. I can see her striding up the tunnels in the brush on the back slope of Beacon Hill — with Koko, Maybbe and Tantrum bounding ahead — to study the light on the strait and, if it's good, make a sketch or a watercolour.

Among the gifts of her art and literature is a vision she laboured to communicate of the indwelling spirit of nature.

Advice to artists from the journal for November 3, 1932:

> *Search for the reality of each object, that is, its real and only beauty; recognize our relationship with all life; say to every animate and in-animate thing 'brother;' be at one with all things, finding the divine in all; when one can do all this, maybe then one can paint. In the meantime one must go steadily on with open mind, courageously alert, waiting always for a lead, constantly watching, constantly praying, meditating much and not worrying.*

Not worrying about, for instance, success? She must have cared. The next lines of the entry are from the poem "Song of the Rolling Earth" by Walt Whitman. It's an exhortation to artists to "pile up the words of the earth!/Work on, age after age, nothing is to be lost." Out rolls this William Blakean prophesy: "When the materials are all prepared and ready, the architects shall appear."

Whitman's poem, faithfully transcribed, composes the triumph of art:

> *I swear to you the architects shall appear without fail,*
> *I swear to you they will understand you and justify you,*
> *The greatest thing among them shall be he who best knows you,*
> *   and encloses all and is faithful to all,*
> *He and the rest shall not forget you, they shall perceive that you are*
> *   not an iota less than they.*

You shall be fully glorified in them.

Glory came, a little, in her lifetime — first for her writing. After her time, it was much more about her painting. Now Carr's circle just widens and widens.

Beacon Hill Park is spacious and diverse, with spectacular displays of flowers in season, a petting zoo for children, a children's playground, a much-used cricket pitch, a remnant Garry oak meadow, ponds and fountains and a bandshell where you can hear concerts on summer afternoons.

A linear waterfront park extends 4.6 km/2.9 mi between Ogden Pt and the east end of Ross Bay, taking in Holland Pt, Finlayson Pt, below Beacon Hill, and **Clover Point**. Everyone and their dog is out there, plus when the wind is up hang-gliders, kite-flyers, wind-surfers and who knows what-all flying machines.

En route or returning, follow your food-finder up Cook St, shaded by spreading chestnut trees, to the **Cook Street Village**. Side streets worth exploring include the neighbourhood east of Cook St and north of Dallas. **Moss St** is famous for its **Saturday market** (seasonal) at Sir James Douglas School, corner Moss and Fairfield Rd, and for its **art walk** on a Saturday in mid-July (see #12).

Details

- About Beacon Hill Park: victoria.ca.
- **Emily Carr House**, 207 Government St, 250-383-5843; emilycarr.com. Emily Carr's birthplace, built 1863; open seasonally; guided tours, occasional events; gift shop.
- Hill House, aka House of All Sorts, Carr's rooming house, is at 217 Simcoe St. It is a suite of private residences not open to the public. Alice Carr's schoolhouse, where Carr lived 1939-41, is just around the corner at 218-220 St Andrews St.
- Carr's written works are published by Douglas & McIntyre (douglas-mcintyre.com). Three classics published in Carr's time: *Klee Wyck* (1941), *The Book of Small* (1942) and *The House of All Sorts* (1944).
- Emily Carr's memoir of her 70th birthday party, on my Oak Bay Chronicles website: oakbaychronicles.ca.
- *From the Forest to the Sea*, the first major European solo exhibition of Emily Carr's work, was mounted at the Dulwich Picture Gallery, London from November 2014 to March 2015, and then at the Art Gallery of Ontario, Toronto: canadianart.ca.
- Fairfield Heritage Walking Tour of the neighbourhood near lower Cook St: victoriaheritagefoundation.ca.

Craigdarroch Castle 11

Craigdarroch Castle is a Victoria landmark, a sandstone apparition of turrets and red tile roofs rising out of the oaks of Rockland, once a posh neighbourhood. It was the city's finest home when completed in 1890 for the Joan and Robert Dunsmuir family. The five-storey, 39-room castle was surrounded by 11 ha/27 ac of gardens and woods. Robert did not live to see it finished, but Joan lived there for 18 years with some of her eight daughters.

Much reduced and after many changes of hands, the Castle now pays its way as a heritage museum with sumptuous architectural details and interesting displays of Dunsmuir family history. The exhibits also reflect the Castle's several institutional uses. It was a convalescent hospital during World War I. During the Great Depression, it was Victoria College. Author Pierre Berton was a notable alumnus. Later it was the Victoria School District office.

During the 1960s, the Castle was the home of the Victoria School (now Conservatory) of Music. There were concerts in the spacious front parlour. I fell in love with string quartets there. At the helm was a team of gifted teachers, Robin Wood and Winnifred Scott Wood. He was from Esquimalt, she from Winnipeg. They met on a ship en route to England. Both were bound for the Royal College of Music to study piano. They were upper-echelon musicians, and they fell in love. They launched a brilliant concert career together, playing duets in the capitals of Europe. Then they gave it all up to take charge of the newly-formed school of music here. The Woods devoted 35 years to building a pillar of community education with some 1,800 students and alumni the likes of pianist Jon Kimura Parker, singer Richard Margison and violinist Timothy Chooi.

The Castle has an outstanding record of public service. Considering it was built as a tycoon's advertisement of wealth, isn't that ironic?

Accolades to the society that has made it a museum. Proceeds go into further restoration work, as for example the painstaking replication of the wallpapers in the 75-foot living room.

Details

- Craigdarroch Castle, 1050 Joan Crescent, Victoria; 250-592-5323; thecastle.ca. Not wheelchair accessible.
- Craigdarroch National Historic Site of Canada: historicplaces.ca.
- Reading: *The Dunsmuir Saga*, by Terry Reksten (Douglas & McIntyre, 1994).
- Victoria Conservatory of Music, 900 Johnson St, Victoria; 250-386-5311; vcm.bc.ca. Alix Goolden Performance Hall, 907 Pandora Ave, has great acoustics.

TAKE 5 *Villages in the City*

Shopping districts away from downtown Victoria, in order of distance.

1. **Cook St Village, between Oscar St and Park Rd.**
Foodie paradise, shaded by spreading chestnut trees, in Fairfield district: **Pizzeria Prima Strada** (pizzeriaprimastrada.com), sensational Neapolitan thin crust pies; **Bubby's Kitchen** (bubbyskitchen.ca), fresh, local, sustainable, green, open all day; **Big Wheel Burger** (bigwheelburger.com) makes the best $5 milkshake in the city, and everything but everything ends up in the composter; **Moka House** (mokahouse.com), locally owned coffee hangout, across from that other one; plus **Pic-a-Flic** (picaflic.net), an outstanding video store.

2. **Fernwood, corner of Fernwood Rd and Gladstone Ave.**
Urbane intersection with thriving cultural life: **Stage Wine Bar** (stagewinebar.com), one of the best restaurants on the island; **Picot** (picotcollective.com), modern handcrafted gifts and goods; **7 Rays New Age Store** (7rays.ca), metaphysical gift shop; two centres of the thespian arts, the well-established mainstream **Belfry Theatre** (belfry.bc.ca) and the brash, inventive **Theatre Inconnu** (theatreinconnu.com).

3. **Oak Bay Ave, between Bank St and Clive Dr.**
Among many shops in this six- block linear village: **Good Things Consignments** (good-things.ca), very good used stuff for cheap; **The Whole Beast Artisan Salumeria** (thewholebeast.ca), the best cured and smoked meats; **Nicholas Randall** (@NicholasRandall.OakBay), top of the line stuff for women; **Ivy's Bookshop** (ivysbookshop.com), Can lit, arts, children's, local interest books in a neighbourhood fixture since the 60s; **Side Street Studio** (sidestreetstudio.com), pottery and other local crafts; **Winchester Galleries** (winchestergalleriesltd.com) and **Ottavio Italian Bakery & Deli** (ottaviovictoria.com), a great pairing, on an eminence; and every 2nd Wed in summer months the avenue is closed to vehicles for the Oak Bay Village Night Market.

4. **Estevan Ave, between Musgrave and Dunlevy aves.**
Nice little shopping-dining area in the Willows neighbourhood of Oak Bay: **Bungalow** (@bungalowvictoria), a home décor gift shop; **Padella Italian Bistro** (padellakitchenandwine.com), fresh and original cooking; **The Village Restaurant** (thevillagerestaurant.ca), casual, friendly, popular.

5. **Cadboro Bay Village, Cadboro Bay Rd, Sinclair-Penrhyn Sts, Saanich.**
Near gorgeous Cadboro Bay beach, this commercial enclave was once a seaside resort. **Gyro Beach Board Shop** (gyrobeachboards.com) for stand-up paddleboarding; **Olive Olio's Pasta & Espresso Bar** in a nicely converted gas station; **Thai Lemongrass Restaurant** (thailemongrass.ca), **Mutsuki-An** Japanese Restaurant (mutsuki-an-restaurant.com).

12 Art Gallery of Greater Victoria

Home of the largest public collection of art in the province — some 19,000 works, including the biggest array of Japanese art in Canada — the Art Gallery of Greater Victoria (AGGV) exhibits them and mounts interesting travelling and special exhibitions in a seven-room gallery attached to one of the city's premier heritage residences.

Two of the exhibition rooms display the amazing Asian collections, while Victoria's iconic 20th-century artist Emily Carr merits a room of her own for the standing exhibition *Emily Carr and the Young Generation*. It's a survey of her life and work that draws on the AGGV's holdings of Carr's art and those of such following artists as Jack Shadbolt, Max Maynard, Ina U. U. Uthoff and Myfawny Pavelic.

One of the AGGV website's several virtual exhibits, *To the Totem Forests: Emily Carr and Contemporaries Interpret Coastal Villages*, recapitulates a 1999 exhibition of paintings of First Nations villages that was accompanied by archival photographs of the subjects and fascinating commentary by First Nations residents of the places. The online searchable database of 12,000 images of the AGGV's huge collection includes just 41 works of Carr's. Some of them — *Big Eagle, Skidegate, B.C.* (1929), *Above the Gravel Pit* (1936), *B.C. Forest* (circa 1938/1939) and *Odds and Ends* (1939) — while not among her most famous works, convey thrillingly Carr's vision of the spirit in nature and Aboriginal art.

Colin Graham, the gallery's founding director (1951-72), also an artist of standing, worked tirelessly to give local and regional artists more exposure. His vision is reflected in the 2017 exhibition *Moving Forward by Looking Back: The First 30 Years of Collecting Art at the AGGV*.

Spencer Mansion, aka Gyppeswyk, aka Llan Derwen, built in 1889, and home of the locally-prominent Spencer family beginning in 1903, was donated by the family in 1951 to establish the Victoria Art Centre, embryo of the AGGV. Today, the mansion's gorgeous paneled front hall and elegant drawing room, hung with paintings by Sophie Pemberton and other artists, embellish its use as a venue for lectures and concerts. Behind Gyppeswyk, in a tiny but charming fragment of the original 2.4-ha/6-ac property, stands an authentic Japanese Shinto shrine, the only such in North America.

The AGGV website includes its substantial e-magazine, a busy events calendar, including lectures and tours, and information about its extensive education and community outreach programs. The annual **TD Bank/ Art Gallery Paint In** draws thousands on a Saturday in July, to stroll the length of Moss St, view (and hopefully buy) the work of dozens of artists and crafters, visit the Moss St Market and join in the organized merriment.

Plans to replace the AGGV's existing exhibition building are at an advanced stage. At time of writing, funding is not in place, so the timetable is uncertain, but at some point, the gallery will close for 18-24 months. The website will keep patrons informed of any changes in accessibility.

Details

- Art Gallery of Greater Victoria, 1040 Moss St, Victoria; 250-384-4171; aggv.ca.
- Parking. Gallery shop. Admission by donation first Tuesday of every month.
- TD Art Gallery Paint-In: aggv.ca/ 30th-annual-td-art-gallery-paint-2017.
- Reading: *The Spencer Mansion: A House, a Home, and an Art Gallery*, by Robert Ratcliffe Taylor (Touchwood Editions, 2012).

Government House Grounds | 13

Government House is a 100-room mansion surrounded by 14.6 hectares/ 36 acres of gardens and woodlands in the Rockland district of Victoria. It is the residence of the Lieutenant-Governor (LG) of British Columbia. Parts of the mansion are open to visitors in occasional guided group tours. The grounds, however, are open during daylight hours. And what a piece of heaven they are: a magnificent, free public resource, a leisurely half-hour walk from downtown Victoria.

Informative plaques scattered around the grounds tell the story of BC's governors and their several houses. The post of governor has evolved from the dictatorship of a tiny colony, appointed from England, to a parliamentary figurehead appointed for five years by the Prime Minister of Canada. The LG is the Queen's Representative in BC and our head of state. (Canada's *Constitution Act* says nothing of the real decision-makers — the province's *premier* and her or his *ministers* — but rather of the *Lieutenant-Governor-in-Council*.) British Columbia's LGs have typically been chosen from the province's business élite. The 29th incumbent, the Honourable Judith Guichon, is a cattle rancher from a pioneer family in the Nicola Valley in BC's southern interior. During sessions of the legislature, the LG makes many short journeys to the Parliament Buildings (#2) to open and close the sessions, read the Throne Speech (written by the premier) and sign bills into law.

The front and sides of Government House grounds comprise 5.7 ha/14 ac of duck ponds, rockeries, rose gardens, herb gardens, cut flower gardens, amazing borders of perennials shaded by graceful walnut and tulip trees along the front wall. Spacious front lawns are edged by Douglas firs. There is a field with a bandshell, a nursery, pathways and benches.

The LG's informative website has an interactive map detailing the many contributions to the dazzling botanical arrays by citizens, horticultural groups and lieutenants-governor.

One of my favorite spots is the Sunken Garden, overlooking serpentine Lotbinière Ave with its rockery walls and a lovely Garry oak meadow below.

Government House stands near the edge of a rocky escarpment with one of the best views in town, overlooking the seaside suburb of Fairfield and the Strait of Juan de Fuca. There are some charming grassy spots. To sit on a rocky knoll amid the dwarf Garry oaks is very Vancouver Island.

Below the escarpment is nearly 9 ha/22 ac of Garry oak woodland with pathways and interpretive signs. It is ecologically significant as the closest thing to an intact Garry oak ecosystem in the city.

Most inspiring to me is the small army of volunteer gardeners in the Friends of Government House Gardens Society. The group was formed in the 1990s to restore the gardens after a period of government belt-tightening and neglect. Under the care of its 400 plus members, the gardens are flourishing.

Thanks to recent restoration of the buildings on the southeast side of the grounds, you can get a bite to eat at the Tea Room. It's the only eatery in Rockland, I believe.

Details

■ Government House, 1401 Rockland Ave, Victoria: ltgov.bc.ca. The Tea Room (open May-Sept) is in the Cary Castle Mews, where there's also an Interpretive Centre, Costume Museum and Heraldry Exhibit. Public toilets are nearby. Tours of Government House start at 9:30 and 11:00 am one Saturday a month, on a first-come-first serve basis. Consult the website for dates.

 ## Ross Bay Cemetery

The shady 11-ha/27-ac Ross Bay Cemetery in the waterfront suburb of Fairfield is the resting place of James Douglas, Emily Carr and a who's who of Victorians. It is one of the most interesting and well-loved landscapes in the city.

Ross Bay Cemetery was established in 1872 on land purchased from Isabella Mainville Ross (1808-1885). The Bay and the cemetery were named for Mrs Ross, a Métis from Lac la Pluie in what is now Ontario. At the age of 14, she married Charles Ross of the Hudson's Bay Company. She birthed ten children and raised them all to adulthood, alone. When she bought farmland on nearby Fowl (Foul) Bay in 1853, she became the first woman to own land in British Columbia.

The chronology is important because, in times past, the places named Ross were assumed to memorialize her husband. But no, the Rosses came to Fort Victoria in 1843. Charles, a Hudson's Bay Company chief trader from Scotland, was in charge of building the fort. In June 1844, he had an attack of appendicitis and died. Ross Bay is a landform bordering Fowl Bay Farm, which belonged to Mrs Ross, and Ross Bay was named for her, end of story. At the cemetery named after her, Mrs Ross was long in her grave — an unmarked grave — when in 1994 the Old Cemeteries Society of Victoria put up a memorial to her.

Among many fascinating gravestones at Ross Bay, my nominee for the one bearing the most interesting inscription is John Dean's:

*IT IS A ROTTEN WORLD, ^ARTFUL POLITICIANS ARE ITS BANE^*
IT'S SAVING GRACE IS THE ARTLESSNESS OF THE YOUNG
AND THE WONDERS OF THE SKY.

Even with a comma splice, a spelling error and an afterthought chiseled into the stone with a carat (^), Dean's epitaph makes a powerful statement. When it was finished, and the gravestone set in place at Ross Bay Cemetery, Dean posed beside it. At 86, he still had a few years left to practice his eccentricities.

A native of England, John Dean (1850-1943) arrived in Victoria in 1884 and worked as a carpenter before rambling around the province. He was a confirmed bachelor and inveterate traveler. He was a some-time politician, elected mayor of Rossland, BC in 1903-04. He returned to Victoria and took up real estate, operating out of his room at the New England Hotel before moving into a house he had built in Esquimalt in 1922/23. His many candidacies in local elections came to nothing. Dean is best known for a park bearing his name on the slopes of Mt Newton in North Saanich. He bought 32 ha/80 ac of mostly old-growth forest there and built a handsome log cabin he named *Illahie*, where he stayed in the summer. He donated the land to the Province in 1921. Some neighbours followed suit, and **John Dean Provincial Park** now protects 174 ha/430 ac of forests. The park is embellished with WWII-era steps and other stonework.

Sad to say, the burial ground has suffered greatly at the hands of vandals. The City hauled many a smashed gravestone and monument to the landfill before the Old Cemeteries Society was formed in the 1980s to draw attention to the cemetery's extraordinary heritage value and take steps to halt the destruction. Part of the strategy is to maintain a presence. The society now sponsors regular Sunday afternoon tours in the more than twenty cemeteries in greater Victoria.

South across Dallas Rd is Ross Bay. From the causeway, behold the altered beach. Groins and tonnes of gravel have been added to retard erosion by hard-hitting seas. The views across the Strait of Juan de Fuca to the Olympic Mountains are sublime. An exquisite pebble beach is beyond the steps at the east end of the bay. To the west is a long causeway and **Clover Point**. A bit inland and west of the cemetery is **Moss Rock**, a gem of an outcrop with vistas of Victoria's south coast.

Details

- Ross Bay Cemetery, 1516 Fairfield Rd, Victoria: victoria.ca (includes a search engine of residents).
- A shopping centre across Fairfield Rd has every convenience.
- Old Cemeteries Society of Victoria website (oldcem.bc.ca) provides historical information and a schedule of its guided tours of Victoria's cemeteries; also a map and self-guiding tour of Ross Bay Cemetery, and instructions for finding graves.
- Isabella Mainville Ross's grave is at C 9 E 22 – section C, row 9, column 22 east.
- John Dean's grave is A 39/40 W 31 – section A, between or straddling rows 39 and 40, column 31 west.
- A useful *Historic Guide to Ross Bay Cemetery*, by John Adams (Sono Nis Press, rev ed 1998) has maps that locate permanent residents of note; out of print; copies can be found in the Greater Victoria Public Library (gvpl.ca).
- John Dean Provincial Park, maps, directions: env.gov.bc.ca. You can drive almost to the top of Mt Newton.
- Jarrett Teague has self-published three devotional books about John Dean and his park: *Blessings in Plenty from John Dean: A Life and Park History: John Dean Provincial Park, Vancouver Island*, (1998), *Sacred Heart: John Dean Provincial Park: History - Photographs – Trails*, (2004) and *John Dean's Cabin Diary: Illahie, Mount Newton 1895 & 1906-1937* (2009).
- Moss Rock: Trails up the south face from May St (a bit of scrambling involved); or enter the park via Masters Rd, off Fairfield Rd.

Gonzales Hill 15

Gonzales Hill is a rocky ridge that rises 66 m/217 ft above sea level and extends about 600 m/1,300 ft along Victoria's south coast, overlooking the Strait of Juan Fuca. To the west, the ridge looms over Gonzales Bay (Foul Bay) and to the east, over McNeill Bay (Shoal Bay). Even tamed into a suburb, Gonzales Hill is an elemental place. The landscape and its setting are of unrivalled beauty. The hill and the point have terrific energy. The overused adjective *breathtaking* applies here, buffeted as it is by winds off the strait. The whole area is eminently walkable. Little lanes run up the north side and along the ridge. (The steep pathways up the south side require some fitness and surefootedness.)

The white meteorological **observatory** is a prominent landmark high on the rocks at the west end of Gonzales Hill. Built in 1914, it was the city's weather station for decades. Today, a 1.8-ha/4.4-ac park surrounds it. For a bird's-eye views of Gonzales Bay and the charming neighbourhood, make your way through a clump of shore pines on the west side of the building and onto the rocks.

At the east end of the ridge is rugged 2 ha/5 ac **Walbran Park**, with little Garry oaks, arbutus and Douglas fir. At the foot of the steps to a cairn is a large bronze **plaque** with a remarkably detailed historical sketch of the exploration of Juan de Fuca Strait. The park commemorates Captain John Walbran, author of *British Columbia Coast Names*, first published in 1909 and still in print.

Across the road is a **lookout** dating from World War II, with 360-degree views, the best on Victoria's south coast, taking in King George Terrace, Harling Point and the Trial Islands 1 km/0.6 mi offshore, much of south Oak Bay district, the varied distant landscapes of Haro Strait to the east and north, and the beginnings of the Vancouver Island mountains to the west.

King George Terrace is the roadway that links the waterfront drives to west and east. The parking pullout is one of the city's favorite spots to show visitors the splendid views of Juan de Fuca Strait.

A granite **cairn** here and others around Oak Bay commemorate First Nations names, occupations and use of resources. Each cairn has a bronze graphic designed and cast by Charles Elliott (Temoseng) of the Tsartlip Nation. The cairn on King George Terrace commemorates the ancient village of *Chikawich* on McNeill Bay.

Harling Point is a flat apron of land accessible by Crescent Road and a path down from King George Terrace. There's a cairn identifying *Sahsima*, a large granitic rock at tideline, the subject of the Salish legend Boss of the Seals.

A stroll through the historic waterfront **Chinese Cemetery**, with its ceremonial altar, is highly recommended. The cemetery was established in 1903 and closed to burials in 1950. Informative plaques tell the fascinating story of Victoria's Chinese settlers, their beliefs and burial practices.

Here, the very rocks have stories to tell. Just 20,000 years ago, the whole area visible from here was covered in ice. Within about 5,000 years, the ice was north of Gonzales Hill and melting fast. I delight to imagine the passing of that glacier — the grinding and scraping, the waters pouring out. Along the shore of Harling Point, just below the Chinese Cemetery, there are *gneisses* — metamorphosed rock — smooth as a Michelangelo statue and creased like your best pants. The ice did that. Within another 1,000 years, Gonzales Hill and most of Victoria was under water. A thousand years later, the hill was a tiny peninsula with a forest of pines and alders. The whole of Vancouver Island rose, as the weight of ice disappeared. By 10,000 years ago, the shoreline was south of Trial Islands and the land swathed in Douglas fir grassland. The dynamic flow of mass between land and sea stabilized at the present level about 6000 years ago.

Gonzales Hill is surrounded on all sides by residential enclaves pleasant to explore. Among interesting nearby excursions:

- A giant ancient **Garry oak tree** near the foot of Falkland Rd.
- **Abkhazi Garden**, with spectacular shows of rhododendron in spring and a delightfully-situated Tea House that serves light meals.
- **Foul Bay Spine**, Foul Bay Rd north to Oak Bay Ave. Once a place to advertise one's prosperity; mansions behind stone walls and show gardens had names (Mountjoy, Tor Lodge, Blair Gowrie, Ince, Foreen, Kildonan), and many were designed by prestigious Victoria architect Samuel Maclure.

Details

- Gonzales Hill Regional Park: crd.bc.ca. Downloadable map with directions. There's a parking lot off Denison Rd.
- Trails on Gonzales Hill include, on the south side, from the parking area on King George Terr down to Harling Point; from an unnamed lane between 80 and 100 King George Terr up to the Lookout (challenging); on the west side, from Barkley Terr up to the observatory; on the east side, a long flight of stairs near the Lookout down to King George Terr.
- Chinese Cemetery National Historic Site: historicplaces.ca.
- Reading: "The Chinese Cemetery in Victoria", by David Chuenyan Lai, a scholarly 1987 *BC Studies* journal article in pdf: ojs.library.ubc.ca.
- Geoscape Victoria, a geology graphic with maps showing the progress of deglaciation; downloadable at geogratis.gc.ca.
- Guide to the First Nations Monuments of Oak Bay: smartphone app at iTunes/App Store.
- Abkhazi Garden, 1964 Fairfield Rd; hours, directions: conservancy.bc.ca.

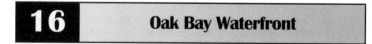

| **16** | **Oak Bay Waterfront** |

The District of Oak Bay is a well-to-do suburb on Victoria's east side with some 12 km/7.5 mi of highly scenic coastline. The walking is delightful, and the views across the straits of Juan de Fuca and Haro are stupendous. This summary of waterfront highlights starts near Gonzales Hill (#15), proceeding east and north along Beach Drive.

McNeill (Shoal) Bay has tidepools in the rocks at its west end. A rocky/pebbly beach extends west to a headland and Kitty Islet, where Adirondack chairs have been anonymously donated for viewing the scenery. Beside the Chikawich First Nations monument (see #15), steps lead down to a two-sided beach providing access to the islet. The

Chikawich family group once had a village on McNeill Bay.

One block inland, on St Patrick St at Central Ave, are a nice grocery store, and **de'lish**, a popular deli and bakery with outdoor seating in a toney residential area.

Anderson Hill is the setting of a charming 2.8-ha/6.9-ac municipal park overlooking McMicking Point and Trial Islands. It can be approached from the north via Island Road, between Central Ave and Newport Ave, from the west via a pathway on Transit Rd, and from the south by a steep path at the top of an alley just east of 500 Beach Dr.

Rocky **McMicking Point** is one of Oak Bay's hidden, little-visited gems, where a bench made of driftwood overlooks Enterprise Channel. The area has great energy when the tide is running and is a good birding spot. It's accessible by way of a trail that begins near the end of Radcliffe Lane, off Hood Lane (just east of 629 Beach Dr), and winds through prickly Scotch gorse. There's a gorgeous pebble beach beyond the end of Radcliffe Lane.

Trial Islands, not far offshore, are the site of a lighthouse and residence built in 1906 to warn ships of the treacherous waters that have landed many a vessel on its shores. The larger island is an ecological reserve established to protect "the most outstanding known assemblage of rare and endangered plant species in British Columbia." Ecological reserves are set aside for science and education. Most are open to the public for no-impact hiking, birding and photography. BC Parks requires visitors to get permission before visiting these islands.

The impossibly scenic **Oak Bay golf links**, known formally as the Victoria Golf Club, was established in 1893, which makes it the "oldest 18-hole golf course in Canada in its original location, and second oldest in North America." *Daily Times* publisher Stuart Keate pronounced the view south from the third green, looking past Trial Islands and the Strait of Juan de Fuca to the Olympic Mountains, his favorite in all the world.

Rugged **Gonzales Point**, adjacent to the 9th tee on the golf links, is of significance to First Nations, whose traditional name for it was *Kukeeluk*, meaning "place of war." The point acquired its present name for the pilot of a Spanish vessel that explored the Victoria coastline in 1790, and it figures prominently on their maps. While the golf course is private property, the owners tolerate public use outside golfing hours. The last time I visited Gonzales Point, a pod of Orca whales swam by just offshore.

Judges' Row is an enclave of stately mansions on Beach Dr. On the boulevard, just south of the entrance to the golf club, stands a **treaty tree** — an old oak that was obviously bent when young, so that it has grown crooked, to memorialize some agreement between First Nations. A plaque memorializes one-time neighbour Gordon M. Sloan, politician and judge best known for his role in creating BC's system of forest management licenses.

The **Oak Bay Beach Hotel** is a recently rebuilt waterfront resort that welcomes casual visitors. The back deck and gardens face east across island-strewn Haro Strait to the Cascade Range, with the snow cone of Mt Baker a glorious view some 115 km/72 mi east.

Visible about 1.7 km/1 mi offshore are Chain Islet and an archipelago of rocks with large gull and cormorant nesting populations. (Protected in the Oak Bay Islands Ecological Reserve, they require permission to visit.) Eastward 3.25 km/2 mi lie the larger, conifer-covered **Discovery Islands**. **Discovery Island Marine Park** spans 2 km/1.2 mi of the island's interesting south coast. There are good campsites in open meadows, but few facilities. The lighthouse at East Point dates from 1886.

The west half of Discovery Island and the two **Chatham Islands** belong to the Songhees First Nation. A village on Discovery Island became a sanctuary from the 1862 smallpox epidemic. It and a settlement on Chatham were populated into the 1960s. The Songhees Nation has closed these islands to visitors.

Oak Bay Marina has a restaurant and coffee house, boat services and rentals and the most scenic parking lot in the city. Overlooking the marina, is grassy Queen Elizabeth Park, with interesting rocks and a pebble beach.

Jimmy Chicken Island, just north of the marina is protected as a municipal park. It has a beautiful little beach edged with outcrops of polished gneisses, and a 360° panorama from its rocky eminence — a good place to watch bald eagles and land-otters. Jimmy Chickens and his wife Jenny were First Nations people who lived on the island before 1900 and legendarily sold seafood and crafted goods door to door. Places here tend to have at least two names. The island's legal name is Mary Tod. Its old Salish name was *Kohweechella*, "where there are many fish." Regrettably, that is no longer the case.

The **Oak Bay Village** shopping district is a short walk west of Beach Drive via Windsor Rd and Newport Ave or a laneway at the east end of Oak Bay Ave. Signs point the way.

Rounding the south shore of Oak Bay proper and proceeding along a causeway, one comes to delightful little **Haynes Park** in a waterfront setting with beach access on two sides.

Glenlyon-Norfolk School, 1723 Beach Dr, was built in 1898 by Francis Rattenbury (see #4) to be the family home.

Scenic **Willows Beach** has a vibrant summertime scene and is much visited year-round. Willows Park has a tea room, toilets and changing rooms and parking. At either end of the sandy beach, it gets rocky. Bald eagles sometimes nest in a tall tree just above the rocks at the south end. You might see a leathery old land-otter on the rocks near Cattle Point.

The nearby **Estevan Ave** commercial block has several good places to eat. Just around the corner at 2564 Heron St is the longest-occupied house in Western Canada and the second oldest building in Victoria. Built in 1851, **Tod House** is still at its original site on a charming property that retains the feel of a farm amid the suburban streets. It's privately owned and occupied, so not accessible.

At the rocky tip of **Cattle Point**, you are close to the lively waters of Baynes Channel. The Cattle Point boat ramp is popular with smokers (i.e, the motorized).

The rocky Garry oak woodland in 31 ha/76 ac **Uplands Park** gives a sense of the distinctive original ecosystem of the drier parts of the island. Entrance, signs and displays on Beach Drive are opposite the trail from Willows Beach.

The Uplands is a park-like subdivision begun in 1907, with sprawling mansions set on winding roads. Three sets of gates (really just pillars) mark the entrances. The northernmost is at Beach Dr and Cadboro Bay Rd.

The intrepid walker can continue down the hill into **Cadboro Bay village**, where there's a gorgeous beach. Beyond that lies **Ten Mile Point**, a rustic enclave of waterfront estates with an inland network of paths.

Details

■ Oak Bay Walking Map and Oak Bay Community Green Map: oakbay.ca.

■ de'lish Fine Foods and Catering, 677 St Patrick St, Oak Bay; 250-598-5614; delishcateringoakbay.ca.

■ Oak Bay Beach Hotel, 1175 Beach Dr, Oak Bay; 1-800-668-7758; oakbaybeachhotel.com; restaurant, café, pub, spa, weekly movie nights.

■ Oak Bay Marina, 1327 Beach Dr; oakbaymarina.com.

■ Padella Kitchen, 2524 Estevan Ave; 250-592-7424, padellakitchenandwine.com; esteemed as a prix-fixe Italian restaurant.

■ Discovery Island Marine Provincial Park, Oak Bay Islands, Trial Islands, Ten Mile Point ecological reserves: env.gov.bc.ca.

■ Friends of Ecological Reserves: ecoreserves.bc.ca.

■ Discovery Island Lighthouse: discoveryisland.ca.

■ Ocean River Sports offers guided kayak tours of Oak Bay and overnight camping trips to Discovery Island Marine Park: oceanriver.com.

■ A word to the wise: while the waters around Oak Bay are popular with kayakers and other boaters, tidal currents and rising winds can be extremely challenging, especially to the self-propelled. Adequate safety equipment and knowledge are a must. Once in the water (typical temperature: 8ºC/46ºF), a boater has about an hour before hypothermia claims another victim. For starters, check out the University of Victoria's Human Powered Vessel Safety Checklist at uvic.ca.

Point Ellice House 17

Victoria's wealth of heritage buildings is unrivalled in Western Canada. A shining jewel in this crown is Point Ellice House, a residence that uniquely displays the furnishings, fixtures, accoutrements and personal effects of the period 1890-1920, amid a cocoon of restored Victorian

TAKE 5 *Oldest Heritage Buildings*

1. **St Ann's schoolhouse**, Victoria, built c. 1844; moved from original location to Elliott St Square, east side of Royal BC Museum; open to the public.

2. **Tod House**, 2564 Heron St, Oak Bay, 1851; believed the oldest house in Western Canada still standing in its original location, although much altered; private home, not open to the public.

3. **Helmcken House**, Elliott St Square, Victoria, 1852; Dr John Sebastian Helmcken family home, in original location, with two additions, originally next door to Governor James Douglas, his father-in-law; operated as a family museum; park setting.

4. **Craigflower Farmhouse**, 1801 Admirals Rd, View Royal, 1853; built by farm servants of the Hudson's Bay Company; not open to the public.

5. **The Bastion**, 94 Front St, Nanaimo, 1853; built by the Hudson's Bay Company to fortify the young mining town; moved from original location and rebuilt (#48).

Others open to the public:

- **Fisgard Lighthouse**, Ocean Blvd, Colwood, 1860; first lighthouse in BC (#18), originally manned, now automatic; two floors of exhibits; spectacular setting.
- **Point Ellice House**, 2616 Pleasant St, Victoria, 1861; uniquely intact late-Victoria O'Reilly family home (#17).
- **Congregation Emanu-El**, 1461 Blanshard St, Victoria, 1863; oldest continuously active synagogue in Canada and western North America; congregationemanuel.ca.
- **Emily Carr House and Garden**, 207 Government St, Victoria, 1863; birthplace of the artist (see #10); home of Richard Carr family; museum, occasional enactments; emilycarr.com.
- **Wentworth Villa**, 1152 Fort St, Victoria, about 1863; restored Ella family home; architectural heritage museum, performance space; wentworthvilla.com.
- **Ross Bay Villa**, 1490 Fairfield Rd, Victoria, 1865; restored Roscoe family home; Saturday tours; rossbayvilla.org.

gardens. Point Ellice House is incongruously located in an industrial zone near the Bay St Bridge, but the riches that await the visitor make it well worth the excursion. You can travel the world over and not find another place where an entire late-Victorian household has been preserved intact.

For preserving the character of Point Ellice House, credit the family that lived in the 1861 Italianate bungalow for more than a century. Originally part of Hudson's Bay Company chief factor John Work's Hillside Farm, Point Ellice House was purchased in 1867 by the O'Reilly family. Peter O'Reilly was, among many other official functions, a gold commissioner. In the rowdy mining communities of early BC, he had the powers of a judge. O'Reilly married Caroline Trutch, a sister of BC's first Lieutenant Governor, and their home was a gathering place for the governing élite. Canada's prime minister, Sir John A. Macdonald, dined at Point Ellice House while on his western swing in the summer of 1886 (see #27). The O'Reilly's daughter Kathleen lived in the house her entire life (1867-1945), during which time the neighbourhood slowly morphed from a fashionable residential enclave into the site of sawmills and, more recently, a metals scrapyard.

Thanks to the efforts of descendants and the provincial heritage authority, the property was preserved and restored. Point Ellice House is in the hands of a society that engages volunteer staff to conduct tours. Among the highlights are the meticulously-restored dining room and the drawing room, whose massed artefacts are guaranteed to amaze.

Also worthwhile is a visit to the Point Ellice House website to take a virtual tour of the O'Reilly family's possessions. Samples of the family's collection of photographs and an interesting essay are also on view.

Details

- Point Ellice House, 2616 Pleasant St, Victoria; 250-380-6506; pointellicehouse.com; Thurs-Mon, May-Sept; audioguides available.
- Point Ellice House/O'Reilly House National Historic Site of Canada: historicplaces.ca.
- The Harbour Ferry stops at Point Ellice House; $10 one way from the Empress Dock — easily the best way to approach it: victoriaharbourferry.com.
- Two dining spots around the corner from Point Ellice House: **Saltchuck Pie Company**, 360 Bay St; saltchuckpies.com (closes at 6 pm most days); and **Moon Under Water Brewpub**, 350B Bay, moonunderwater.ca, with local fare and award-winning suds.

18 — Fisgard Light and Esquimalt Harbour

British Columbia's first lighthouse, built 1860, stands at the entrance to Esquimalt Harbour, marking the rocks on the west shore. Accessible by land, Fisgard is the only functioning west coast lighthouse open to the public. Situated on a photogenic rocky islet, Fisgard Light has a spectacular prospect of the straits and approaches to Esquimalt Harbour.

The former lightkeeper's house has handsome exhibits of the technology of the day. The light was automated in 1929, when an electric light replaced an acetylene flame.

Directly opposite the harbourmouth is Duntze Head, named after Captain John Duntze, master HM frigate *Fisgard*, 42 guns. *Fisgard* and other Royal Navy warships called in there during the first years of Fort Victoria.

Esquimalt Harbour is spacious and deep with a defensible entrance, and as a result, the Royal Navy established a presence here. Their presence helped dull the American appetite for ever more land. The 1844 American election slogan "54-40 or fight" summarized the US claim to possess the entire northwest coast to Alaska (54º40' N latitude). More than 40 warships and gunboats were stationed here during the first decades of the colony.

The Fisgard light was the first permanent construction in the naval precinct. By 1864, a functioning naval yard was established in the lee of Duntze Head. It became the Royal Navy's Pacific Station — squadron headquarters — in 1865. Today, it is still known as HMC Dockyard, and it is the heart of **Canadian Forces Base Esquimalt**.

On the south side of Duntze Head, a well-cultivated waterfront property surrounds the 1885 red brick Admiral's House. A number of heritage buildings from that period survive in Dockyard.

By BC's terms of union, Canada agreed to build a drydock in Esquimalt Harbour. After much delay, it was completed in 1887. The drydock was of vital use for Royal Navy vessels in the North Pacific. It was used until a much larger drydock was built across the harbour in the 1920s.

The harbour's strategic value increased with the establishment of an Admiralty coaling station — the only one in the eastern Pacific — supplied by Nanaimo coal.

Pacific Station became a likely target for seizure by foreign navies. In 1877, England and Russia were rattling sabres. Russia's Pacific naval base at Vladivostok was heavily armed. The war scare resulted in construction of the first shoreline batteries of heavy guns along the Victoria waterfront.

Fort Rodd Hill, constructed in the 1890s above Fisgard Light at the entrance of the harbour, was the culminating fortification. The battery was in service until the 1950s. During World War II, it was the head-quarters of an elaborate system of sea-lane surveillance, with lookouts posted on prominences from East Sooke to Oak Bay.

The Royal Navy maintained the Esquimalt base until 1905. A five-year hiatus ensued before the Canadian Navy took possession in 1910. In 2010, CFB Esquimalt celebrated the base's centenary, and Fisgard Light marked 150 years of service. They stand on guard for the community their presence did much to shape.

Details

- Fisgard Lighthouse National Historic Site: fisgardlighthouse.com.
- Fort Rodd Hill National Historic Site: fortroddhill.com.
- Entrance to both is via Ocean Blvd, Colwood.

TAKE 5 *Canada's Warmest Places*

Victoria weather researcher Steven Murray used a database of Environment *Canada's Canadian Climate Normals and Averages, 1981-2010*, to assemble the following data. A simpler version is on that agency's website climate.weather.gc.ca. Steven keeps the *Victoria Weather and Climate* blog (victoriaweatherandclimate.blogspot.ca).

Weather stations on the islands with the highest annual mean temperature averaged over 30 years 1981-2010

	° Celsius	° Fahrenheit
1. **University of Victoria**	11.14	52.05
2. **Chemainus**	11.09	51.96
3. **St Mary Lake, Salt Spring Island**	10.67	51.21
4. **Esquimalt Harbour**	10.66	51.19
5. **Gonzales Observatory, Victoria**	10.65	51.17

Close behind: Galiano Island North, 10.64°C; William Head, Metchosin, 10.45°C; Saanichton CDA, 10.31°C; Mayne Id, Nootka Island, Lighthouse, Saturna Island, Capmon, all 10.2°C; Nanaimo Airport 10.1°C; Victoria Airport 10.0°C.

The University of Victoria station's average annual mean temperature of 11.14°C turns out to be the highest in Canada; Delta Tsawwassen Beach, south of Vancouver, had the second highest, 11.10°C; and Chemainus, on the southeast coast of Vancouver Island, just a shade lower at 11.09°C.

What's it like in the zone of Canada's highest average annual temperatures? There's plenty of sunshine, especially in summer; moderate temperatures year round; a long frost-free season; moderate precipitation, with little snowfall. The wind blows off the ocean in all seasons.

- **CFB Esquimalt Naval and Military Museum**, Naden (accessible via Admirals Rd, Esquimalt): navalandmilitarymuseum.org.
- Royal Canadian Navy's Maritime Forces Pacific (MARPAC) overview: navy-marine.forces.gc.ca.

Galloping Goose and Lochside Trails · 19

The Galloping Goose and Lochside Regional Trails are among Victoria's best-loved amenities. The low grades and smooth roadbeds of our linear parks are a great gift from the past.

Four railways once served Victoria. Three didn't survive, and the fourth, the Esquimalt & Nanaimo Railway (E&N), is on the ropes. Along the way, one railbed became Interurban Road, two have been recycled as multi-use trails, and parts of the E&N right-of-way are now half railroad, half trail.

The 29 km/18 mi **Lochside Trail** follows old railbeds between Victoria and North Saanich en route to BC Ferries' Swartz Bay terminal.

On the way (Km 5), it passes the delightful **Swan Lake Christmas Hill Nature Sanctuary**. This 58 ha/143 ac urban preserve, a Saanich municipal park, is in two parts. Swan Lake (48 ha/119 ac) is an eutrophying lake — filling in with vegetation. It's pretty much the domain of the feathered and the furry. The Swan Lake nature house has regular programs for kids. Across busy Mackenzie Av are delightfully fashioned walkways and stairs to the rocky summit of Christmas Hill, with 360° views of the city's north side.

The **Galloping Goose** uses 55 km/37 mi of mostly railbed on a line that ran west to Sooke and north to Cowichan Lake. The original Galloping Goose was a self-propelled railcar that provided daily passenger service between Victoria, Milnes Landing (Sooke), West Shawnigan Lake and Cowichan Lake, 1924-31.

For a longer biking day trip passing through increasingly rural landscapes, we would choose from two rides on The Goose.

The nearer route begins at Atkins Rd and winds through Victoria's Western Communities en route to Sooke. We drive (or bus) to the Atkins Road parking lot, near Km 10, in Colwood, to avoid the haul from downtown and a stretch along Highway 1. A friendlier route to the Atkins Rd launch is under construction — the **E&N Rail Trail** between downtown Victoria and Langford. It has recently been extended to Esquimalt Rd but remains stopped at the Songhees reserve in View Royal.

Metchosin is particularly scenic, with small farms and four exquisite regional parks at **Witty's Lagoon**, **Devonian Beach**, **Matheson Lake** and **Roche Cove**. Round trip Atkins Rd to Roche Cove: 50 km/31 mi.

The farther route begins near Roche Cove. Drive or bus the Sooke

Road to Gillespie Road. West from Roche Cove (Km 35) the trail follows Sooke Harbour, then climbs into the Sooke Hills, past the **Sooke Potholes** (Km 48) (#24) to the terminus at **Leechtown** (Km 55). There are long inclines and some challenging crossings. Round trip is 40 km/25 mi.

Leechtown is a mélange of forest, brush and open meadow at the juncture of the Sooke and Leech rivers. Besides an old plaque and a display, there's not much left of the railroad, or the 1864 Leechtown gold rush towns, or the logging operations of the Kapoor family and other Sikh immigrants. When logging began hereabouts in the 1920s, operators typically bought the land they intended to log. Fast forward to 1999. The Capital Regional District (CRD) was looking to provide a buffer around the Sooke Lake reservoir, where Victoria gets most of its drinking water. The CRD acquired 1,300 ha/3,212 ac of Kapoor lands through a land swap. The Kapoor family also donated 13 ha/32 ac of land at Leechtown, between the railbed and the Sooke River, for a Capital Region District park.

Details

- Capital Regional Parks' website (crd.bc.ca/parks) has maps, directions and descriptions of the Lochside, Galloping Goose and E&N rail trails, Kapoor Regional Park and parks in Metchosin.
- Swan Lake Christmas Hill Nature Sanctuary: swanlake.bc.ca. No biking or dogs allowed.
- Leechtown was named for Lieut. Peter Leech, second-in-command in Robert Brown's 1864 exploring party. Brown's 28-page narrative, *Vancouver Island: Exploration, 1864*, published the following year, can be acquired at archive.org.

 The Butchart Gardens

In Victoria, City of Gardens, The Butchart Gardens is the centerpiece — indeed, the very icon of southeastern Vancouver Island, a place abounding in beautiful sights in a salubrious environment where flowers flourish. The 22 ha/55 ac Butchart family's show gardens, on a 53-ha/130-ac estate near Brentwood Bay, 23 km/14 mi north of downtown Victoria, include the signature Sunken Garden (a spectacularly reclaimed limestone quarry) and Japanese, Rose, Italian and Mediterranean gardens (featuring plantings native to places with a so-called *Mediterranean* climate). There are thousands of species of flowers, shrubs and trees, presented in season, amid spacious lawns, fountains, bronze statues, hanging flower baskets and many amenities.

Like most Victorians, I have been to The Gardens many times, in all seasons, in daylight and at dusk. It's one of the first places you take out-of-town visitors. At Christmas time, you go towards dusk to see the extensive lighting. Pressed to name a favorite spot, I would choose the Rose Garden in mid-summer. It's beautifully sited on a slope overlooking the Butchart family home, *Benvenuto*, with benches near a curious spherical mirror, the so-called Gazing Ball, all surrounded by a profusion of *rosaceae* of every description.

The story of Mrs Butchart's Sunken Garden smacks of myth or fairy tale or some green *Book of Genesis*. The Butchart family was prominent in the cement business. Robert Butchart was working in his father's hardware store in Owen Sound, Ontario when he met Jennie Kennedy. After they married, Robert joined a local manufacturing business that produced Canada's first portland cement.

In 1902, he visited Victoria to check out deposits of limestone and clay at Tod Inlet. They were of high quality and located right next to tidewater. The Butcharts moved from Ontario and built a handsome residence, *Benvenuto*, in 1904, a stone's throw from the cement plant and port. Cement manufacture is not the cleanest operation in town. Huge amounts of energy had to be generated by burning gasified coal — plentiful on Vancouver Island — to raise the temperature of rotating cylindrical kilns to 1,482°C/2,700°F and fuse the ingredients (lime, sand, gypsum and water) into *clinkers*, which were then ground up to produce powdery cement. Then the limestone ran out, and soon after the Great War the cement plant closed.

Tod Inlet, where a community of workers and their families had grown up, slowly returned to nature … and Jennie Butchart got busy. She had already engaged the noted landscape artist Isaburo Kishida to design the Japanese Garden. The Rose and Italian gardens followed. After the limestone quarry was exhausted she set to work landscaping it. I love the image of the dauntless Mrs Butchart suspended in a bosun's chair, stuffing ferns into cavities along the sheer sidewalls of the quarry. As word spread about their marvelous creation, the Butcharts started serving tea and sundry to all. Soon, The Gardens attracted 50,000 visitors a year, while Mrs Butchart ran a flourishing mail-order seed business. A newspaper clip from 1920:

> *Ex-Mayor Baker, of Prince Albert and Mrs. Baker are very much impressed with Butchart's Gardens.*
> *They have visited Mr. (sic) Butchart's Gardens at Tod Inlet, and they were greatly impressed with what they saw. Mr. Baker declared that the gardens are wonderful, and said that, in his opinion, the famous gardens at Pasadena, California cannot compare with them. The fact that the Tod Inlet gardens have gained their present beauty, when they were originally a stone quarry, struck the visitors as very clever and original.*

In 1941, the ageing Butcharts wanted to move closer to town. They offered to lease The Gardens to the City for ten years, on condition they would be maintained, but that didn't work out. The family kept The Gardens going by charging admission (25 cents to begin) until their grandson, the late Ian Ross, stepped up and took on the responsibility. His children followed in his footsteps, and the rest is history. "Butchart's" has become famous the world over. It's a National Historic Site and a major attraction, with shops (including a descendant of the seed business Mrs Butchart started) and access to *Benvenuto*, where **The Dining Room**, a recent addition, attracts good reviews.

The family has protected The Gardens' character for more than a hundred years, while through three generations, a host of remarkable sidelights have accreted to the main attraction.

- The **fireworks** display, Saturday evenings in the summer, is not to be missed. Watching the unique son-et-lumière show, while savoring your picnic dinner on the grass, just the best. (No blankets? You can buy them there; ditto the picnic repast.) When we were there, the fireworks featured pinwheels and lines of little displays, their firings perfectly matched to a suite of contemporary music, framed by a mountainous blanket of forest, its edge silhouetted against the night sky. A different show is crafted every year.

- There's a **concert stage** with musical performances every evening in summer. Among the highlights of 2016 were concerts by the Mavericks, Great Lake Swimmers and the Victoria Symphony. The website posts the calendar of concerts every spring.

- The **Children's Pavilion and Rose Carousel**, lavishly constructed by the present proprietor, features exquisite hand-crafted animals. An adjoining event room can be rented for birthday parties.

- **Boat tours** are now offered in season around scenic Tod Inlet and Brentwood Bay from The Gardens' docks.

Solitude is usually not part of the Butchart Experience. It's more like the United Nations, with a map-guide available in more than 20 languages. In summer, you'll be rubbing shoulders with a staff of 500, of whom the full-time employees number about 200.

Details

- The Butchart Gardens, 800 Benvenuto Ave, Brentwood Bay, in Central Saanich; 1-866-652-4422; butchartgardens.com; open year round; 2017 adult admission fees range seasonally from $18 to $32.60CDN +GST; includes access to entertainments; parking is efficient and free.

- Dining Room reservations: 250-652-8222; accessible with admission to the Gardens; voted among 100 best restaurants in Canada (one of only two on the islands) by Open Table patrons in 2015 and 2016: opentable.com.

- Blog post about The Gardens' integrated pest management program: butchartgardens.com/blog/pest-management.

- *A Family Garden*, an excellent 22-minute TV Ontario film (2006): tvo.org.
- Butchart Gardens National Historic Site of Canada: historicplaces.ca.
- Tod Inlet is part of Gowlland-Tod Provincial Park; the ruins and remnants of the cement plant and worker housing are accessible by two trails from Wallace Drive (but not from The Gardens); features, maps, directions: env.gov.bc.ca.
- Reading: *Tod Inlet: A Healing Place*, by Gwen Curry (Rocky Mountain Books, 2016).

Sidney by the Sea 21

The seaside town on the Saanich Peninsula owes its growth partly to setting and partly to culture. Sidney occupies a stretch of coastline on a flat, low prairie. There's plenty of access to the waterfront, overlooking the many islands in Haro Strait and Mt Baker looming behind. As one who has rowed and camped among those little islands, I can testify to their high scenic values, whether sparkling in the sun or veiled in mist. Part of the Saanich Peninsula's appeal is its mild climatic regime, with quite a lot of sun and not so much rain, although it can get quite windy.

Sidney's character is on display on its two axes. **Beacon Avenue**, running up to the Pat Bay Highway and down to the waterfront, with offshoots and many pedestrian-friendly touches on the sidewalks, is a shopper's delight. One-way walking time through the shopping district, without stopping, is maybe 15 minutes. There are quite a number of bookstores and art galleries, the Sidney Museum and Archives in the reconstructed post office building, and branches of those venerable Victoria fixtures, Capital Iron (hardware and home furnishings) and W & J Wilson's (clothiers to the gentry). The liquor store in the Sidney Inn stocks Vancouver Island and Gulf Islands wines. From there, you're just a few paces from checking out the local catches at the fish market on the government wharf. If shopping is your thing, you may want to catch the **Sidney Street Market**, every Thursday evening in the high season, when Beacon Ave is closed to traffic.

Sidney's **waterfront walkway** links multiple amenities and has enough benches to satisfy the most resolute *flaneur*. A set of interpretive plaques, as good as any on the island, outlines the many threads in Sidney's fascinating history. The walkway runs across the foot of Beacon, extending north and south for a total of 2.5 km/1.6 mi. Factor in a visit to Sidney's small but excellent museum and one of its many reputable eateries, and you have the makings of a half-day trip.

To the north, the walkway winds past several interesting attractions, beginning with a **garden of sculpture**. (Some of the public art is very good. I love the Picasso-esque metal woman walking her metal dog.)

Nearby, in the glassy Sidney Pier building, is the **Shaw Centre for the Salish Sea**, a well-designed aquarium and education centre for marine ecology and culture that is well worth a visit, especially with kids. The boutique **Victoria Distillers** and restaurant is a new addition to the waterfront near the Port Sidney marina, one of many boaters' facilities in the area. Further along is a boardwalk built out from the waterfront houses and condos that crowd the shore. It ends at a stairway to Third St.

South of Beacon Ave, the waterfront walkway extends a few blocks, with nice brickwork and fixtures. The **fishing pier** at the foot of Bevan Ave reaches quite a way into the elements. The walkway terminates on First St, but then resumes a short distance further south, past the Sidney-Anacortes ferry terminal, through Tulista Park — with the best boat launch in town — and onto the newly completed Lochside Waterfront Park.

Talk to Sidney old timers, as I did when researching a history-in-photographs, *The Story of Sidney*, and you become aware that Sidney has changed dramatically, not once, but again and again.

For millennia, the Saanich Peninsula was the domain of salt-water Salish peoples who maintained strong ties with neighbours along the waterways of the Salish Sea. Members of the W̱SÁNEĆ (Saanich) First Nation live in four villages on the peninsula. The nearest to Sidney is Tseycum, on Patricia Bay, on the west side of Saanich Inlet. In the 1860s, the coastal lowland was bought up by retired gold rush miners, notably the Brethour family, Irish Palatines of Rhineland origin, who farmed it for a time and then converted it to a village, adding a railway connection to Victoria, a wharf with steamer connections to ports on the Salish Sea, and a sawmill. Other industries followed, like the long-vanished Sidney Rubber Roofing plant. The area evolved into a transportation nexus. The Sidney-Anacortes ferry run, winding through the San Juan Islands, started in the 1920s. Today it is served by Washington State Ferries. The giant BC Ferries terminal at Swartz Bay is 6.4 km/4 mi north of Sidney, and Highway 17 has been funneling streams of ferry traffic through the town since the 1960s. Victoria International Airport, which handles more than 100 flights a day, began as the Patricia Bay Aerodrome in 1936. It was the base for the Commonwealth Flyer Training Program that brought thousands of pilots and crews to the area before and during the Second World War. The **BC Aviation Museum** occupies three hangars at the edge of the airport. It evokes the bygone days of biplanes and open cockpits.

During the decades, these facilities evolved and Sidney morphed into a post-industrial condition. Today, the town has a population of 12,000 and a thriving commercial district. It's a place where setting and culture combine to evoke Lifestyle with a capital L.

Details

- Sidney Parks and walkways map, including Seaside Sculpture Walk: sidney.ca.
- Shaw Centre for the Salish Sea, 9811 Seaport Place, Sidney; 250-665-7511; salishseacentre.org.
- Victoria Distillers: 9891 Seaport Place, Sidney; bookings 250-544-8217; victoriadistillers.com; tours and tastings, waterfront lounge; open Wed to Sun.
- Sidney Museum and Archives, 2423 Beacon Ave, Sidney; 250-655-6355; sidneymuseum.ca.
- BC Aviation Museum, 1910 Norseman Rd, Sidney; 250-655-3300; bcam.net.
- Sidney Booktown: sidneybooktown.ca.
- Sidney Days, every July 1 holiday: peninsulacelebrations.ca.

22 Goldstream Provincial Park

Goldstream Provincial Park protects 477 ha/1,179 ac of incredibly varied terrain around the narrow defile of Goldstream River, 26 km/16.7 mi west of downtown Victoria. Goldstream is particularly famous for its salmon run, the most accessible on the island — literally right beside Highway 1.

The annual run of Chum (or Dog) salmon in little Goldstream River is a poignant drama of nature that attracts crowds every fall, typically in November. The fish, weighing perhaps 4-7 kg/9-15 lb, return from three to five years in the open ocean to spawn, making their way upstream in search of gravel, where they mate in that strange no-contact way, females and males depositing in turn their eggs and milt. Then they die, and their mottled remains become objects of competition among gulls and eagles and myriad other feeders — the food chain is wide here. Viewing this pageant of death and new life, one contemplates the gift of the migrating salmon, injecting all that rich biomass into the ecosystem. This phenomenon is repeated in countless rivers, some far from tidewater, for six oceangoing species of Pacific salmon.

The setting for this drama is a section of the park where trails wind through an enchanting coniferous forest with some large western red cedar trees. There are also giant Douglas fir trees, possibly 600 years old, in the park.

A nature house, the **Freeman King Visitor Centre**, sits just above the estuary at the head of Saanich Inlet. It's a busy place, especially on fall weekends and holidays. On the front porch, kids paint fresh salmon carcasses and press sheets of paper over them to imprint the colourful contours of the fish. This highly scenic spot overlooks, to the north, one of Victoria's most interesting landscapes. The views across the estuary and down the narrow, steep-walled fjord are sublime.

The park is popular in summer. From Goldstream, you can climb a trail beside the 47-m/154-ft-high waterfall of the Niagara River to the 1886 iron trestle of the Esquimalt & Nanaimo Railway. The trestle — like the railway, temporarily disused — is some 80 m/262 ft above the floor of the canyon. Among other trails is one of the oldest on the island, the original up-island trail, built in 1861, that followed the upper Goldstream en route to Shawnigan Lake.

Mt Finlayson, 419 m/1,375 ft in elevation, is the highest point in the Victoria area, with magnificent views in three directions. The trail up Mt Finlayson is a locals' favorite — challenging, with some steep bits and some scrambling over smooth rock. The west face has dangerous cliffs. The trail starts near the east bank of the river, on Finlayson Arm Rd.

Goldstream Park has one of the island's most popular campgrounds, with individual sites on the west side of Highway 1 and group sites to the east. The day-use section beside the lower river has a picnic area with sheltered facilities.

Details

■ Goldstream Provincial Park: env.gov.bc.ca.

East Sooke Park   23

Peninsular East Sooke is a rural enclave west of Victoria with one tiny through-road and some amazing dead-ends. East Sooke Park, a 1,434-ha/3,543 ac block of the peninsula facing Juan de Fuca Strait, provides a taste of the wild west coast within an hour's drive from the city. The park is laced with some 50 km/31 mi of trails. Some are easy, but others make for difficult going, in broken terrain, with steep climbs and uneven surfaces.

The park has four points of access. Aylard Farm, at the end of Becher Bay Rd, is the closest to town and the gateway to the park's most accessible features. Among its pleasures is the short walk to Creyke Point, with exhilarating views across Becher Bay. Alldridge Point, less than half an hour one-way, is the site of mysterious waterfront petroglyphs — ancient figures incised into the rock. There's an amazing sort of petrified beach, made of 20-million-year-old conglomerate rock. The lookout at Beechey Head, less than an hour's walk, provides views across the strait that are simply spectacular. There's ample parking at Aylard Farm.

An equally accessible trailhead is at the end of Pike Rd, on the park's western edge. More driving is involved, parking is limited, and the trail is less used than Aylard. The 1.5-km/0.9-mi Iron Mine Bay trail is smooth and gentle, and the reward is a charming pebble beach. From there a short but more challenging trail leads to Pike Point, where the views are superb.

The rugged 10-km/6.2-mi coast trail between the Aylard Farm and Pike Pt is the centerpiece of East Sooke Park. The coast is rocky, with windswept forests of pine, fir, spruce and cedar. From many prominences, there are spectacular views across the Strait of Juan de Fuca. It's a full day's hike one way.

The network of interior trails is notable for climbs to two heights-of-land. They're accessible from the park's northeast side. The Anderson Cove trailhead, on East Sooke Road, has parking. A rough trail leads to Mount Maguire, elevation 268 m/879 ft. The more challenging Endurance Ridge trail leads to Babbington Hill, elevation 230 m/755 ft. Consult the online park map at the Capital Regional District website for points of access.

Details

- East Sooke is accessible via Gillespie Rd, off the Sooke Rd (Highway 14) or by East Sooke Rd, off Rocky Point Rd, Metchosin.
- East Sooke Regional Park: crd.bc.ca/parks.
- **Race Rocks**, a tiny islet and surrounding reefs 1.5 km/0.9 mi southeast of Christopher Point, is the southernmost point in British Columbia. The Race Rocks light has warned ships off the rocks since 1860 — it came into service days after the Fisgard light (#17). Race Rocks' high-current channels support abundant sea-life that is attractive to feeding sea mammals. Two species of sea lions gather by the hundreds on the rocks in winter. Enormous sea elephants breed there. Orca whales often visit in summer. It's an internationally known marine biology research site. Protected as an ecological reserve since 1980, and a marine protected area besides, Race Rocks is under the watchful eye of Pearson College, a prestigious United World College in nearby Pedder Bay. Marine science students at Pearson are the volunteer wardens of the ecological reserve. They study changes in the ecosystem and run an experimental installation that uses current to generate electricity. They keep a detailed website chronicling their interventions. The college employs the lightkeepers. Try to land without a permit and you will quickly be shooed away. No permit? You can watch and listen to the wildlife at Race Rocks real-time through a cam on the college website. Pearson College sponsors occasional field trips to the reserve, which I highly recommend. It's an elemental place, and the advanced work of the high school diver researchers is amazing. Pearson College Race Rocks website: racerocks.com.

24 Sooke Potholes

The Sooke River is the second largest river on southern Vancouver Island, draining an area of nearly 280 sq km/108 sq mi west of Victoria. A lot of water hits the bluish rocks of the Sooke Hills. The cool, clear water tumbles through fluted galleries, falls into black pools and flattens into ponds with gravelly beaches.

These are the famous Sooke Potholes that have delighted generations of swimmers. On a hot day, watch them fill up with grateful bathers of all ages. As a kid, my favorite place in the world was the Potholes. Now as then, my very favorite place is the series of pools in a canyon overlooked by the ruins of a never-completed lodge. Near the upper parking lot is a steep trail with stairs into the canyon. Then the going gets tough. The rocks surrounding the pools are exceedingly rough underfoot. The rewards include crystal-clear views to the bottom of a deep, sheer-sided circular pool.

Sooke Potholes Regional Park protects an 8.5-km/5.3-mi-long stretch of the river. There's pay parking and some facilities. The gorgeous 67 site Spring Salmon Place campground fronts the river at the north end of the park. The Galloping Goose Regional Trail runs right by it.

The endlessly beautiful rock formations of the Sooke Potholes tell an interesting story. It looks like the river must have been carving the hard, hard rock for millions of years. In fact, geologists believe the potholes were formed about 15,000 years ago. The rock itself is basalt and has been dated to between 55.8 and 33.9 million years ago. It began on the ocean floor, where molten magma squirts or oozes out and instantly solidifies. It built up into seamounts and islands, becoming part of what geologists call the Metchosin Igneous Complex.

Now the story gets interesting. Earth's crust comprises a few big continent-sized plates and many small terranes that actually move around, pushed by seafloor spreading — so goes the theory of plate tectonics. Seafloor spreading pushed the Crescent Terrane, bearing those basalts, northward. The leading edge of the terrane apparently subducted — got pushed under — older rock. Eventually it ground to a halt. Behind it, however, seafloor spreading seems to have continued to push the terrane north. The basalts of the Metchosin Igneous Complex had only one way to go — up. They were uplifted.

A mere 15,000 years ago, kilometer-high ice blanketed most of the island, but when it began to disappear, meltwater poured out of the hollowing glacier. Torrents of water — full of boulders, rocks, gravel, sand — descended in a thundering vortex, scraping and scouring away at the rock, creating one of the island's most enchanting landscapes.

Details

- Sooke Potholes Regional Park, Sooke River Rd, off Highway 14; information, map, directions, and a video of the campground: crd.bc.ca/parks. Parking can be at a premium on hot days.
- Spectacular drone video, The Ruins and Cliffs of the Sooke Potholes: youtube.com.
- Spring Salmon Place (KWL-UCHUN) Campground is operated by the T'Sou-ke First Nation (250-642-3957) seasonally, in partnership with the CRD, on a first-come, first-served basis.
- Geological History of Vancouver Island: an overview with links to more detailed information: crd.bc.ca/education.

Sooke 25

Sooke is a maritime community 35 km/22 mi southwest of Victoria, poised on the threshold of the wilder west coast (see #64). The village sits on snug, picturesque Sooke Harbour, opening onto the Strait of Juan de Fuca. Sooke's eastern approach winds past Sooke Basin. The harbour and the basin divide at the estuary of the Sooke River. East Sooke (#23) forms the south shore of the waters.

Sandy, winding **Whiffen Spit** is an interesting landform near the mouth of Sooke Harbour. A walk to the end of the spit (1.3 km/0.8 mi from a little parking area) is a great way to take in Sooke Harbour, the East Sooke coast and the Straits.

Nearby, stands the venerable waterfront resort **Sooke Harbour House**, which has done more to put Sooke on the map than any natural attraction. The 28-room boutique hotel looks out on Juan de Fuca Strait, just where the west coast begins to catch the flavour of the open Pacific Ocean. The centerpiece is a charming old house that has borne the same name since 1929. The Philip family took over in 1979 and turned it into something grand. There are meeting rooms, a spa and an art gallery which shows the work of the region's artists. The dining room is a culinary destination in its own right, its kitchen the very fountainhead of slow food culture on Vancouver Island. Its practice of using local sources of food induced a small agricultural revival in the Sooke area. **Wild Mountain Food and Drink** advances the trend of presenting locally-sourced food creatively; the restaurant opened near the Sooke waterfront in 2015.

A shorter seaside stroll is via the 290-m/950-ft-long **Marine Boardwalk** and **Rotary Pier**. The pier is below the foot of Murray Rd, where there's a small parking lot. The pier is a popular place with crab fishers, who drop baited traps into the chuck. At the west end of the boardwalk, an access trail leads through Ed Macgregor Park, on the harbour side of the

6700 block West Coast Road. The attractive little park is well signed, but there's no parking nearby.

Sooke was long the domain of the T'Sou-ke First Nation, a Coast Salish people who flourished on the bounty of the sea. They sold their lands to the Hudson's Bay Company for 58 blankets in 1850. Today, their community at the mouth of the Sooke River is noted for its dedication to renewable energy sources. Meanwhile, Walter Colquhoun Grant, the first European settler on Vancouver Island independent of the Hudson's Bay Company, was hired to be the colonial surveyor. He bought land in Sooke, but soon tired of the place, quit his job and sold his land. Fellow Scot John Muir was the buyer, and with his family Muir settled in Sooke and built a sawmill. The Muirs might better be considered the founders of Sooke. Salmon was the area's long-time economic mainstay. Giant traps stood offshore where migrating fish were hoovered up, and the salmon were processed in local canneries. Sport fishing charters are now the order of the day. Sooke has long been a logging community. It was incorporated as a district municipality in 1999.

The place to delve into the area's history is at the excellent **Sooke Region Museum**. On the grounds are Moss Cottage, a relocated pioneer home dating from 1869, and the dome of the historic Triangle Island lighthouse, which operated from 1910-20, far off the northwestern tip of Vancouver Island. The museum also functions as the local **visitor centre**.

Details

- Sooke Region Museum, 2070 Phillips Rd, Sooke: sookeregionmuseum.ca. Visitor centre: 1-866-888-4748.
- Sooke Harbour House, 1528 Whiffen Spit Rd, Sooke, is a 30- to 45-minute drive from Victoria; 1-800-889-9688; sookeharbourhouse.com. Reservations recommended for dinner.
- Wild Mountain Food & Drink, 1831 Maple Ave S, Sooke; 250-642-3596; wildmountaindinners.com. Open 5 to 9, Tues-Sat.
- T'Sou-ke Nation: tsoukenation.com.

Students in the University of British Columbia's Masters program in Sustainable Forest Management, class of 2013, visiting Cathedral Grove. Photo by Deborah DeLong.

II. Southeast Vancouver Island and the Gulf Islands

Southeast Vancouver Island is on the dry side of the mountain spine, facing the Strait of Georgia and, south of Nanaimo, the Gulf Islands. More than 300,000 people live along the sunny, scenic coastal margin between the Cowichan and Comox valleys, including fast-growing residential enclaves around Duncan-North Cowichan, Nanaimo, Parksville-Qualicum and Courtenay-Comox. Unceded traditional lands of Salish First Nations, the region became the base for the Island's first industry, coal mining, while the heartland of the Douglas fir forest supported logging, sawmilling, pulp and paper industries. Today, the warm lands of the southeast Island nurture heritage farms and vineyards off bucolic back roads. Nearby, and yet a world apart, are the Gulf Islands, a mariner's paradise by sea, by land the gourmandiser's happy hunting ground.

26 | Malahat Lookouts

If you're driving up-Island from Victoria, you pretty much have to take the Malahat Drive, a mountainous and scenic 25-km/15-mi stretch of Highway 1 that is usually referred to simply as The Malahat. Beginning in the canyon of Goldstream River, near sea-level, the road winds across the face of Malahat Ridge as it climbs to a 352-m/1,155-ft summit.

Two lookouts provide spectacular views of Saanich Inlet and a respite from the traffic. If visibility is good, the views are not to be missed. The lookouts are, however, accessible only from the northbound lane.

The first stop, about 10 km/6 mi north of Goldstream, looks south toward Finlayson Arm. The tapering body of water, edged by walls of rock, is the head of a fjord — the only one on the north side of the Island. Opposite Malahat Ridge is the rugged expanse known as the Highlands, dominated by Mt Finlayson. Much of the Highlands bordering Finlayson Arm is protected in Gowlland-Tod Provincial Park; beyond, the rolling green of Victoria's western borders is framed by the distant Olympic Mountains.

The second lookout, about 3 km/2 mi further north, provides gorgeous vistas to the east and north. Across Saanich Inlet lies the mostly agricultural Saanich Peninsula, a verdant greenspace broken by the suburb of Brentwood Bay and the forested slopes of Mt Newton. Further east lie the American San Juan Islands, with snow-capped Mt Baker beyond. The Canadian Gulf Islands are sometimes framed by the Coast Mountains, north of Vancouver.

At this rock bound spot it's possible to visualize what the original Malahat Drive was like. Completed in 1911 after decades of work, the first, tiny road was a hair-raising adventure to drive. The lookout preserves a tiny fragment of the original route. Just imagine it without railings.

You may spot the tiny Brentwood Bay-Mill Bay ferry as it plies Saanich Inlet, linking the Malahat with the Saanich Peninsula. See the suggested circuit in #43. Some bound for Victoria from up-Island prefer the more leisurely ferry route to driving the busy Malahat.

Details

Current road conditions on the Malahat Drive: malahatdrive.ca.

Shawnigan Lake 27

Shawnigan Lake is a lovely summer resort area nestled in rollercoaster foothills. Historic Shawnigan Lake Rd, originally a trail blazed in 1861, winds past cottages and docks and through the tiny village. In the vicinity are beaches great for summertime family outings; the vineyards and cideries of Cobble Hill; the Trans-Canada Trail and iconic Kinsol Trestle (#28); and several decent restaurants, bakeries and pubs.

Below the village, the disused Esquimalt and Nanaimo Railway (E&N) track skirts the shore. The E&N was of vital importance to the island's development. At **Cliffside**, 4 km/2.5 mi south of the village, there's a cairn commemorating the inauguration of the 116-km/72-mi railway. On August 13, 1886 the Prime Minister of Canada, Sir John A. Macdonald — Mr National Dream himself — hammered in the E&N's last spike, made of gold. With that the hinterland of the Island's richly endowed southeastern quarter, an 8,000 sq km/3,089 sq mi swathe given to coal magnate Robert Dunsmuir as an incentive to build the line, opened for business.

One km/0.6 mi south of the village, where the tracks run close to the shore, is 7-ha/17 ac **Old Mill Park**. Pathways wind through a lacustrine landscape shaded by mostly deciduous forest. There's a viewing platform on the shore. It's a good place to view waterfowl, sunsets and the old dolphins of the Shawnigan Lake Lumber Company. Shawnigan Lake had one of the first sawmills along the E&N, built by the Losee family in 1890. The company changed hands several times, and the mill burned down three times. Twice the enterprise bounced back, and the owners

TAKE 5 *John Schreiner's Favorite Island Wineries*

Author of BC Coastal Wine Tour: The Wineries of the Fraser Valley, Vancouver, Vancouver Island, and the Gulf Islands (Whitecap Books, 2011) *and 13 other books on wine, keeps a blog,* John Schreiner on Wine *(johnschreiner.blogspot.ca) and publishes articles in periodicals. A native of Saskatchewan, he was a career business writer with* The Financial Post. *He lives in North Vancouver, BC.*

Winemaking in British Columbia began with the making of berry wines on Vancouver Island in the 1920s. The modern era of island winemaking began in 1992 with the opening of Vigneti Zanatta. Since then about 40 wineries have been established, making everything from berry and grape wines to cider and mead. Here are my favorites.

1. Averill Creek Vineyard

6552 North Rd, Duncan; 250-709-9986; averillcreek.ca.
Grape grower and former doctor Andy Johnston offers fine Pinot Noir and Pinot Gris in an elegant Cowichan Valley tasting room.

2. 40 Knots Vineyard & Estate Winery

2400 Anderton Rd, Comox; 250-941-8810; 40knotswinery.com.
Layne Craig and Brenda Hetman-Craig, his wife, have re-energized this winery since buying it in 2014. The expanded wine list now includes several sparkling wines, table wines made with estate grapes and Okanagan grapes, and even an "orange" wine.

3. Sea Star Estate Farm & Vineyard

6621 Harbour Hill Dr, N Pender Id; 250-629-6960; seastarvineyards.ca.
David Goudge and his winemaker, Ian Baker, have transformed the former Morning Bay Vineyard. The whites and rose wins all have a pristine freshness; the big red is made with Okanagan grapes.

4. Blue Grouse Estate Winery

2182 Lakeside Rd, Duncan; 250-743-3834; bluegrouse.ca.
In 2015, owner Paul Brunner, a former mining executive, funded the most spectacular new winery and tasting room on Vancouver Island. A must visit, the stylish building's roof line mimics the back of a grouse. The wines match the spectacle.

5. Venturi-Schulze Vineyards

4235 Vineyard Rd, Cobble Hill; 250-743-5630; venturischulze.com.
Notable for creative wines (great sparkling, Pinot Noir and dry whites) and balsamic vinegar true in style to those of Modena, where winemaker Giordano Venturi was born.

John is also keeping an eye on **Symphony Vineyard**, 6409B Oldfield Rd, Saanichton, 250-208-8784, symphonyvineyard.com, which has taken up where Starling Lane left off; **Unsworth Vineyards**, 2915 Cameron Taggart Rd, Mill Bay, 250-929-2292, unsworthvineyards.com, where there is an esteemed restaurant; and **Chateau Wolff Estate**, 2534 Maxey Rd, Nanaimo, 778-441-2625, reopened two years by a youthful couple from Ontario, Natalie and Matt Riga.

were always able to buy more timber west of Shawnigan Lake. The mill became a mainstay of the local economy. In its peak years in the 1920s, it employed 150 workers and another 100 in the woods. Geared locomotives brought logs down the slopes and onto a long wooden trestle where West Shawnigan Lake Park is today. The logs were dumped into the lake, to be towed to the mill by steam tugs. The finished lumber was loaded onto E&N railcars and off to market. In 1942, Vancouver's budding industrial magnate H.R. MacMillan bought the Shawnigan Lake Lumber Company. He needed timber for his much bigger sawmills. He soon considered the mill not worth fixing up and shut it down, triggering widespread fears that forestry in the E&N Lands had created future ghost towns.

Favoured by nature, Shawnigan Lake survived on seasonal tourism and recreation. The first hotel, long-gone Morton House, opened in 1885. There has been a succession of resorts ever since. The Strathcona Hotel, built in 1900 (twice), went bust in the 1920s and was for decades a girl's private school. In the 1950s, it was an adventure to drive up The Malahat. Shawnigan Lake was appealingly remote from Victoria. Enclosed by second growth forest, it certainly wasn't peaceful, with speedboats and float planes buzzing up and down in summer. More recently, Shawnigan Lake has developed into a bedroom community. The lake retains its charm, and at Old Mill Park, the human past glints through the world of nature.

Details

- Old Mill Park access, facilities, map: cvrd.bc.ca. Parking lot off Recreation Rd, W of Shawnigan Lake Rd.
- E&N passenger service Victoria-Courtenay turned on a point of history: the land grant that went with the railway contract carried an obligation to keep it running. Sadly, VIA Rail "temporarily" terminated service in 2011 owing to safety concerns, and despite promises to the contrary, has not revived it.
- Shawnigan Heritage Fair, community event every August: shawniganlakemuseum.com.
- **Unsworth Vineyards Restaurant**, 2915 Cameron Taggert Rd, Mill Bay; unsworthvineyards.com; notable cuisine in a heritage house; 4.8 km/3 mi from Shawnigan Lake village.

28 | **Kinsol Trestle**

A towering wooden construction spans the Koksilah River near Shawnigan Lake. It's the keystone in the rail trail between Shawnigan Lake and the Cowichan Valley. It opened in 2011, after years of rotting neglect and miraculous reconstruction. Bikers and walkers and horseback riders now flock to the iconic bridge to admire its hugeness — 44 m/144 ft high and 188 m/617 ft long — and the views over the little river valley. How the Kinsol Trestle was resurrected is a story of local initiative powered by the fusion of history and self-propelled tourism.

Construction of a railbed from Victoria to Port Alberni began in 1911 as part of the Canadian Northern Pacific Railway (CNPR). Local farmers and loggers furnished the labour, but little track was laid. The Esquimalt & Nanaimo Railway completed a branch line to Cowichan Lake in 1913. That railway jump-started the logging industry there. CNPR's Cowichan Lake line cashed in on the boom. In 1917, the company became the publicly-owned Canadian National Railway (CNR). The Kinsol Trestle, completed in 1920, was a vital link in the Cowichan line. It took the name of the train station near the short-lived King Solomon mine. Wooden railway trestles were once common on Vancouver Island, built to traverse its many carved river valleys. The Bear Creek trestle was 76 m/249 ft high and Haslam Creek, 60 m/197 ft.

The gas-powered Galloping Goose passenger car started operating from Victoria as far as Milnes Landing in 1922, to Lake Cowichan in 1924 and the following year to Youbou (see #38). The service lasted only until 1931. Logging companies started operating near the CNR line. The logs went to Cowichan Bay tidewater on a CNR spur line. The Cowichan line continued to serve the logging industry until the 50s. The last train rolled across the Kinsol Trestle in 1979.

The trestles disappeared with the railways. Today the Kinsol is the largest remaining *Howe truss pile-bent trestle*, and it's believed to be one of largest wooden structures anywhere. The long-abandoned bridge was until recently a wreck, hazardous and closed to public use. We could only gaze at the massive ruins and imagine biking from Shawnigan Lake to the Cowichan Valley.

The vision of a reconstructed Kinsol Trestle evolved in the 1990s, guided by Jack Peake, mayor of Lake Cowichan 1999-2008, and a passionate railroad buff. He considered the trestle a feat of engineering and a potential world-class attraction. A local campaign fundraised to match pledges by governments and the Trans Canada Trail society. The Cowichan Valley Regional District was the lead agency, the Province of BC the largest contributor to the project's $5.7 million budget. In charge was Macdonald and Lawrence Timber Framing, a heritage restoration company based in Mill Bay with clientele world-wide. They used original CNR plans and created a database of every one of the trestle's 6,000 pieces of timber. Steel trusses were used to ensure the integrity of the structure, most of the original wood was replaced, and a solid deck and railings were added. The project was completed in 2011. Thousands turned out for the grand opening. The trestle is now part of the 22,000-km/13,670-mi-long **Trans Canada Trail**. Once again it provides vital linkage on this mountainous Island.

Details

- Kinsol Trestle map and description: cvrd.bc.ca.
- Directions to the north end of the Kinsol Trestle: Trans-Canada Highway to Koksilah Rd heading W; left on Riverside Rd just past Koksilah River bridge; at 8.5 km, parking on left; 5-minute walk.
- To the south end: From the Village of Shawnigan Lake, follow Renfrew Road W; right on Glen Eagles Rd; parking lot at corner of Glen Eagles and Shelby Rd; follow Trans Canada Trail N.

Merridale Cidery and Distillery 29

Merridale Cidery entices a stream of customers to the countryside of Cobble Hill, offering the experience, unusual in North America, of English-style dry ciders, made on the premises with apples from the orchard. The apples are heritage old-country cider-making varieties. Unlike eating or dessert apples, they have high tannin content, like wine grapes, and are therefore quite acidic. Merridale's splendid website has detailed notes on the varieties and processes it employs.

The time-tested techniques practiced in the ciderworks, which can be toured during working hours, include fermenting *to dry*, to take out the sugars. The result is "a heck of a lot different," says co-proprietor Janet Docherty, "from what we were used to in BC."

Our neighbours Jim and Dawn drive up to Merridale for lunch occasionally. In his youth, on a farm near Creston, Jim tried to make cider with eating apples. "It was never anything like this." He considers the dry ciders comparable to wine as an accompaniment to food. Jim especially likes the strong Somerset cider.

BC's first estate cidery began under the previous owner, with plantings of cider apples from England, France and Germany. Cobble Hill was chosen for its growing conditions — a microclimate that has, Docherty says, "a tremendous amount of sunshine, but is usually not too hot or too cold."

Docherty and husband Rick Pipes purchased the cidery in 2000. They knew nothing about cider but — both business graduates, with a family — were looking for an investment that involved a healthy lifestyle. From their serendipitous discovery of Merrridale, the vision evolved of an agricultural operation people would want to visit.

Merridale's cidery makes seven ciders, eau de vie, apple juice and cider vinegar, while the distillery, added in 2007, makes cider, pear and grape brandy, several gins, vodka and whiskey. Distribution is limited — there's another inducement to go there.

Visitors can also tour the orchard. There is a spacious tasting room and a convivial bistro that features local ingredients and tends to the creative. It is also open weekend evenings in the winter months.

Do read the Cider House Rules. It's all there — "Always designate a driver to get you home safely." Should that prove unworkable, you can stay in one of Merridale's two yurts (April-Oct).

Details

■ Merridale Cidery and Distillery, 1230 Merridale Road, Cobble Hill; 1-800-998-9908; merrIslandaleclslander.com.

 Mt Tzouhalem

Mt Tzouhalem is a rampart of rock on the north side of Cowichan Bay. A white cross, visible from across the bay, stands at the edge of a cliff a few hundred metres short of the 536-m/1,759-ft-high summit of Mt Tzouhalem. It's an hour's easy climb through forest to the cross. (The cross has been known to disappear, only to be returned.)

What you find there is a little grassy flat, sheltered by outcrops of knobby conglomerate, a Garry oak tree ringed by red-barked arbutus trees in the middle and manzanita bushes at the fringes. It overlooks the Cowichan Valley and is an excellent place to get the lie of the land. The panoramic view in three directions is simply breathtaking.

Far to the west, over a ridge, is Cowichan Lake (#38). The lake is 31 km/19 mi long, and from its outlet the Cowichan River flows east on a 47-km/29 mi path to tidewater, while dropping 164 m/538 ft. The narrow valley opens onto a floodplain.

You can see the Cowichan River flowing through the city of Duncan, picking up the tributary watersheds of Quamichan and Somenos lakes — visible past Tzouhalem's western flank — and, near its mouth, joined by the Koksilah River, which drains the other side of the valley. The rivers meet salt water in a large and exceedingly beautiful estuary 2.5 km/1.6 mi wide and 1 km/0.6 mi deep (#33).

This is the richly fertile land Hul'q'umi'num-speaking Salish peoples have owned and occupied "since time immemorial" and have never surrendered.

First Nations didn't have a name for the whole valley, but the traditional name of the Mt Tzouhalem is *Shquw'utsun* (Cowichan), meaning "a giant frog who lay on his side basking in the warm sun." The mountain is an important setting in the First People's creation myths.

Beginning in the 1850s, the valley was settled by European farmers after its agricultural potential was advertised by the Hudson's Bay Company.

The Europeans appropriated the name Cowichan, using it for the entire valley. They gave the word a new twist of meaning — "the warm land."

The settlers gave the mountain a new name as well. *Ts'uwxxilem*

(Tzouhalem) was an historical resident of the valley whose violent way of collecting wives became legendary. *Ts'uwxxilem* had lived with his wives in a stronghold at the base of the mountain. That may account for the use of his name. His violence was an object of deep fear and loathing in some First Nations families. In others, his strong medicine excites reverence even today.

In the book *Two Houses Half-Buried in Sand* there's a narrative of *Ts'uwxxilem* acquiring spiritual powers. Supernatural events occurred on Cowichan Mountain/Mt Tzouhalem. It's a gripping tale.

You certainly do get a long view from Mt Tzouhalem.

Details
- Mount Tzouhalem guide and map of approach from north: northcowichan.ca.

TAKE 5 *Garry Oak Woodlands*

The sight of spring and summer wildflowers in a woodland of mature Garry oak trees is a vision not soon forgotten. Garry oak meadows are a signature landscape of the islands. The drier lowlands of southeast Vancouver Island and the Gulf Islands are in its northern range. Garry oaks grow in the Comox Valley on Vancouver Island, latitude 49°N, and as far south as 35°N in California, where the acorn-bearing angiosperm is known as *Oregon white oak*. Here the tree inhabits two ecosystems, deep soil and rocky outcrops. Some trees spread gnarly branches in stoic isolation. Others form a grove and close a canopy. Garry oaks often grow with Douglas fir and arbutus. Even in a suburb you may come across a tree of magnificent girth, with the deeply fluted bark that suggests it is quite old. Sometimes windshear and terrible pruning — all too common near wires — render an oak tree homely as broccoli.

Because their habitat coincides with prized suburban real estate, intact Garry oak ecosystems are now rare. Only five percent of the islands' original Garry oak habitat are intact, and of the deep-soil ecosystem, less than 1.5 percent. That's the conclusion of research by the Garry Oak Ecosystems Recovery Team. In the Cowichan Valley, 4.5 percent of the deep-soil ecosystem are intact, and nearly half the scrub oak ecosystem. Only a tiny fraction of that is protected from residential or commercial uses. Volunteers with the Cowichan Valley Naturalists and other groups turn out to pull broom and other invasive species and rebuild native plant communities. Their work is restoring these beautiful places to a semblance of their original glory.

1. The **Mount Tzuhalem Ecological Reserve** is an 18-ha/44-ac area of rocky outcrops and scrubby oaks on the northwest side of the mountain in North

- Mt Tzouhalem's western slope can easily be climbed by road and trail from the gravel parking lot just south of St Ann's Church, 1775 Tzouhalem Rd. The trail is unmarked, and much of the mountain is criss-crossed with bike trails and logging roads — it's both a working municipal forest and a popular mountain biking destination. Best make a first climb with someone who knows the route.
- The east side of Mt Tzouhalem can be hiked by a trail that begins near the end of Khenipsen Road.
- Reading: *Two Houses Half-Buried in Sand: Oral Traditions of the Hul'q'umi'num' Coast Salish of Kuper Island and Vancouver Island*, by Chris Arnett (Talonbooks, 2007).
- "Two Houses Half-Buried in Sand: Reviving the Legacies of 1930s-era Hul'qumi'num Story-tellers:" a University of Victoria (uvic.ca) mapping project.
- Way cute video *Once Upon a Day… Cowichan* on YouTube (youtube.com).

Cowichan. In the 1980s, Emily and Syd Watts helped rescue the site from subdivision and get it protected.

2. The **Cowichan Garry Oak Preserve** is a 10.8-ha/26.7-ac site purchased from the Elkington pioneer farm estate by the Nature Conservancy of Canada.

3. The **Somenos Garry Oak Protected Area** is a 9-ha/22-ac site east of Somenos Marsh in North Cowichan with a rare deep-soil Garry oak forest, rescued from development by local action and purchased by BC Parks; open to public use and not to be missed, especially in spring.

4. In Victoria's **Beacon Hill Park** (#10), the remnants of a Garry oak woodland on the east side, bordering Heywood Ave, are following Nature's path: when old trees topple, the City lets them be. The fallen giants make a grand and moving tableau.

5. On the southwest corner of the **Government House grounds** in Victoria (#13), stands the best remaining fragment of Garry oak woodland in the city; open to the public every day from dawn to dusk.

Details
- Cowichan Garry Oak Preserve: natureconservancy.ca.
- Mt Tzuhalem Ecological Reserve: env.gov.bc.ca.
- Somenos Garry Oak Protected Area on the excellent Garry Oak Ecosystems Recovery Team website: goert.ca.
- Somenos Garry Oak Protected Area parking is at the west end of York Rd, Duncan.

Providence Farm   31

This working organic farm, nestled under Mt Tzouhalem in the lower Cowichan Valley, is the centre of a therapeutic community "dedicated to restoring the spirit and skills of those with physical, mental and emotional challenges." Providence is what is called a care farm or social farm. There are few in Canada, but perhaps 1,000 in Europe, where it is a genuine movement.

The farm welcomes visitors. You can take a self-guided tour and even come for lunch and dinner. A store sells its produce (in season): jams and preserves, furniture, apparel and crafted goods.

The visual centrepiece is steepled Providence House, built in 1921. Spacious lawns in front are the setting for large gatherings. There is a charming sitting garden in back, allotment gardens — one of many links Providence Farm has created with the larger community — numerous outbuildings with workshops and meeting rooms, stables for horses, fields, country roads and forests laced with trails.

The historic 162-ha/400-ac farm has been an education centre for much of its nearly 150-year history. For 100 years it was St Ann's School, operated by Sisters of Saint Ann, a teaching order of Catholic nuns. The Sisters bought the property in 1864, and until 1876 St Ann's School was a residential school for First Nations girls. The students apparently shunned it. The school population increased when girls attending St Ann's Academy in Victoria were orphaned and the Sisters started sending them to Cowichan.

The institution was the setting for a notable cultural exchange. First Nations girls learned to knit there. Sister Marie-Angèle is said to have been the agent of technology transfer, which the women adapted to an ancient Salish knowledge of textiles. They started making handsome waterproof wool sweaters — the basis of the flourishing Cowichan sweater industry and its many imitators. The Sister, born Marie Gauthier, learned knitting in her native Quebec.

In 1904, the farm became St Ann's Boy's School, with 30-50 boarding students. When the central block was built, the school started taking day students. By 1950, it evolved into a co-ed day school. The school closed forever in June 1964.

Since opening in 1979, Providence Farm has developed an extensive vocational training program. Some are here on a more casual basis for emotional healing. There's a culture — and a program — of horticultural therapy, "people caring for the soil, and the soil nurturing the people." The environment itself is a mode of healing. Every week, some 60 volunteers come to the farm to assist.

I've sat in the garden on a warm summer evening, looking across the fields at Mt Tzouhalem. The farm's very wholesomeness is therapeutic. "Damn braces, bless relaxes," the poet William Blake wrote. Would the sisters not agree?

Details

- Providence Farm, 1843 Tzouhalem Rd, North Cowichan; 250-746-4204; provIslandencefarm.wildapricot.org. Visitors are requested to check in at the main office in Providence House, and to call ahead for lunch. The Farm Table restaurant, open Wed-Fri: 250-597-0599.

- An annual fixture at the farm since 1984 is the delightfully low-key *Islands Folk Festival* (Islandsfolkfestival.ca), with performances on five or six stages over two days in July. Some music lovers bike in and camp in a nearby field.

32   The Emptiness of the Butter Church

The abandoned stone church on Comiaken Hill near Cowichan Bay has always been called the Butter Church. A popular subject for photography, the handsome building looks like a symbol of something — but what?

The church was built in 1870 near the ancient village of *Qwumi'iqun'* (Comiaken, pronounced with the stress on the "a"). It was a testament to the community's hard work and to the vision of pioneer missionary Peter Rondeault.

Fresh out of a Quebec Catholic seminary, Father Rondeault arrived in Cowichan Bay in 1858, by canoe, alone. His way of winning the hearts and minds of First Nations people was to throw himself headlong into the life of the community.

He was a skilled carpenter. He grew and milled wheat. He even grew tobacco. By 1870, legend has it, sales of butter from the dairy farm were enough to pay a mason and First Nations construction workers to build the church. Or maybe it was just that Rondeault just paid the workers in butter. Either way, it was the church that butter built. Its real name was St Ann's.

Within ten years, the Catholic diocese in Victoria purchased land on Tzouhalem Rd and built another St Ann's Church. Why? One story is that Rondeault's congregation grew so rapidly the stone church became too small.

The Butter Church was on what became an Indian Reserve, and that may be part of the story. It was a special category of federal property that could not be bought or sold — which didn't sit well with the diocese. Either way, the Butter Church was de-consecrated in 1880. Its windows and doors went to a church on Salt Spring Island, and it has mostly stood empty ever since.

SOUTHEAST VANCOUVER ISLAND AND THE GULF ISLANDS

A darker story about relations between First Nations and Europeans has the abandoned church for a setting.

A crowd gathered on the grassy slopes of Comiaken Hill on May 27, 1913. The Royal Commission on Indian Affairs staged an open-air hearing in front of the church. The joint federal-provincial undertaking was to identify BC Indian Reserves that were bigger than the requirements of the population, which had declined precipitously. Unoccupied lands in Indian Reserves would revert to the Crown provincial. British Columbia wanted, in other words, to take away some of what little land had been allotted to First Nations.

A remarkable photograph in *Those Who Fell From the Sky* (a must-read book) shows a picture bearer retained by Chief *Tsulpi'multw* (Khenipsen) holding a picture of King Edward VII who he had visited in 1906.

Chief *Tsulpi'multw* had been one of three BC Indian Chiefs who made a 10,000 km/6,000 mi journey to London, England where, on August 13, 1906, they were granted an audience with King Edward VII. It was a rare opportunity to make a case for redress of the land policies.

"They took the very best of our land," their petition asserted, "and gave us rock and gravel."

"I went to the King a few years ago," Chief *Tsulpi'multw*'s said to the commission, "to try and get some settlement from the King, and when I got there, the King gave me this photograph. His Majesty promised to do something for us, and said he would send somebody out to look into the matter."

Other chiefs joined in the representation. Chief *Suhilton* (Seehaillton) said, "I myself only occupy 3½ acres [1.4 ha], and yet the white man says I have got too much." Charley Kutsowat told the commission that "whenever he goes to get his food he gets into trouble the same as the rest, and when his cattle get out on the road they are placed in the pound, and afterwards sold."

To this day, nobody has looked into those grievances. For the Cowichans and other Hul'qumi'num' (Halkomelem) Salish people, there was no buy and sell, "we" just moved in. There remains no treaty. That silence, that indifference — maybe that's what the emptiness of the Butter Church represents.

Details

- Butter Church, 5455 Lemo Rd, off Tzouhalem Rd. Church and adjoining cemetery are maintained for visitors. Parking.
- St. Ann's First Nations Parish, 1775 Tzouhalem Rd, has a large graveyard; Father Rondeault is buried under the chapel behind the church.
- Readings: "The Cowichan Tribes' Historical Narrative of their Search for Justice" is in a commissioned work, *Those Who Fell from the Sky: A History of the Cowichan Peoples*, by Daniel P. Marshall (1999).
  The Great Land Grab in Hul'qumi'num Territory, an account of the

Cowichan Bay 33

In Cowichan Bay village, shops and eateries crowd along gloriously scenic waterfront back of a cluster of docks where float homes rub bumpers with fishing boats and yachts. Old-time wooden façades recall the village's history as a port for the Cowichan Valley. Beginning in the 1860s, Cowichan Bay evolved into an industrial service centre and, later, a world-renowned salmon sport-fishing base. The fish are pretty much gone, but the taste for fine food lives on.

Cowichan Bay is a *slow-food centre* — the first community in North America so designated (in 2009) by Cittaslow, an Italian organization that promotes the use of local produce, organically grown where possible. Several shops along the bay have a culinary theme.

True Grain Bread is a bakery which takes organic grains, mostly grown on the island, some their own, mills them on the premises, and rises them with organic starter yeasts. True Grain's wheat of choice is un-hybridized Red Fife. It uses others such as spelt and kamut, an ancestor of durum wheat. This is some serious bread. In contrast, the gorgeous pastry display tends to the shiny and shapely.

Hilary's Cheese uses local organic cow and goat milk to craft an impressive assortment of cheeses — fresh-made cream cheese, white camembert-style, several tangy blues and a rinded cheese washed with local dessert cordials.

Crowe & Appel Fine Foods is a newcomer on the bay, a combination seasonal eatery, deli and grocery delivery service. The enterprise moved into a vacated seafood retailer's space and continues to be devoted to fresh foods.

Every May, on a weekend when the local wild prawns are in season — which lasts only six weeks — Cowichan Bay hosts a **Spot Prawn Festival**. One of several such in the region, Cow Bay's is wildly successful. Parking is in short supply, lineups are long, and prices are increasing (expect to pay close to $20CDN a pound on the wharf, $30 in stores).

A sturdy 82-m/269-ft-long former oil company jetty houses the **Cowichan Bay Maritime Centre**. It's the showpiece of the Cowichan Wooden Boat Society, dedicated to the restoration of old wooden boats and the construction of new ones. The centre's purpose-built pods have displays of the bay's marine history. Visitors are welcome to stroll around.

The village is perched on the southern edge of the **Cowichan Estuary**, a rare coastal ecosystem 4.9 sq km/1.9 sq mi in area. Land, salt water and fresh water mingle in the estuary, nurturing a web of marine and terrestrial life. The Cowichan Estuary Nature Centre is an educational resource sustained by the estuary's local defenders against industrial incursions. Misuse of the estuary stretches back to the earliest days of European settlement. It has been dyked and dammed, been the site of a seaport and sawmills, and used to store log booms. (Yet recently, a local group building a low-impact nature trail through the estuary has been restrained by one of the industrial users, claiming concern about liability in case of accidents. The trail remains closed.)

Just west of a picturesque row of waterfront cottages is a little park overlooking the industrial port and the Cowichan River estuary. There are tables and benches. Weather permitting, it's a great place for a picnic.

Details

- True Grain Bread & Mill, 1725 Cowichan Bay Rd; 250-746-7664; truegrain.ca; closed Mondays.
- Hilary's Cheese, 1737 Cowichan Bay Rd; 250-748-5992; hccheese.com and on Facebook.
- Crowe & Appel Fine Foods, 1751 Cowichan Bay Rd; 250-748-0020; croweandappel.ca.
- CittaSlow: cittaslow.net.
- Cowichan Bay Maritime Centre: classicboats.org. Admission by donation.
- Cowichan Estuary Nature Centre, 1845 Cowichan Bay Rd, Cowichan Bay; 250-597-2288; cowichanestuary.ca; open afternoons Wed-Sun, holiday Mondays.
- Cowichan Estuary Restoration and Conservation Association (CERCA): cowichanestuary.com.

34 Duncan, City of Totems

Duncan is the little city in the middle of the Cowichan Valley, with a nice shopping district in a grid of narrow streets west of the Trans-Canada Highway.

Duncan is The City of Totems. The civic initiative kicked off in 1986 and to date has nurtured the creation of 40 poles. Thirty-seven poles embellish numerous places around town — one of the largest outdoor public displays anywhere of the art of carving and painting poles. A tour of the poles makes for a pleasant hour's (or so) walk. The majority were made by local Salish carvers. The giant figure of Kwa'mutsun (Quamichan) artist Simon Charlie (1919-2005) hovers over the project — he carved three of the poles and taught several of the artists working today. His pole Cedar Woman and Man (no. 1 of the series) exemplifies to me the spare, progressive character of Salish carving, little resembling the familiar poles of northern First Nations that display family crests.

There are works by noted Kwakiutl carvers Richard Hunt and Calvin Hunt, of northeast Vancouver Island, and by a Nuu-Chah-Nulth carver of the Island's west coast. Three of the carvers were from other regions. Many, if not all, of the poles represent metaphysical themes of origin, genesis, transformation. Canadian ethnologist Marius Barbeau explained the nature of the figures on totem poles this way in his two volume study of the art:

> The figures on totem poles consisted of symbols and illustrations, many of them comparable to our heraldry, and others commemorating historical events. They were not pagan gods or demons as is commonly supposed; they were never worshipped. Usually they illustrated myths or tribal traditions. Their meaning and associations inspired veneration rather than actual religious devotion.

The city's website has a descriptive guide to the installations, and the same information is provided on plaques beside each pole. The centerpiece is the two groupings on either side of the old railway station, now the Cowichan Valley Museum, in an inviting park of greenspace and informative displays with the daunting name Charles Hoey, VC, Memorial Park. The most recent addition, commissioned to commemorate the city's centennial in 2012, can be found in this space. Carved and painted by Calvin Hunt of Fort Rupert, it is magnitudes larger and more complex than any of the city's other poles.

The Cowichan Valley has a long history of Aboriginal ownership (see #s 30 and 32). One of Duncan's most attractive features is the green-swathed river running through. For that we can thank the indigenous people: most of the Lower Cowichan on both sides is reserve land. The Cowichan River was the traditional domain of this Nation. They are a people of the river as much as of the ocean. Most of their villages were on the river, and they operated as many as 21 weirs for trapping salmon. Today, the Cowichan Tribes form the largest First Nations community in the province, with nearly 5,000 registered members.

Duncan was originally named Alderlea after the name of William Duncan's farm. It became Duncan's Crossing and, after the farmer successfully petitioned the builder of the Esquimalt and Nanaimo Railway to put a station there, Duncan's Station. The station that stands today was built in 1912, the year Duncan was incorporated. Reminders of the Cowichan Valley's notably English heritage are evident in, for example, the cenotaph in the park that lists nearly 300 local men who died or went missing in action in the Great War, 1914-18.

Duncan's working-class character is based largely on forestry. It was once the home base of Sikh businessman Herb Doman's logging and milling empire. Hobby-farmers, retirees and refugees from city life have given Duncan a veneer of sophistication, as evidenced by the fine dining establishment Hudson's on First, located in a handsome 1906 residence, and several upscale interior décor shops downtown. Residents manifest a fondness for history, for which the centerpiece is the Cowichan Valley Museum.

Details

- Totem Tour Walk: duncan.ca.
- Cowichan Valley Museum and Archives: 130 Canada Ave, Duncan; 250-746-6612; cowichanvalleymuseum.bc.ca.
- Hudson's on First, 163 First St, Duncan; 250-597-0066; hudsonsonfirst.ca.

TAKE 5 *Good Guidebooks*

1. *The BC Coast Explorer and Marine Trail Guide. Vol 2 South Vancouver Island Bamfield to Comox Harbour* by John Kimantas. Nanaimo: Wild Coast Publishing, 2015. Kimantis is the unfatiguable publisher (irregularly) of *Coast&Kayak* and *Wild Coast* magazines (coastandkayak.com, wildcoast-magazine.com). Fantastic photos, maps, wonderful coverage; website sells waterproof maps.

2. *Hiking the Gulf Islands of British Columbia* by Charles Kahn. Madiera Park BC: Harbour Publishing, 3rd edition 2011. Ranks the trails 1-5 but curiously not the beaches and many other destinations; good maps.

3. *Hiking the West Coast of Vancouver Island* by Tim Leadem. Vancouver: Greystone Books, 3rd edition, 2015. West Coast Trail 47-80.

4. *Secret Beaches* series by Theo Dombrowski. Heritage House. *Greater Victoria: View Royal to Sidney* (2010) ¶ *Southern Vancouver Island: Qualicum to the Malahat* (2010) ¶ *Central Vancouver Island: Campbell River to Qualicum* (2011) ¶ *Southern Gulf Islands* (2012) ¶ *Northern Gulf Islands* (2012). Full colour; quite expensive: $20-27. Also $10 Kindle eds. Cookie-cutter format, rather plodding style. I lose interest. Doesn't always discriminate the casually interesting from the must-see. Great coverage though. Lists of top tens in many categories. ¶ By the same author: *Popular Day Hikes 4: Vancouver Island* ¶ *Seaside Walks on Vancouver Island* (both Rocky Mountain Books, 2014; both $15).

5. *Hiking Trails* series published by the Vancouver Island Trails Information Society: *1 Victoria & Vicinity* (13th edition, 2007, compiled and edited by Richard K. Blier, $20) ¶ *2 South Central Vancouver Island and the Gulf Islands* (9th edition, 2010, edited by Richard K. Blier, $31); ¶ *3 Northern Vancouver Island* (10th edition, 2008, revised and expanded by Gil Parker, $31) ¶ Website has trail updates: hikingtrailsbooks.com.

Not a guidebook, but indispensable for the adventurous: *Vancouver Island BC, Victoria & Gulf Islands Backroad Mapbook*. 8th edition, 2017; backroadmapbooks.com; $26.

Farm Stays and Visits 35

The bucolic Cowichan Valley was settled by farmers in the 1850s and remains extensively farmed. For those who dig the atmosphere of barnyard, farmhouse and field, here are a few local destinations wherein to shop, to dine, and perchance to stay.

Fairburn Farm is the mother of farmstays on the island. It offers comfortable lodgings in five rooms in an 1880s farmhouse on a working, organic, dairy farm near Duncan. A herd of water buffalo delivers the butterfat. The ample front porch looks to the west, across a garden of produce and flowers to fields that slope down to a forested creek. Mountains loom beyond. On the higher back side stand photogenic old farm buildings, relics of the original spread of nearly 500 ha/1,236 ac. (It's about one-tenth that size now.) The Archer family has owned Fairburn Farm since 1954, and the third generation is involved in its operation as a farm destination. It's open year-round as a bed and breakfast, with a two-night minimum stay. There are tours of the farm in season.

Alderlea Farm is a 4-ha/10-ac producer of organic foods and flowers grown by "biodynamic farming." The Farm Café reputedly serves the best pizza in the valley. Saison Market Vineyard operates a market and café highly esteemed by locals, open only on weekends (9 am-4 pm) from May to December.

Westholme Tea Farm grows organic teas and blends "microbatches" to make half a dozen products for sale on site or online. The tea room serves them up in artistic style — partner Margit Nellemann is a potter who employs a quirky imagination in crafting teapots and cups: her work is exhibited in an adjacent gallery.

Damali Lavender & Winery grows more than 25 varieties of lavender and makes them into oils, flower waters, lotions, creams, soaps, and dried flower buds. It is even used to flavor the wine the proprietors make from local grapes, berries and rhubarb. There's a shop and wine tasting room. Damali welcomes picnickers and curious visitors.

Hillcrest Farm Bed and Breakfast offers a suite and adjoining room in a 1930s farmhouse on a working farm around a hilltop in Cobble Hill. You can bring your pets, even your horse — it's close to a network of riding trails and has a sand ring.

Farmstays elsewhere on the islands:

Gordon's Beach Farm Stay Bed & Breakfast, near Sooke, offers two rooms and a self-contained cabin on a 4-ha/10-ac hobby farm.

Bold Point Farmstay B&B and Cottage has two farmhouse rooms and a self-contained cottage on a 4-ha/10-ac organic sheep and poultry farm on the secluded east coast of Quadra Island. Serves dinner by arrangement.

Details

- Fairburn Farm Guesthouse, 3310 Jackson Rd, Duncan; 250-746-4637; fairburnfarm.bc.ca.
- Alderlea Farm Café, 3390 Glenora Rd, Duncan; 250-597-3438; alderleafarm.com. Thurs 4-8, Fri-Sun 11-8; pizza Thurs & Sun evenings.
- Saison Market Vineyard, 7575 Mays Road, North Cowichan; 250-597-0484; saisonmarket.ca; Facebook page.
- Westholme Tea Farm, 8350 Richards Trail, North Cowichan; 1-855-748-3811; teafarm.ca; tea shop, tea room, Wed-Sun 10-5.
- Damali Lavender & Winery, 3500 Telegraph Rd, Cobble Hill; 250-743-4100; damali.ca.
- Hillcrest Farm Bed and Breakfast, 3915 Cobble Hill Road, Cobble Hill; 250-743-3843; hillcrestfarm.ca.
- Gordon's Beach Farm Stay Bed & Breakfast, 4537 Otter Point Road, Sooke; 778-425-1312; gordonsbeach.com.
- Bold Point Farmstay B&B and Cottage, 250-285-2272; farmstay-ca.com.

36   Deerholme Farm

Forage, v.: Search (a place) so as to obtain food. From Old French *fourrager*. (Oxford). The latest buzzword in foodie circles is humanity's oldest means of getting dinner. At Deerholme Farm, Bill Jones walks the talk, as a seasoned forager and foraging workshop leader, an acclaimed chef and dining host, a cooking class instructor and author of several books of cookery that incorporate foraged ingredients. Bill is one of a kind, and Deerholme Farm is, too.

Like everything forageous, dinner at Deerholme is a seasonal event that Bill offers once a month in fall and spring. Our visit in November was long on mushrooms. The passthrough in Bill's kitchen was heaped with fungi, including a humungous cauliflower mushroom and hard-to-find pine mushrooms, all from the vicinity in the Cowichan Valley. The season's menus are posted on the Deerholme website. We paid $90CDN+tax each in advance — Bill's dinners often sell out well in advance — and brought our own beverages. The dining room, which seats 28 at shared tables, resounded with the convivial talk of people enjoying something out-of-the-ordinary. The ambience is more like someone's dining room than a restaurant. You can watch Bill, big, bluff and sometimes gruff, at work in the semi-open kitchen. The whole affair — amuse-bouches, starters, soup, salad, main course and dessert, all sublime — stretched out for four hours. The conversation at our table of six was intense, and three couples who were strangers at the get-go were not by the wrap up.

I read Bill's menu for a recent spring dinner as a sensuous poem:

Grilled Humboldt squid with ox-eye daisy and chili oil
*Rillete of seared alabacore tuna and oyster mushrooms
   with rosehip jelly*
Spring soup of white fava beans, morels and wild herbs
*Crispy stinging nettle pancake with smoked salmon tartar and
   water buffalo yoghurt*
*Japanese braised duck with gobo, wild greens and sake kasu
   served over grand fir rice.*
*Wild blueberry and caramel custard parfait, big leaf maple cream
   and sumac sponge toffee.*

The lines suggest writerly skills, and Bill is indeed a seasoned scribbler. His three Deerholme forage-and-cookbooks are big and bountiful, lavishly illustrated with Bill's own photographs.

Bill's cooking classes are often paired with foraging workshops — as for example, the morel mushroom theme in April. The price of the "wild food weekend" combo is $215+GST; for just the foraging workshop, $135+tax. Again, they often sell out early. Spring is also the time of new growth in the world of photosynthesis, while in fall foraging is largely focused on the world of the fungus.

Deerholme Farm is literally next door to the Trans-Canada Trail, in a rural corner of Duncan. If you're unfamiliar with the neighbourhood and approaching by road in the dark, be sure you're packing GPS, or you will surely get lost. All one could wish for is a handy bed and breakfast. Fairburn Farm (#35) is a 15-minute drive, and Bill has listed other nearby lodgings on his website.

Details

- Deerholme Farm, 4830 Stelfox Rd, Duncan; 250-748-7450; deerholme.com.
- Books: *The Deerholme Vegetable Cookbook* (Touchwood Editions, 2015), *The Deerholme Foraging Book: Wild Foods and Recipes from the Pacific Northwest*, (Touchwood, 2014); *The Deerholme Mushroom Book: From Foraging to Feasting*, (Touchwood, 2013).

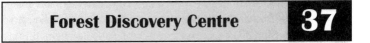

Forest Discovery Centre — 37

A working steam locomotive named Samson chuffs around a pleasant 3 km/1.9 mi of track by Somenos Lake. That alone is worth a stop to visit to this 40-ha/100-ac *open air museum* on Highway 1 north of Duncan.

The museum's collection of 12 steam locies recap the industrial history of the Island. Among the treasures is the Hillcrest Lumber Co. No. 1 Shay, which worked in the Cowichan Valley (#38) beginning in 1920.

The real discovery is how profoundly steam power altered the southeastern island. Steam made it possible to move the giant trees where before only animal power was available. *Railway logging* had a twin named *high-lead yarding*, where stationary *donkey engines* were used to pull the logs to trackside.

In its heyday, in the 1920s, more than 1,300 km/808 mi of logging railway were used at any time on the BC coast, and almost all the track was on Vancouver Island. After World War II, the *hi-baller* era quickly gave way to the internal combustion engine.

The museum started as one man's hobby. Gerry Wellburn (1900-1992) was a Cowichan valley logging operator who saw the writing on the wall and amassed a huge collection of abandoned machinery. Wellburn's name is equally well-known in stamp-collecting circles. His Vancouver Island collection is one of the greats.

Details

- British Columbia Forest Discovery Centre, 2892 Drinkwater Rd, Duncan; 250-715-1113; bcforestdiscoverycentre.com; hours vary by season; steam locomotive operates summer weekends and Christmas special events; food concession, gift shop.

- *From Camp to Community: Cowichan Forestry Life*: an informative, if not entirely functional, online feature about the Cowichan Valley logging camps: camptocommunity.ca.

- Reading: *The Stamps & Postal History of Colonial Vancouver Island and British Columbia*, a lavish, privately-published coffee-table book displaying Gerry Wellburn's amazing collection, with his meticulously hand-lettered notations; privately published in the 80s.

 38   **Cowichan Lake**

Cowichan Lake occupies a narrow valley in the heart of the south Island. Hemmed with steep slopes, the 31-km/19-mi-long lake has a haunting beauty and a certain grandeur. It's the picture of serenity until summer, when the lakeshore comes alive with campers and cottagers and boaters of every stripe. Dusty through-roads carry outdoor adventurers on to the west coast — Nitinat Lake, Carmanah-Walbran Park, Bamfield to southwest, while southeast from the South Shore Road a paved surface leads through a low pass into the San Juan Valley and Port Renfrew. The town of Lake Cowichan (2016 pop 3,226), at the head of the winding Cowichan River, is the service centre. Legions of tubers use the river in summer.

Lake Cowichan and Youbou are nice little towns. The whole valley has a relaxed vibe, quite distinct from what is commonly called the Cowichan Valley, the lowland between Duncan and Cowichan Bay. For summer recreation, the valley of Cowichan Lake is tops. As the staging place for wilderness adventure, it's situated excitingly close to the action.

Cowichan Lake was traditionally a resource base of First Nations on both the east coast (the Cowichan people) and the west (the Didaht people). In 1883, the whole valley became part of the stupendous Esquimalt & Nanaimo Railway land grant to coal tycoon Robert Dunsmuir, and started to be sold off to loggers and sawmill operators. The first loggers used oxen to yard the logs. During this period, the valley was the haunt of rich hunters and fishers. The adventurous took First Nations canoe rides down the river.

The era of industrial logging began when the Esquimalt & Nanaimo Railway spur reached Lake Cowichan in 1912. Youbou (pronounced *You bo*) is 10 km/6 mi west of Lake Cowichan, on the north side of the lake. The name memorializes the Messrs **You**nt (general manager) and **Bou**ten (president) of the Empire Lumber Company, operators of the first sawmill there, beginning in 1914. Youbou acquired by degrees a bank, a police station, a jail, a doctor's office, a theatre, a community hall and a school. It was one of several villages sustained by sawmills in the valley. Others were Honeymoon Bay, Mesachie Lake and Paldi. In 1925, the Canadian National Railway line opened from Victoria to Youbou, sparking construction of a state-of-the-art sawmill. For its time, the mill was advanced — it supplied some of the town's power by using waste wood to fuel a generator.

In its heyday, logging and milling supported 5,000 jobs in the valley. The whine of the cables and chuff of the steam donkeys resounded from end to end. The steam-powered logging system of the day combined high-lead yarding with "donkeys" (sledded winches, their tackle anchored to a spar tree) and hauling logs on flatcars to tidewater with "locies" (geared locomotives). Industrial logging cleaned out the entire valley, from lakeshore to height of land, one end to the other. For decades, Cowichan Lake was known for moonscapes of stunning proportions, a monument to unsustainable forestry. (Actually, it was the Great Depression that killed the boom.) The era of bleak landscapes is past, the valley has greened up and the second crop is being logged, but in little patches.

After World War II, truck logging took forestry into public forestlands on the west coast. In the 1950s, Camp 6 on the south shore was home for a thousand loggers and family members. One by one, the camps closed. The mills closed too, leaving Honeymoon Bay and Mesachie Lake decimated. TimberWest Corporation's Youbou sawmill closed in 2001, after more than 70 years sawing dimension and specialty lumber.

Youbou, still unincorporated, is now a quiet community of 1,000 arranged around a little hourglass of a peninsula. Cottages crowd the nearby north shore, on the sunny side of the lake. (For much of the year and for some of most days, the south shore loses sun.) Three small parks provide public access to the waterfront. Two-hectare Mile 77 Park commemorates a CNR section manager's home. Price Park occupies 5.5 ha/13.6 ac on a quiet bit of shore. Arbutus Park is busy in summer with a beach and a pool, lifeguards and picnic tables. Views up the valley are magnificent.

The **Kaatza Station Museum and Archives**, in the 1913 E&N railway station at Lake Cowichan, is the must-see attraction in the valley. Representative and well-presented, this little gem lays out the whole history in meticulous reconstructions of a kitchen, an office, and other features of life in the glory days of logging and milling. Among its holdings are 1,000 plates of Wilmer Gold's forest industry photography, information and records of 50 local forestry companies and much more. It's attractively sited in lakeside Saywell Park, next to the visitor information centre.

A sense of the transient lingers here. The **Gordon Bay Provincial Park** campground, on the south shore, is a case in point. It's very popular in summer, with a beach area protected from speedboats that roar around the lake. On a nice hot summer day, family recreation doesn't get much better. Campsites are set amid gracefully growing Douglas fir trees. The forest provides respite from the heat. But, poignantly, you sense the campground will someday prove more valuable as lumber and will cease to exist when someone in an office decides it's time to "harvest" the "timber."

Some of the 230 workers who lost their jobs when the Youbou mill closed put up a fight. They formed the Youbou TimberLess Society to protest the accelerated extraction of old-growth forests and their export as raw logs. They counted the logging trucks leaving the valley loaded with wood — 450 in four days. Raw log exports have continued to rise: 2016 was a record year. On the North Shore Road, the village's main street, TimberWest logging trucks continue to rumble on through. Here's to the citizens of Youbou who are standing up for a better deal.

Details

- Kaatza Station Museum and Archives, 125 South Shore Rd, Lake Cowichan; 250-749-6142; Facebook page.
- Community parks in Youbou: cvrd.bc.ca. The following distances are west of the Youbou Rd exit to Lake Cowichan on Highway 18.
  - Mile 77 Park, on Creekside Dr, 7.6 km
  - Price Park, at end of Miracle Way, intersection at 9.5 km.
  - Arbutus Park, end of Alder Cresc, intersection at 14.5 km.
- Gordon Bay Provincial Park, 122 reservable campsites on 104 ha/257 ac at Honeymoon Bay: env.gov.bc.ca.
- Reading: *Those Lake People: Stories of Cowichan Lake*, by Lynne Bowen (Douglas & McIntyre, 1996).

The Gulf Islands

An archipelago of 15 greater and more than 200 lesser islands between the east coast of Vancouver Island and Georgia Strait, the Gulf Islands are rugged and even wild in spots, with bits of flat arable land on valley bottoms. They comprise many irregular landforms within a unified geological domain of sandstone and shale where there's great upland hiking and wonderful mountaintop scenery (see #40). With their indented coastlines on the Salish Sea (#41), the islands are a boater's delight, and much of the shoreline is protected in a world-class network of protected areas (see #44). The Gulf Islands are lightly populated, and it's quite a dispersed population. Food-farming is one of the principal occupations, with its roots in the 1850s. The islands are well-known as cottage country, and for their many lodgings and purveyors of food and drink (see #s 42 and 43). The population swells and abates with the seasons. Nine of the islands are served by BC Ferries, and among the main southern Gulf Islands, service is frequent between Vancouver Island and Salt Spring Island, even more with Gabriola Island, somewhat less frequent between Vancouver Island and the other Gulf Islands and between the mainland terminal at Tsawwassen and the Southern Gulf Islands.

Salt Spring Island is the largest Gulf Island (182.7 sq km/70.5 sq mi) and the most populated (2016 census pop: 10,557). Ferry traffic through the charming hamlet of **Fulford Harbour** supports a tiny, busy commercial enclave. The colorful village of **Ganges** is the island's shopping centre — gone way upmarket in recent years — with three good bookstores and the seasonal, venerable, must-see **Saturday Market** (#42). Tiny **Vesuvius** on the sandstoned west side of Salt Spring benefits commercially from the terminus of the Crofton ferry. Salt Spring is the Gulf Island I know best, having visited since I was knee-high — see #42.

On the other biggest southern Gulf Islands — North and South Pender, Galiano, Mayne and Saturna — and smaller islands to the south, the permanent population totaled 4,732 in 2016; their aggregated area is 191.2 sq km/73.8 sq mi. Their census count was down 2.8% from 2011. Salt Spring's population, by contrast, gained by 3.8% between censuses. The reason for the disparity may be as simple as ferry fare increases for residents of remoter islands.

The port of **Galiano Island** is the excellent hamlet of **Sturdies Bay**, with a wonderful bookstore and a funky soi-disant resort that hosts a great literary fest every February. It's the island's shopping centre. The restaurant **Pilgrimme**, already a legend, is a ways distant, on the approach to beautiful Montague Harbour.

On **North Pender Island** are tiny enclaves near Browning Harbour (the islands' shopping centre), at Port Washington and Hope Bay. **South**

SOUTHEAST VANCOUVER ISLAND AND THE GULF ISLANDS

Pender has a resort and marina on scenic Bedwell Harbour.

On **Mayne Island**, all roads lead to the commercial enclave at Miner's Bay, on Active Pass. The much-photographed lighthouse on Georgina Point stands on the brink of the Strait of Georgia.

Access to **Saturna Island**'s well-off-the-beaten-track roads begins at the port on Lyell Harbour. Nearby is a whimsical coffee house in a double-decker bus, and up the road is a modest shopping centre.

Thetis Island, accessed from Chemainus, has a couple of B&Bs and a colourful marina.

Further north, fronting Nanaimo Harbour, is **Gabriola Island** (2016 census pop: 4,033). There is no there there — folks do their shopping in Nanaimo, a stone's throw away, but it has many scenic delights and the venerable Haven "centre for transformative learning."

Lasqueti Island, in the middle of the Strait of Georgia, is accessible by passenger-only ferry from French Creek, near Parksville; its 400 residents pride themselves on energy self-sufficiency.

The sunny pair **Denman Island** and **Hornby Island** (#58), combined 2016 population 2,181, lie off the east coast mid-Island. Access is by way of the cable ferry at Buckley Bay. To get to Hornby, a second ferry hop is necessary. Hornby has a funky shopping centre at Tribune Bay, and there's a community centre en route.

As to why they're called the Gulf Islands, the story begins with Captain George Vancouver. The surveyor named the inland sea the *Gulphe of Georgia* in 1792. The geography-minded might say that's a misnomer, since a *gulf* is a body of water open on one side, whereas Georgia Strait is open at both ends. But it's a fact that Captain Vancouver encountered the strait after his ships sailed *in* via the Strait of Juan de Fuca, but before he discovered Discovery Passage, through which, at the northwest end of Georgia Strait, he sailed *out*. In 1865, Captain Richards renamed it the Strait of Georgia. Today, the entire inland waterway is known as the *Salish Sea*, while the different parts retain their old names.

Nobody, it seems, named the Gulf Islands. According to historian Michael Layland, the name came into common use after the settlement of the San Juan Boundary Dispute in 1872. When the 49th parallel latitude was established in 1846, and because Britain and the United States both presented claims to possessing San Juan Island, the boundary was left undetermined in the waters between the straits of Georgia and Juan de Fuca. The German Kaiser was arbiter of the dispute, and he awarded the San Juan Islands to the United States. The new international boundary isolated the Canadian islands. (Geographers sometimes group the Gulf and San Juan Islands under the single name San Juan Archipelago.) In time, the Canadian group acquired its collective identity as the Gulf Islands. In the Victoria *British Colonist* newspaper, the name first turns up on June 27, 1883, in lower case: "The steamer Hope, which carries the mails between the gulf Islands, blew out her cylinder head on Monday."

40 Gulf Islands: Natural History

The best way to experience the lie of the Gulf Islands is to fly over them on a clear day. Regular float plane service between Victoria and Vancouver provides that opportunity. It's not cheap, but on a clear day the views are unbeatable. You'll see little farms cradled in narrow valleys, with parallel lines of sandstone forming the ridges. Lines of exposed shale run into a saddle of forest, and then continue into a bay on the other side. You will note little shell beaches with red-barked arbutus trees overhanging, somehow rooted in those edgewise strata of shale.

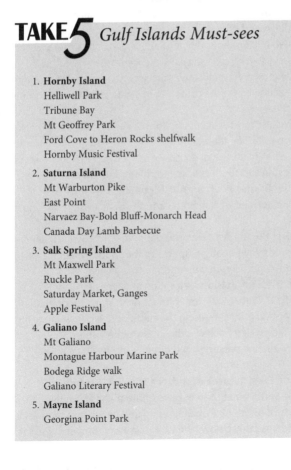

TAKE 5 *Gulf Islands Must-sees*

1. **Hornby Island**
   Helliwell Park
   Tribune Bay
   Mt Geoffrey Park
   Ford Cove to Heron Rocks shelfwalk
   Hornby Music Festival

2. **Saturna Island**
   Mt Warburton Pike
   East Point
   Narvaez Bay-Bold Bluff-Monarch Head
   Canada Day Lamb Barbecue

3. **Salk Spring Island**
   Mt Maxwell Park
   Ruckle Park
   Saturday Market, Ganges
   Apple Festival

4. **Galiano Island**
   Mt Galiano
   Montague Harbour Marine Park
   Bodega Ridge walk
   Galiano Literary Festival

5. **Mayne Island**
   Georgina Point Park

SOUTHEAST VANCOUVER ISLAND AND THE GULF ISLANDS

You'll see, too, how much of the bigger islands are rocky, rugged, thickly forested, impassible to vehicles. Overall, you will see that the southern Gulf Islands are strongly aligned on a northwest-southeast vector.

Geologists have pieced together the forces that created the Islands' distinctive lineaments. About 100 million years ago, Wrangellia Terrane accreted to earlier arrivals along the western edge of the North American Plate. The core of central Salt Spring Island is metamorphosed rocks — igneous granites and sedimentary argillites — that are about 350 million years old. Over time, a basin formed between Wrangellia and the continental plate. Sand and other sediments built up.

During the Upper Cretaceous Age, 86-65 million years ago, the deposited sediments turned into the shale, sandstone and conglomerate rocks known collectively as the Nanaimo Group. Most of the southern Gulf Islands and the eastern margins of Vancouver Island are of the Nanaimo Group. The formation created the coal belt that figures so hugely in Vancouver Island's history. Over the aeons, more terranes moved into place. The result was much crunching and compacting and the uplifting of both Wrangellia and Nanaimo Group rocks. Layers of sedimentary rock folded into either arches or basins, forming the Gulf Islands' distinctive alternation of valleys and ridges.

For the last two million years, down to about 15-12,000 years ago, the whole area was overlain by glacial ice. As the ice retreated northward, it scoured valleys, exposed the sandstones and sculpted the shales and conglomerates. The action of the sea continues to erode shoreline sandstone into fantastic façades.

Salt Spring has the most striking landforms. The island's three blocks of upland are separated by fault lines that have formed into two fertile valleys running parallel, northeast-southwest. The west side of the island rises to its highest in the south block, and the middle block is nearly as high, crowned by Baynes Peak, with its dramatic lookout. The northern block is lower, formed of Nanaimo Group rock. It's where the most people live.

As is general, in this area of recent glacial retreat, many prominences on the larger islands have open prospects to the south, while the north sides are forested. Especially worth visiting for the views:

- **Mt Maxwell, Salt Spring Island**, elevation at Baynes Peak lookout 552 m/1,812 ft; 11.4 km/7.1 mi from Ganges, with some rough road. A delightful option is to walk along the contour (link below) through a southwest-facing Garry oak woodland. Exquisite vistas unfold of ridges, narrow marine passages, and directly south, a little valley of farms.

- **Mt Warburton Pike, Saturna Island**, el 403 m/1,322 ft (according to Google Earth; other sources give different elevations, eg, 497 m/1,631 ft). Drive or hike up Staples Rd and park near the tower, or hike up the nose (see below). We walk east along Brown Ridge for panoramic views across the Gulf and (US) San Juan Islands. The views are by many accounted the best in the Gulf Islands.

- **Mt Galiano, Galiano Island**, el 314 m/1,030 ft; is a 3/4 to 1 hour hike from several trailheads. Here there are dramatic views of Active Pass and Mayne, Pender and Prevost Islands beyond, and in the far distance, Vancouver Island and the Olympic Mountains.

The climate of the Gulf Islands is mild year-round and relatively dry, within the rain shadows of the Vancouver Island Mountains and the Olympics (see Take 5: Canada's Warmest Places).

Ecologically, much of the lower elevations of the Gulf Islands are belts and pockets of Garry oak woodland within the domain of the Douglas fir. Meadows of wildflowers are associated with Garry oaks as well as the tree species arbutus and Douglas fir. Much of the land under protection in National or Provincial parks aim to conserve what little of the Garry oak ecosystems remain (see Take 5: Garry Oak Woodlands). The three south-facing eminences described above are clothed in Garry oak meadows.

Details

- Harbour Air: harbour-air.com; many float-planes daily between Victoria and Vancouver harbours and to Gulf Island destinations.
- *The Gulf Islands Ecosystem Community Atlas* (Canadian Parks and Wilderness Society, 2005); cpaws.org; has a good overview of geologic processes in the southern Gulf Islands, and great maps of biodiversity and protective assessment.
- Saltspring Island Geology, map and notes: empr.gov.bc.ca.
- Mt Maxwell Provincial Park road and trail map: env.gov.bc.ca; trail #6/6A to/from Baynes Peak highly recommended, as is #9, a shoreline walk from the end of Burgoyne Bay Rd.
- Mt Galiano trail map: galiander.ca.
- Saturna Island road map: lyallharbour.com.
- Alternate hike up Mt Warburton Pike: a steep climb up the nose of the mountain; this is a condensed version of a posting on waymarking.com: drive south on Harris Rd; just before the stone gate of Saturna Island Vineyard, look on left for an old community trail, sometime logging and power-line access road; follow flagging and cairns; where the power-line access road swings to the left, continue straight ~20 m/66 ft, then turn left; dirt road at cottage leads to summit; cross the road and follow goat trails through the open areas to the ridge.

The actual summit, with communication towers and parking lot, is unattractive; the Brown Ridge trail extends along the rim of the ridge for ~3 km/2 mi, past gnarled trees and rocky bluffs; ridge trail is in the National Park Reserve except for private property around a red-roofed cabin, whose owners permit hikers to cross their property.

Upon the Salish Sea | 41

Active Pass is the narrow, Z-shaped passage on the BC Ferries' route between Swartz Bay, Vancouver Island and Tsawwassen, on the mainland. It's the most used of BC Ferries' 25 routes. Some five million passengers and 1.6 million vehicles thread the narrow channel every year. Indeed, generations of local ferryboats, beginning in the 19th century, have used Active Pass on routes between Victoria and the lower mainland. The scenic narrows, with its looming rocky shores and mountainous reaches, always draw travellers onto the decks. In the colder months, the channel comes alive with feathered migrants, especially near the elbows at either end. The waterfowl rise in thousands as the ferry passes, only to settle back in sheets on the swirling chuck.

In the summer, when travellers lie all over the decks, soaking up the sun, that's when you're likely to see Them. You want to be on deck at the Georgia Strait (north) end of Active Pass. There are nice views along the outer coasts of Galiano and Mayne Islands. I've seen Orca whales several times there. Once, we all crowded to the port side, making the vessel list noticeably, to marvel at a pod of Orcas leaping and cavorting a stone's throw away. The ferry stopped there for a good ten minutes. I doubt if anyone minded its late arrival.

As the boat traverses the middle section of the pass, a view unfolds of the low hump of Helen Point on Mayne Island, to the south. There, a First Nations village site has been excavated and its artifacts dated to 5,000 years before present.

The grand offshoot of the North Pacific Ocean known as the Salish Sea comprises all the waterways between Vancouver Island and the mainland and Puget Sound as well. Ringed by mountains, in forms wild and rugged, mild of climate, teeming with fish (not so much any more) and birds, home range of Orcas and other large mammals, it was the traditional domain of Salishan-speaking peoples.

The origins of the Salish people is lost in the mists of time. For a long time, archaeologists supposed there was a migration to the coast from the interior of BC sometime between 3,000 and 2,000 years ago. A rival theory, whose currency is rising, holds that the ancestors immigrated into the northwest Pacific coast much earlier, perhaps 10,000 years ago, soon after the retreat of glacial ice. The oldest artifacts found on Vancouver Island and nearby Islands date from about 9,000 years ago. Earlier sites may now be under water.

Salish territory extended throughout the inland sea, well north of present-day Campbell River, all of both sides of Georgia Strait, all of Puget Sound, all of the islands and passages north of Puget Sound and most of Juan de Fuca Strait, excepting Wakashan-speakers of the Ditidaht First

Nation territory on the Canadian side and Makah on the American. The traditional territories of Coast Salish First Nations was much about salt water. The sea was food locker and garden, highway, medium of commerce, trade and war. Their villages were sited on tidewater or beside major rivers. They might move seasonally between several places, depending on local patterns of food supply.

The name Salish Sea is of recent coinage — the indigenous peoples evidently did not have a name for the whole inland waterway — and it serves an urgent need. The name was proposed by marine scientist Bert Webber of Western Washington University in 1988. The way Dr Webber explains it, human impacts on the marine ecosystem have been considerable, in some places catastrophic — witness the precipitous decline of the Orca population resident in the southern Salish Sea; witness the declining stocks of wild salmon. Marine ecosystems are no respecters of jurisdictional boundaries — yet the respective governments of Washington, BC, the US and Canada have not even begun to collaborate on addressing ecological impacts. The catchy name Salish Sea was intended to raise public consciousness of the unitary nature of the waterway and stimulate more effective trans-boundary planning. The university's Salish Sea website has a text that reads in part: "Having a name to identify the entire area calls attention to the trans-border commonality of water, air, wildlife and history." At a celebration in Victoria in 2010, Webber told a newspaper reporter: "A name allows you to develop a sense of place, and a knowledge of that. There are about nine million people who live on the Salish Sea, and it's crucial that we have that sense of place."

Details

- Active Pass: named for the US revenue cutter/surveying vessel Active, a 2-gun paddle-steamer, passed through in 1855. Captain Richards, RN, of the surveying vessel *Plumper*, discovered in 1858 that it was not the first boat of the European hegemon to navigate the pass. He did the right thing, naming it in honour of the American boat.

- Facts & figures: the saltwater surface area of the Salish Sea totals 18,000 sq km/7,000 sq mi. Tumwater, Washington marks its southern limit at about 47°N latitude; the northern boundary is the head of Bute Inlet, BC, at 50°55' N; the western is near Campbell River, BC, longitude 125°10'W; while its easternmost is at Everett, Wa, longitude 122°11'W. The coastline of the Salish Sea, including 419 Islands, totals 7,470 km/4,642 mi. When the areas of all the rivers draining into the Salish Sea are considered, the total area multiplies six times to include some 110,000 sq km/42,000 sq mi.

- History of "Salish Sea," description of ecosystems, maps: wwu.edu/salishsea.

- Reflections on the Water: Conversations about the Salish Sea:

salishreflections.wordpress.com.
- Salish house at the Canadian Museum of History, Gatineau PQ: historymuseum.ca.
- The W̱SÁNEĆ people, traditional proprietors of much of the Gulf Islands, on the SENĆOŦEN language portal at firstvoices.ca.
- Reading: *The W̱SÁNEĆ and Their Neighbours: Diamond Jenness on the Coast Salish of Vancouver Island*, 1935 (Rock's Mills Press, 2016).
- "An introduction to First Nations' history in the Gulf Islands" by Chris Arnett: saltspringarchives.com.
- Guidebook to the natural and human history of the Swartz Bay-Tsawwassen route: *What's That Island? A Ferry Travel Guide*, by Bruce Whittington (Stray Feathers Press, 2010): strayfeathers.ca.

42 Edible Islands

Salt Spring Island is accessible from Victoria in little more than an hour. Easy access and fame have changed the island and, no question, it has lost some of its rural character. Traffic on the highway and in Ganges has hugely increased. Suburban developments have sprung up around the village. There's even bus service (infrequent). Much remains unchanged. Rugged Salt Spring is still largely uninhabitable. Strips of smallhold agriculture still inhabit the valleys and gentler upland. Wherever there's a bit of level ground and accessible shore, waterfront enclaves have filled in.

Food continues to be a huge attraction on the Gulf Islands — eating it, cooking it, growing it.

The seasonal **Saturday market in Ganges** showcases local produce and some of the Island's many artists and crafters. Organic cheeses are but one of the Island's specialities. Galiano, Pender, Saturna, Mayne and Gabriola also have farm markets Saturdays during the growing season.

Salt Spring is famous for its apples. Every fall there's a one-day **Apple Festival** showcasing more than 350 varieties grown here. You can guide yourself around 30 farms and orchards on the tour.

Some farms are open to visits and lodging. **Salt Spring Seeds** does most of its business by mail-order. Proprietor Dan Jason gladly (by arrangement) shows visitors the organic farm, part of the **Salt Spring Centre of Yoga**.

On the slopes of Mt Maxwell, Michael Ableman, organic farmer and author of several gorgeous books about farming, operates with his family **Foxglove Farm** — a working organic farm, a retreat with cabins to rent and the home of the Centre for Arts, Ecology and Agriculture.

The devotion to good food has taken root elsewhere on the Gulf Islands. On nearby Galiano Island, there's the **Pilgrimme Restaurant**, voted #3 on the 2015 *EnRoute* (Air Canada) Canada's Best New

Restaurants, and in *Vancouver Magazine*'s 2016 best restaurant awards for Vancouver Island outside Victoria, it was Number one.

Carnivores congregate on Saturna Island every Canada Day (July 1) for the **lamb barbecue**, a big affair at Winter Cove, near scenic narrow Boat Passage. It's a fund-raiser for services not provided to Saturna Islanders by the regional district. Last year, I walked in from the ferry dock to the barbecue, 5.2 km/3 mi of up and down. At least ten cars and the shuttle bus stopped to ask if I wanted a ride. The community field was packed, and the succulent lamb, splayed on racks planted around great blazing fires tended by a dozen cooks, so juicy and tender. The cuter they are, as the saying goes, the better they taste.

Some of my earliest memories are of Salt Spring island lambs. In the 1950s, my family visited the Island on occasional weekends. We would catch the ferry *Cy Peck* from the tiny slip at Swartz Bay, and then drive from Fulford Harbour across sylvan terrain, opening into farms, sheep grazing the golf course, finally just about losing our stomachs on the twisty-hilly dirt road down to Booth Bay on the west side of the island. The shingled lodge at Acland's Guest House was surrounded by more than 100 acres of gardens, pasture and forest, with hundreds of feet of waterfront on the excellent bay. Across the water were the mountains of Vancouver Island. For a child, it was paradise — water warm enough to swim in summer, log rafts and a rowboat, and meadows and forest to play in. And they had sheep. Most of their food was local, if not grown in their spacious, well-fenced backyard garden.

The Aclands' impossibly picturesque old boathouse of bleached planks stood on a little spit at the mouth of the Canal. Just inside the spit, the water was deep enough that you could jump off the heaped shell beach into the swirling sand-warm current of an incoming tide. That spit was full of clams. Early one morning, I opened the door of the boathouse to discover a lot of people asleep on the floor — First Nations people, clammers from Vancouver Island, I was told. The Canal was a narrow tidal reach a few hundred yards long — called that, I guess, because of its shape. Maybe in the old days the Canal went right through to Ganges. This Canal is so shallow it empties at low tide, leaving small boats sitting on mud.

The rocky part of the beach teemed with life. There were crabs under every rock. Occasionally at low tide we came upon a pool made by rocks arranged in a crescent. In the pool would be a dogfish or sculpin, trapped by an ebbing tide. This was likely a First Nations sea-ranching installation.

Presiding over that magic kingdom were Marge and Bevill Acland. They were gracious and kindly and of English descent. Marge was born in the United States and grew up in the Okanagan Valley but spoke in distinctly British tones. Bevill was the grandson of the second son of Sir Thomas Dyke, 10th Baronet Acland. Not that they ever mentioned their origins. Marge turned out amazing meals on the wood stove. Her cooking was heavenly. Puffy golden muffins of Yorkshire pudding with the roast beast on Saturday night. In late summer, warm blackberry pudding with fresh whipped cream. Marge turned out bread and buns in that wood stove that remain the best I ever tasted. (Sorry, mum.)

I would go into Ganges with Bevill on Saturday morning in his old Austin. At the general store, the Salt Spring Island Trading Company, you went up to a wide counter and ordered your supplies. A clerk would climb up a ladder with runners on the floor and ceiling to fetch your items. That charmingly retro way of shopping is long gone, like the old telephone on the wall in the hall at Acland's, black bakelite with a separate earpiece and a crank that you turned to get the operator. You would give her a number to call. The Aclands' phone number was 8-7-Y. I didn't know it at the time, but I was privileged to glimpse a way of life that was fast disappearing from a thousand cities.

Details

- Salt Spring Island Saturday Market: saltspringmarket.com.
- Salt Spring Island Apple Festival: saltspringmarket.com. The farm tour is fascinating; maps are available only on the day of the festival.
- Salt Spring Seeds has a world-wide mail-order service: 250-537-5269; saltspringseeds.com.
- Salt Spring Centre of Yoga, 355 Blackburn Rd, Salt Spring Island; 250-537-2326; saltspringcentre.com.
- Foxglove Farm, 1200 Mt Maxwell Rd, Salt Spring Island; 250-537-1989 (accommodations), 250-931-5336 (farm office); foxglovefarmbc.ca.
- Michael Ableman, farmer, author, urban and local food systems advocate: michaelableman.com.
- Booth Bay: public access via steps at the foot of Baker Rd, W of Lower Ganges Rd, 3 km N of the centre of Ganges. Booth Canal is to the left. (In Canada all foreshore below mean high tide is public.) The boathouse is long gone; the spit much changed.
- Pilgrimme restaurant: 2806 Montague Rd, Galiano Island; 250-539-5392; pilgrimme.ca.
- Canada Day Lamb Barbecue: Hunter Field at Winter Cove Day Use Area, part of the Gulf Islands National Park Reserve: saturnalambbarbeque.com.
- Saturna Island ferries: two are sometimes required to/from Vancouver Island or mainland BC: bcferries.com.
- Reading: *Trauma Farm: A Rebel History of Rural Life*, by Brian Brett (Douglas & McIntyre, 2009).

The islands' agricultural heart is a belt of sunny lowland straddling the **Cowichan Valley**, the **Gulf Islands** and the **Saanich Peninsula**. These largely rural areas can be linked by short ferry routes and back roads into a circuit that takes you to centres of local cuisine and a flourishing wine industry.

The circuit of about 100 km/62 mi is a three-day excursion (at least) by bike. It's best undertaken toward the end of summer. Bikers face several long steep hills and unavoidable bits of highway travel. Whether you bike or drive, the rewards are many and marvellous. Amid this region's bucolic beauties are many distinctive lodgings, organic dining rooms, open farms and wineries. Beckoning you to explore along the way are beaches and parks and heights of land with sweeping views. Three ferry rides offer their own scenic experiences.

Ferry: Swartz Bay–Fulford Harbour.

At BC Ferries' Swartz Bay terminal there's long-term parking, and sailings every two hours to Salt Spring Island.

Coming into Fulford Harbour, you get a fine view up the valley towards Mt Maxwell's rocky brow.

In **Fulford Harbour**, the place to dine or have a coffee is **Rock Salt Restaurant & Café**, beside the ferry terminal.

Fulford Harbour to Ganges: we can follow the Fulford–Ganges Rd toward Mt Maxwell, and stop in at one of the wineries on the first hill, but in my honest opinion, the traffic gets pretty bad, just saying. Bikers can take a shorter back route by angling right onto Beaver Point Rd at the top of the hill. The reward for a fair amount of uphill work is charming, swimmable Stowell Lake. Then we go left on Stewart Rd and onto Cusheon Lake Rd, where we can either turn left and hook up with the Ganges Rd before the long hill, or go right and transition to Beddis Rd, where we turn left and enjoy the views across Ganges Harbour as we navigate a long straightaway and pick up the Ganges Rd near the last precipitous hill into the village. It's 12.5 km/7.8 mi by the shortest route.

Ganges, Salt Spring's tiny metropolis, has many places to eat and stay. I've always enjoyed the outdoor ambience of the **Tree House Café**, and it's a good place to get your morning beverage. If possible, plan to be in Ganges for the **Saturday Market**, for the people-watching. Everyone turns out, it seems.

Ganges to Vesuvius Bay: we're stuck with traffic arteries, unfortunately, Upper or Lower Ganges and Vesuvius Bay roads. Upper is the shorter (7.3 km/4.5 mi), Lower the less travelled. In gorgeous **Vesuvius Bay**, you can walk on the sandstone beach, sit on the deck at the **Seaside Restaurant**, and enjoy some serious seafood.

SOUTHEAST VANCOUVER ISLAND AND THE GULF ISLANDS

Ferry: Vesuvius–Crofton.

Crofton is a quiet gem of a community in North Cowichan. The town was built (1902) on a hillside to house workers in a copper mine and smelter. Falling copper prices closed it in six years, and the town languished until 1957, when it became a bedroom community for workers at the nearby pulp mill. A heritage schoolhouse has been moved there and converted to a museum. A boardwalk along the shore provides views across the water.

Crofton to Mill Bay: the longest stretch of the circuit, about 40 km/ 25 mi by these back roads: Osborne Bay Rd; Herd R; Maple Bay Rd — past scenic Quamichan Lake — Tzouhalem Rd, which skirts the amazing Cowichan Estuary; Cowichan Bay Rd, through Cowichan Bay village, where they take food seriously, and Telegraph and Kilmalu Rds to Highway 1. Turn left onto a short stretch of heavy traffic on Highway 1 across the bridge, then follow Deloume and Mill Bay Rds.

Besides the culinary attractions of Cowichan Bay, the Cowichan Valley invites side trips for food, drink and lodging. North of the Cowichan River, there are half a dozen wineries, and a dozen in South Cowichan and Cobble Hill. In the *Take 5: John Schreiner's Favorite Island Wineries*, note the three vineyards in Cowichan district.

Ferry: Mill Bay–Brentwood Bay.

Brentwood Bay to Swartz Bay: the scenic waterfront of Brentwood Bay, so popular with boaters, is worth exploring, with its little beaches overhung with ruddy arbutus trees.

To return to our point of origin, Swartz Bay, we have options. An east side route that's about 20 km/12 mi proceeds via a left turn onto Peden Ln and a right on Stelly's Cross Rd, which we follow to E Saanich Rd, then turn right. At Island View Rd turn left, cross Highway 17 and make a left onto the Lochside Trail. Note, there are a clutch of vineyards south of Stelly's Cross Rd.

A west side route goes north along Tsartlip Dr, W Saanich Rd, Birch Rd, Chalet Dr and Lands End Rd to Swartz Bay. It's longer (24 km/15 mi), along narrow roads, but the rewards include, if you're lucky and feeling flush, a meal at **Deep Cove Chalet**, the legendary bastion of rich French cookery. The Chalet was once an inn at a railway-ferry nexus. The dining room overlooks Deep Cove and across Saanich Inlet to South Cowichan. Sublime.

Bon appétit!

Details

- BC Ferries: bcferries.com. Long-term parking only at Swartz Bay. Only cash or travellers' cheques are accepted on the Brentwood Bay-Mill Bay ferry.
- Maps and guides for the biker: cyclevancouverlsland.ca.
- Reading: *Food Artisans of Vancouver Island and the Gulf Islands,*

by Don Genova (Touchstone Editions, 2014).

- Guidebook: *An Edible Journey: Exploring the Islands' Fine Foods, Farms and Vineyards*, by Elizabeth Levinson (Heritage House, 3rd ed. 2009).
- Rock Salt Restaurant & Café, Fulford Harbour; 250-653-4833; rocksaltrestaurant.com.
- Should we slug our guts up Mt Maxwell? *Ride with GPS* profile: rlslandewithgps.com/routes/2255006.
- Tree House Café, Purvis Lane, Ganges; 250-537-5379; treehousecafe.ca
- Seaside Restaurant, Vesuvius Bay; 250-537-2249; seaslslanderestaurantsaltspring.com.
- Cowichan bike routes: naturecowichan.net.
- Deep Cove Chalet, 11190 Chalet Rd, North Saanich; 250-656-3541; deepcovechalet.com.

44 Gulf Islands Protected Areas

The better part of the Gulf Islands experience is provided by nature, whether on land or sea. There's excellent hiking in a multitude of settings, whether climbing the highest hill, meandering along the waterfront, or (my particular favorite) ridge-walking. Almost everybody seems to be messing about in boats. For recreation, the parklands of the Gulf Islands make an embarrassment of riches. In summer, the islands' many campgrounds do a busy trade. The waters swirl with a thousand paddles.

The **Gulf Islands National Park Reserve**, created in 2003, is a patchwork of 36 sq km/14 sq mi of land on 15 Islands and more than 50 islets, and 26 sq km/10 sq mi of intertidal and nearshore subtidal marine areas. The lands include 43 percent of the total area of Saturna Island and 30 percent of South Pender Island. Five complete Islands — Tumbo, Georgeson, Russell, Portland and D'Arcy — are protected. A paddler could spend nearly two weeks in the islands and camp in a different part of the park every night. A few campgrounds have reservable sites.

One of my favorites is a few primitive sites back of a sandy beach on tiny **Cabbage Island**, near Saturna Island. Another is in gorgeous **Narvaez Bay**, on the south side of Saturna's East Point. (Experienced paddlers give the turbulent waters of East Point a wide berth.) In contrast to the serenity of Saturna is busy **Sidney Spit** park, on Sidney Island, with foot-passenger ferry connection to the town of Sidney. It's heavily used by yachters, but ideally situated for paddlers exploring the many little islands in Haro Strait. Complementing the network of national park sites are a number of fine provincial parks. One of the most popular with boaters, bikers and car campers is **Ruckle Park**, a grassy meadow near Beaver Pt, on the east side of Salt Spring Island, with 78 walk-in sites (only a few reservable). The 529-ha/1,307-ac park has

15 km/9 mi of trails, including 7 km/4.3 mi of fabulous shoreline of little coves and shell beaches. The campground gets busy in summer: bring your earplugs. The very popular **Montague Harbour Marine Provincial Park**, on Galiano Island, has 15 walk-in sites that you can reserve.

It pays to plan waterborne excursions. Herewith, a cautionary tale. We set out to circumnavigate Salt Spring Island, Paula by kayak and I in my dory. It's about 80 km/50 mi around the Island. We allowed three nights. We put in at Deep Cove, crossed choppy Satellite Channel and decided to take the route less travelled, up Sansum Narrows, on the west side of the Island. We assumed we would find a campsite along the way. The Gulf Islands have so many.

We landed on a little beach for relief and refreshment. Within moments, a power boat launched from a float across the bay. A polite but firm security chap told us to move on. A syndicate owns all the Salt Spring foreshore for several kilometres. We told him we were sitting on the intertidal, which is public land, Her Majesty and all that. It didn't seem to register.

The passage through Sansum Narrows was indeed narrow, rock-walled in spots, and beautiful, with the panorama of Cowichan Bay, Mt Tzouhalem and Maple Bay unfolding to the west. A lively current carried us along. Then the current suddenly reversed. I was too busy rowing like hell to reflect on this strange phenomenon. It slackened as the narrows opened out into Burgoyne Bay.

The head of Burgoyne Bay is overhung with mountains. It's gorgeous. We crossed the bay and looked for a campsite along the rocky north shore, a flat spot with a haul-out nearby. We found a sun-drenched grassy bluff. The land behind sweeps up and up to the sheer rock face of Mt Maxwell. There were no signs posted. We saw few people that evening, none the next morning. Consulting a land-use map, I discovered our campsite was on a triangular piece of private property. There are no designated campsites on the west side of Salt Spring Island. No wonder there were no other paddlers.

The upland around Burgoyne Bay was the focus of intensive efforts to protect rare and endangered Garry oak ecosystems. Provincial parks protect about 750 ha/1,850 ac of the bay. Mt Maxwell Ecological Reserve protects nearly 400 ha/ 988 ac. Day use is welcome in the provincial parks. You're supposed to need permission from BC Parks to visit the ecological reserve. I'm not sure that regulation isn't winked at by users of Mt Maxwell.

Next day we proceeded to Wallace Island, off Salt Spring's north point. A pencil of furrowed, whalebacked sandstone, Wallace has a provincial campground with a few nice sites near the little bay and a lot of gloomy ones behind.

We spent a day exploring the area, and the following morning picked up a skookum current running along Salt Spring's well-populated northeast shore. We crossed from Nose Point to Prevost Island, hoping to cross back to Salt Spring's most popular campground, Ruckle Park. We never made it, and that was okay with us. A tiny islet, barely 100x250 m/300x800 ft, hove into view, with a little meadow above an exquisite shell beach. A platform of wooden slats invited us to have a rest. No nails marred the smooth surface. We unfurled our Therm-a-Rests and listened to the susurration of the wind in the firs. We looked for property signs; there were none. Later I asked Bristol Foster, a noted conservationist and Salt Springer, about the little gem. He said it's known as Owl Islet and was once a popular rendezvous — dancing naked in the moonlight, that sort of thing. The following year we were in the vicinity and paddled past Owl Islet. A dock had been installed, and No Trespassing signs were posted. Owl Islet was on the list for purchase to become part of the Gulf Islands National Park, and I understand that owner has recently indicated a willingness to sell it.

Details

- BC Marine Trails Network website has an interactive map and trip planning features: bcmarinetrails.org.
- Maps, information about Mt Maxwell, Burgoyne Bay and Ruckle provincial parks and Wallace Island Marine Provincial Park: env.gov.bc.ca/bcparks, under Find a Park.
- About Mt Maxwell Ecological Reserve: on the same site, under Conservation, choose link to alphabetic listing of ecological reserves.
- Mt Maxwell, Burgoyne Bay and Ruckle parks are all accessible by road. Mt Maxwell has one of the best viewpoints in the Gulf Islands, overlooking Burgoyne Bay and valley.
- Portland Island and Prevost Island protected areas in the Gulf Islands National Park Reserve: pc.gc.ca.

Chemainus River Estuary | 45

The estuary of the Chemainus River and Bonsall Creek is the major coastal feature between Crofton (see #43) and Chemainus (#46). This ecological jewel is sheltered from Georgia Strait by sandstone islets and rocks that follow a NW-SE trend, precisely parallel to the Gulf Islands. The estuary spreads across 4.5 km/2.8 mi of coast and is as much as 2.5 km/1.6 mi wide. Despite having an uber-industrial neighbor, the estuary is relatively untouched. Just north of Crofton, you pass the yards and plants of the Catalyst pulp and paper mill. The estuarine tide laps at its feet, but the estuary is separate from the mill's busy log handling waters.

Estuaries are intertidal and subtidal spaces at the mouths of some rivers. They are among the most productive of all ecosystems, places where fauna and flora, the terrestrial and the marine, congregate and mingle. When Environment Canada and Ducks Unlimited Canada ranked 442 BC estuaries according to their productivity and value, the estuaries of the Chemainus, Courtenay, Cowichan and Nanaimo rivers were in the top ten. The Chemainus estuary occupies a central location within the mosaic of wetlands along Vancouver Island's east coast. It is important habitat for migrating waterfowl along the Pacific Flyway. During the migration and wintering periods, daily averages of 1,000 waterfowl have been reported on the Chemainus.

In 2009, Ducks Unlimited spearheaded the purchase of 210.5 ha/520 ac of the estuary: a patchwork of farmland, forest and intertidal flats. The federal and provincial governments, land trusts, foundations and local businesses helped support the $3 million price tag. The purchase provides for access for all, including the Halalt First Nation, who live above the estuary and tried unsuccessfully to buy the land. Hunting is allowed.

This little-visited birder's paradise is worth anyone's while to make a detour, just to take in the sweep of the land and ponder its value. But the estuary can't be properly viewed from the Crofton-Chemainus road. The following directions provide access to highly scenic overviews just a few minutes' walk from Swallowfield Rd. Mill Point, near the mill, is a short walk from MacDonald Rd. Needless to say, the estuary is also accessible by water from Crofton or Chemainus.

Details

- Swallowfield Rd access:

  From Crofton: From the Chaplin St intersection (km 0), follow Crofton Road north past the Catalyst pulp mill (1 km); bear right on Crofton/Chemainus Rd (Route 1A) (3.5 km) and take 1st right east onto Swallowfield Rd (3.7 km). From Route 1, turn east at lights onto Mt Sicker Rd/Route 1A (km 0); turn north (L) at Westholme Rd (0.6 km); bear straight onto Crofton Rd (2.3 km) and take 1st right onto Swallowfield (2.4).

  "About 100 yds [yards=91 m] up Swallowfield," writes Robert Kissinger in a posting on March 20, 2014, "Chemainus Estuary," on the Island Waters Flyfishers website (iwff1.ca), "There is a yellow gate and a parking area. Park there, do not drive through the gate even if it's open as you could be locked in. Walk up the gravel road, and after about 10 minutes, you will reach a 'Y' junction. Take the left road. After about another 10 minutes, you will come to the river and a nice deep hole. On your right, is a grassy field where you will find a trail leading to the estuary."

- MacDonald Rd access:

  MacDonald Rd is 1.5 km N of Chaplin St on the Crofton Rd, or 2 km S of the intersection of Westholme and Crofton rds. Turn N onto MacDonald, take a right fork and park off the road near the gate. The road is a haul road, and can be busy during working hours; a 10-minute walk leads to a delightful picnic area overlooking the estuary.

- Ducks Unlimited factsheet and map: ecoreserves.bc.ca/misc/BC_FS_VitalEstuaries.pdf.
- Estuaries in British Columbia: env.gov.bc.ca/wld/documents/Estuaries06_20.pdf.
- Blog of a 2015 visit to "the best kept secret," the Chemainus estuary: vibigyear.ca/2015/04/22/the-best-kept-secret/.
- Flickr album of birding visit: flickr.com/photos/60612262@N08/23433755459.

46 Chemainus

Chemainus is the North Cowichan district sawmill town that discovered how to turn sawdust to gold. Forty-two **murals** festoon the outsides of

TAKE 5 *Gary Kaiser's Wildlife Spectacles*

Gary W. Kaiser is a retired seabird biologist with the Canadian Wildlife Service based in Victoria. He is a co-author of Birds of British Columbia *(4 vols, 1992-2001) and* Seabirds of the Russian Far East *(CWS 2000), and author of* The Inner Bird: Anatomy and Evolution *(UBC Press, 2007).*

These are great places to see masses of water birds at particular times. A birder would likely choose places with greater diversity.

1. Qualicum Beach and Parksville during the northward migration of **Black Brant and White-fronted Geese from the second half of March to mid-April.**

2. Comox Harbour and south to Denman Island during April-May when herring spawn attracts a huge collection of sea ducks, **Surf Scoters**, **White-winged Scoters** and **Long-tailed Duck (Oldsquaw)**.

3. Cleland Island, off Vargas Island, north of Torino, best-known for gulls and oystercatchers, it is the only place in southern BC where you can see **Tufted Puffins**, and there's also a big colony of **Rhinoceros Auklets** June-July. It's an ecological reserve, so you can't go on the island, but you can go around it.

4. Active Pass, between Galiano and Mayne Islands, has a big population of **Brandt's Cormorants** during the winter, January-March, at the Victoria end, while at the far end, perhaps 1000 **Arctic Loons** will gather in Miner's Bay and toward the lighthouse. They moult their wing feathers in January-February and can't fly.

5. Courtenay farms have **Trumpeter Swans** sitting in the fields in winter. They were endangered in the 1970s, but now it is easy to find spectacular flocks of 100-200, especially in potato fields!

its buildings, depicting the several threads of Chemainus's history. And the murals don't just tell the town's story — *they are the story*. The murals have put Chemainus, population about 4,000, on the map.

A tour of this phenomenon begins at Waterwheel Park. There's a map and display beside an artistic reconstruction of the 1862 water wheel that powered Chemainus's first sawmill. Besides the murals, there are eleven history-themed sculptures in the town and two interesting pieces using the art of Emily Carr to present forests, forestry and First Nations themes. A block away is the tiny Chemainus Valley Museum, with a parking lot and a lookout. The busy sawmill is directly below.

The overall quality of the project is very high. Artistically speaking, some of the murals are strikingly good. Of those representing the town's commercial history, **The Hong Hing Waterfront Store** has an iconic simplicity, its weathered wooden façade hung with old ads for cigarettes and soft drinks. **Letters from the Front**, the epic collage on the wall of the post office, evokes the rivers of correspondence between Chemainus and the battlefields of World War I.

The town does have a long industrial pedigree, and at least a dozen murals take up the forestry theme. Western Forest Products' sawmill is the fifth on the property — the longest-occupied mill site in BC. Chemainus was the island's first forestry community. The first railway logging operation on the island used the fresh-laid track of the Esquimalt & Nanaimo Railway to haul logs to Chemainus, in the 1880s.

The third mill (1891-1923) marked the advent of American capital to the island in the person of John A Humbird from Wisconsin. Washington timber tycoon Frederick Weyerhaeuser, a shareholder, visited every year. He would ride out and sit near the cold deck, studying the piles of logs.

The fourth mill (1925-82) was once, during H. R. MacMillan's tenure, the largest sawmill in the British Empire. When the old, big-log mill closed forever in the downturn of the early 1980s, Chemainus's future looked dim. During that period, the mural project took shape. The originator of the idea, local retailer Karl Schutz, had been trying for a decade to get the district interested. *Paint It*, he said, *and They Will Come*.

Schutz came to my Victoria office once in the first year of the murals. He was working hard to spread the word. Bubbling with good humour and confidence, he motivated me to publish a piece about the murals — probably one of the first.

Karl went on to become a consultant to postindustrial communities worldwide. More than 60 towns have adopted Chemainus's use of a distinctive marketing brand to attract tourists.

Across Chemainus (Horseshoe) Bay and a bit of the Salish Sea are Thetis and Penelakut (Kuper) Islands. They're super-scenic, and BC Ferries has regular service, but … Penelakut is a First Nations reserve, and visits are by invitation. Thetis Island is entirely private, and there are no parks.

■ Chemainus Festival of Murals Society website has profiles of all 55 pieces of art: muraltown.com.

Joseph Mairs Memorial, Ladysmith — 47

Ladysmith flourishes as a residential enclave while retaining one of the island's few working sawmills. A heritage streetscape forms the core of a revitalized commercial district.

Incorporated in 1904, the town was the creation of James Dunsmuir, and was based on the model of Dunsmuir coal centres Wellington and Cumberland. When the Wellington mine approached exhaustion, he had some of the town's buildings relocated — at the tenants' own expense, of course — to Ladysmith.

Ladysmith was the epicentre of the island's most prolonged episode of civil strife — the coal miners' strike of 1912. The Great Strike started over safety issues at the Extension mine — Dunsmuir, by this time, had sold it to eastern railway interests — and quickly spread to Nanaimo and Cumberland. A pitched battle between strikers and scabs came to a head in Ladysmith on a hot August night in 1913.

After the disturbance, Ladysmith and other coal towns were occupied by militia and under martial law for months. To this day, every January, a group of old-line social democrats march to the Ladysmith Cemetery and gather at the memorial to Joseph Mairs. An immigrant coal miner from Scotland, just 21 and living with his parents, Mairs was the only participant to die during the two-year strike.

He joined the Mine Workers Union of America in trying to sway the hard hearts of the mineowners and stop the ceaseless slaughter in the mines. (Methane explosions were the most common of many ways to die.)

Young Mairs was arrested for taking part in the Ladysmith uprising. He copped a guilty plea, whereupon Judge Howay sentenced him to 16 months' hard labour in Oakalla Prison. There he soon died of a rupture in an untreated tubercular intestine.

The union raised the money for the fine monument we are visiting today. They sold postcards showing Mairs posing beside his bicycle and the prizes he had won in races.

Mairs' relations live on there today, but it's thanks chiefly to hard stone that he is remembered. There are many on the island for whom Ladysmith's industrial strife is a badge of honour. Folks in Ladysmith are crazy about history. Strange — how few traces of the Great Strike there are.

Details

- Ladysmith Cemetery, 4th Ave at Christie Rd; the Joseph Mairs memorial is at plot P-R08B-10.
- Joseph Mairs Memorial Committee, with a history of the Great Strike: josephmairs.ca.
- "Joseph Mairs" article in the Dictionary of Canadian Biography: biographi.ca.
- Ladysmith & District Historical Society, with a local history and inventory of heritage buildings: ladysmithhistoricalsociety.ca.

 Nanaimo Bastion and Museum

A whitewashed octagonal tower in downtown Nanaimo is the city's oldest standing building and one of the island's oldest, too. Built in 1853, the Nanaimo Bastion is the only remaining free-standing fort of the Hudson's Bay Company (HBC), and one of few such structures remaining anywhere. And it's the only fort in the HBC's far-flung fur-trading empire where coal was traded. Had it not been moved, several times, the Bastion would surely be a National Heritage Site.

Well worth experiencing for its unusual three-storey inside space, the Bastion has a symbolic quality that is central to the story of Nanaimo's founding.

The first chapter of that story belongs to the Suquash Mine (#100).

Chapter 2 begins with a legendary conversation in the blacksmith's shop at HBC Fort Victoria. A Snuneymuxw First Nation chief was in having his rifle repaired. The smith threw some coal on the fire. The chief remarked there was plenty of that where he came from. The smith sent for Joseph McKay, second in command at the fort. The chief was invited to bring some *klale* (pronounced *CLA lay*, Chinook for *black*) stones to the fort. That was late 1849.

At length, the chief returned, and forever after he was known as *Coal Tyee*. (*Tyee* is Chinook for *chief*.) Joseph McKay made a bee-line for Winthuysen Inlet — Nanaimo Harbour — and started searching. In June 1852, he found a seam nearly a metre wide. McKay did a little dance on it.

James Douglas, governor and HBC chief factor, dropped everything and paddled up the east coast. With him were surveyor Joseph Pemberton, mine-manager John Muir and the governor's personal secretary. The shores and the harbour were *"one vast coal-field,"* Douglas wrote.

By the end of August, McKay, age 23, was in charge of it. A week later the mining families who had evacuated Fort Rupert began arriving. The first shipment of coal cleared the harbour September 10.

As the failed colony at Fort Rupert was being abandoned, Colviletown sprang into life. It was named for a London HBC bigwig. The name was dropped within a few years. It was always called Nanaimo — after the Hul'qumi'num Salish name for the domain of the Snuneymuxw First Nation.

McKay was a force of nature. Houses, stores, a school and a saltery went up in short order. Nanaimo's instant success put the colony back on course to having a settlement within five years. Had it not, Vancouver Island might have gone American.

Getting the Snuneymuxw First Nation to sell the coalbeds and townsite was not so simple. It took Douglas nearly two years of negotiation, and then the purchase of about 2,500 ha/6,178 ac "from Commercial Inlet 12 miles [19 km] up the Nanaimo River" was documented with the marks of First Nations leaders on blank paper. James Douglas signed as chief factor of the company.

Construction of the Bastion started in February 1853, soon after the hangings at **Gallows Point, Protection Island** (#49). The Bastion was the local office of the HBC, an arsenal and a refuge for miners and their families in case of an attack. That never happened, and the company didn't last long there. The HBC pulled out of the coal business in 1862.

In short order, Nanaimo was a city — a community where people lived right on top of their livelihood. Nanaimo remained a coal-mining town for a century. The downtown is laced with tunnels. There were shaft openings and slopes all around the Bastion. More than 50 million tonnes/55 million tons of bituminous coal came from the Nanaimo Coalfield.

The Bastion is one of few reminders of that heritage, a relatively unchanging thing in an ever-changing city. It overlooks the lively **Nanaimo Harbour** scene, with a promenade, visitor-friendly docks, float plane terminal, ferries to Protection Island and Newcastle Island (#50) and, a bit of a walk north, the well-used waterfront Maffeo-Sutton Park. Across the tiny inner harbour is the tallest building on the island, which occupies the peninsular site of the Snuneymuxw people's principal village.

The **Nanaimo Museum**, three short blocks from the Bastion, memorializes the history of the city, with a replica coal mine, an overview of the harbour's many aspects, an exhibit of Snuneymuxw First Nation history, even a paean to the **Nanaimo bar**, arguably the city's most famous export, all sharing a well-wrought space.

Details

- The Nanaimo Bastion, Front St opposite the foot of Bastion St, is open to visitors May-Sept. Outside, a cannon is fired every noon in season.
- Nanaimo Museum, 100 Museum Way; 250-753-1821; nanaimomuseum.ca: website has an interactive virtual tour of the Bastion, good graphics, old photos.
- List of coal mines and landmarks in the Nanaimo area, with precise co-ordinates: wikipedia.org.
- Nanaimo coalfields map: em.gov.bc.ca/DL/arcview1/terrain/

Nanaimo_landsat.pdf
- Snuneymuxw First Nation: snuneymuxw.ca.
- Readings: Jan Peterson's trilogy, *Black Diamond City: Nanaimo, the Victorian Era* (2002), *Hub City: Nanaimo, 1886-1920* (2003) and *Harbour City: Nanaimo in Transition, 1920-1967*, (2006), published by Heritage House.

Gallows Point 49

Protection Island is a hidden jewel in Nanaimo Harbour. The island, closest of the three that enclose the harbour, is a residential enclave with a decidedly rustic feel. Just 1.5 km/0.9 mi across, its flat, forested terrain is crisscrossed with little lanes and pathways. For those who don't paddle to town, there's regular foot ferry service. Visitors are welcome, although there are few amenities beyond the homey **Dinghy Dock Pub** by the ferry slip.

On the south side of Protection is little Gallows Point Park. Beyond expanses of beach (at low tide) are great views of passing vessels and the working harbour. Directly south is the Nanaimo River estuary, bordered by the sandstone finger of Duke Point.

TAKE5 *Lynne Bowen's Literary Places*

Author of seven books of historical nonfiction on Vancouver Island and other Canadian themes, most recently, Those Island People (Rocky Point / Nanaimo Museum, 2014), Lynne Bowen lives in Nanaimo.

1. The Dunsmuir Wellington mine was the model for the industrial setting of John Galsworthy's 1909 play *Strife*. Galsworthy's father was chair of the board of the Vancouver Coal Mining Company, which ran Nanaimo's biggest mine, the No. 1. John, a recent graduate of Oxford law school, was in a state of unrequited love when in 1891 Papa sent him to Vancouver Island to report on the labour situation following a long strike against Wellington Collieries. No doubt doors opened for Galsworthy that would be closed to anyone else.

2. The entire coal belt is the setting of my 1982 oral history *Boss Whistle: The Coal Miners of Vancouver Island Remember*. The originator had conducted nearly 120 hours of interviews, and I was asked to take over the material after I had completed my MA in history. (My thesis was about coal mining on Vancouver Island.) All the contributors are now dead. This is the book I'll be remembered for. On Alan Twigg's list of 200 significant BC works, it was #102. There never was a "boss" whistle, by the way. My husband Dick and I made up the phrase to convey a sense of the mining life. Now, when

Gallows Point commemorates the first executions in the Colony of Vancouver Island. A public hanging there on January 17, 1853 followed the relentless pursuit and speedy trial of two First Nations men.

The story of the gallows speaks volumes about our heritage.

Hudson Bay Company shepherd Peter Brown was killed in November 1852 on Christmas Hill, 5 km/3 mi north of Fort Victoria. A Snuneymuxw First Nation man and a man of Cowichan were said to be the perps.

Fear grew that First Nations were going to attack the tiny settlement of Fort Victoria, or the fledgling HBC farms, or Colviletown (Nanaimo) or Fort Rupert.

James Douglas took charge of a posse, and a motley flotilla departed Esquimalt Harbour on a bitter cold January 5. It comprised the paddle-steamer *Beaver* towing the HBC brigantine *Recovery*, accompanied by three small vessels from a 36-gun warship. On board were 120 British sailors and marines and 20 Voltigeurs, French-Canadian militiamen.

The force arrived in Cowichan Bay the next day. Douglas sent messengers to the villages. The following day, a war party appeared in a fierce show. But no shots were fired, and the residents were persuaded to give up the one suspect they were harbouring.

How? Disciplined intimidation. Douglas had a feel for theatre. With his force deployed behind him, he made a little speech:

there's talk of restoring the mine, they always include it!

3. Nanaimo society was skewered in Jack Hodgins' 1987 satiric novel *The Honorary Patron*. Jack was a Nanaimo high school teacher who had won two Governor General's awards for his comic fiction about Vancouver Island. He doesn't like to admit it, but he was the said figurehead in a local Shakespeare company, a project put together in 1984 as a tourist attraction. Shakespeare Plus contracted the black cop from Barney Miller to play Mercutio in *Romeo and Juliet*. Leon Pownell was artistic director. The festival ended up $250,000 in debt. Hodgins mined it for colourful characters.

4. In Marilyn Bowering's 1989 novel *To All Appearances a Lady*, there is a memorable reconstruction of life among the D'Arcy Island lepers, unfortunate souls whose disease was so feared they were condemned to permanent isolation. The sequence begins when a woman is left stranded on the island and seeks their help.

5. Brian Brett's charming 2009 life-in-a-day memoir *Trauma Farm: a Rebel History of Rural Life* is a brilliant anatomy of the endangered small farm tradition as well as a kaleidoscope of his and his loved ones' 18 years on a Salt Spring Island farm.

Hearken, O Chiefs! I am sent by King George who is your friend, and who desires right only between his tribes and your men. If his men kill an Indian, they are punished. If your men do likewise, they must also suffer. Give up the murderer, and let there be peace between the peoples, or I will burn your lodges and trample out your tribes." (Emphasis added.)

Ponder that threat for a moment. Does it seem more than a little out of proportion to the crime? After all, Brown had, it was bruited, provoked the attack by insulting a woman or women in the First Nations party.

Douglas's policy was to *avoid* using direct force against First Nations groups. He decried the bloody confrontations erupting in the northwest United States. The Brown case was a test — and a showpiece — of Hudson's Bay Company justice.

Douglas isolated the wrongdoers in an almost surgical procedure.

The party arrived in Nanaimo Harbour on the evening of January 9. The Snuneymuxw First Nation leaders were less than forthcoming, and the suspect escaped. Douglas took the chief, his father and "another influential Indian" hostage. The troops deployed. They advanced by land to the suspect's village. It was deserted, the abandoned houses filled with winter provisions. The inhabitants "were now completely in our power," Douglas wrote.

The chase led up a snowy creek bed to a hiding place under a log. The troops withdrew without incident. The two men were tried aboard the *Beaver*, Justice Douglas presiding. Officers of the force served as the jury of peers. The men were hanged the same day with the Snuneymuxw people watching.

Details

- Protection Island ferry, hourly from Nanaimo Harbour dock, Promenade Dr near Front St, opposite the mall.
- Dinghy Dock Pub, Protection Island; 250-753-2373; dinghydockpub.com.
- Map of Protection Island: tourismnanaimo.com.
- Biggs Park and Jack Point Park, at the end of the Duke Pt Peninsula, have more vantage points for views of the harbour; they're a bit of a trek through Nanaimo's heavy industry zone.

50 Saysutshun (Newcastle Island)

Newcastle Island is a 334-ha/825-ac forested oasis near downtown Nanaimo, laced with trails and studded with viewpoints. There are gorgeous views to the east across Georgia Strait to the Coast Mountains. A heritage wooden dancing pavilion is the focal point and information centre for **Newcastle Island Marine Park**. The park has many amenities — swimming beaches and a playground, a store in the pavilion, an 18-site walk-in campground close to the ferry dock (12 sites reservable during summer months) and public moorage. The Snuneymuxw First Nation operator of the park mounts interpretive tours and serves barbecued Sockeye salmon.

The island's 22 km/14 mi of well-marked trails reveal abundant evidence of the indigenous populations' diverse life. There are the shell middens of two Salish winter fishing camps, evidently occupied during the herring season. *Saysutshun*, the Halkomelem name for the island, translates as "training for running," meaning special places where runners, canoe paddlers or warriors would bathe to cleanse themselves before a race or battle.

Several mining industries have called Newcastle Island home. Coal mines were worked for a few years in the 1850s and 1870s. Newcastle sandstone was used in the ornate façades of Romanesque architecture favoured for public buildings of the day. The handsome 1895 **Nanaimo Courthouse**, designed by Francis Rattenbury, is a showpiece of Newcastle sandstone. In the 1920s, giant sandstone millstones were quarried separately for use in groundwood pulp mills.

After 1900, Japanese fishers built salteries on the island. Preserved herring (in winter) and salmon (in summer) found good markets in Asia. Japanese residents started a shipbuilding yard that flourished until World War II.

It's worth a trip just to see the splendid **pavilion**. Built by the Canadian Pacific Steamship Co in the 30s, it was the dance hall that invited folks to have a good time on a summer evening. You can almost hear it — laughter and music floating across the harbour, a chorus of *Happy Days Are Here Again*, lights shimmering on the water, the antique steamship *Charmer* tied up in Mark Bay as a floating hotel.

Details

- Newcastle Island Marine Provincial Park: env.gov.bc.ca/bcparks.
- Visit Newcastle Island, the First Nations park operator's website, with ferry times, rates: newcastleIsland.ca. In high season, the passenger-only ferry leaves the Nanaimo Harbour Ferry dock in Maffeo-Sutton Park half-hourly; last ferry returns from the Island at 8:45 pm; in the shoulder season, 4:30 pm; low season, 2:30 pm.
- Snuneymuxw First Nation: snuneymuxw.ca.
- Nanaimo Courthouse: 36 Front St.

Parksville-Qualicum Sand 51

The scenic stretch of east coast between Parksville and Qualicum Beach is called **Oceanside**. If you're looking for sand, fill your boots. For 20 km/12 mi, a happy succession of sandy beaches faces the Strait of Georgia. This is big sky country. Rathtrevor Beach, on Craig Bay, is easily 1 km/0.6 mi wide at low tide.

The summertime scene in Parksville-Qualicum is tops in family waterfront destinations. It's the atmosphere, the exhilarating views — but mainly the sand. I like the way, on a sunny, summer day, the sand warms the incoming tide — water that is otherwise chilly at anytime of year. On the water are legions of skimboarders and stand-up paddleboarders.

In July, the community focuses on sand fashioned into works of art at the **sand sculpting competition**. This is the real thing, the Canadian Open of sand sculpting. The winner gets a place in the world championships. The sand sculptures are created over a weekend using just sand and water, then on display for a month. They display remarkable detail, and some are true originals. Fantasy is a popular theme. Some memorialize events or causes. The best sculptures deliver powerful impressions. There's a poignancy about their transience — here today, gone tomorrow.

This is campground heartland. **Rathtrevor Beach Provincial Park**, with 174 drive-in sites and 25 walk-ins, is probably the most popular of all BC Parks' campgrounds. You must book in advance in summer. Rathtrevor Park comprises 347 ha/857 ac of forest, fields and the spacious beach on Craig Bay. Some years, the beach is strewn with sand dollars — quite a sight. There are interpretive programs for kids at the Nature House.

South of Highway 19, there's more interesting parkland. The **Top Bridge Regional Trail** for pedestrians and cyclists starts in Rathtrevor Park, crosses the Englishman River on the Top Bridge, and leads into the 207-ha/512-ac **Englishman River Regional Park**.

Two wonderful campgrounds are a bit away from the busy beach scene. **Englishman River Falls Provincial Park** is 13 km/8 mi south of Parksville. It has 103 drive-in campsites, half of them reservable, in a 97-ha/240-ac forested setting. **Little Qualicum Falls Provincial Park**, 20 km/12 mi west on the Port Alberni Rd, has 96 drive-in sites, most reservable, on a beautiful 440 ha/1,087 ac site. Near the campgrounds, the rivers form falls and pools sculpted in bedrock.

Nearby family-oriented attractions include the North Island Wildlife Recovery Centre (#52), goats on the roof at the Coombs Old Country Market (#54), the Horne Lake Caves (#56) and Cathedral Grove (#57).

One might be forgiven for supposing Parksville was named for all those parks. Not so. Nelson Parks bought land on the Englishman River in 1884 and was appointed postmaster of the Englishman's River Post Office in 1886. The following year, it was renamed Parksville Post Office. All this and more at the **Parksville Museum**, located in Craig Heritage Park with eight relocated heritage buildings in a pleasant setting.

Details

- The Oceanside route (Highway 19A) begins at the Parksville off-ramp on Route 19, and it extends 123 km/76 mi to Campbell River.
- Quality Foods Canadian Open Sand Sculpting Competition and Exhibition: parksvillebeachfest.ca. Parking at the Parksville Community Park. Admission by donation to the gated competition exhibition.
- Rathtrevor Beach, Englishman River Falls and Little Qualicum Falls in the Provincial Parks finder for navigation, maps, guides: env.gov.bc.ca.
- Parksville Museum and Craig Heritage Park, 1245 Island Highway East, Parksville; 250-248-6966; parksvillemuseum.ca.

52 North Island Wildlife Recovery Centre

This kid-friendly wildlife rehab and human education centre near Parksville takes care of "ill, injured or orphaned" eagles, falcons, hawks, vultures, wild turkeys, six species of owls, a raven, an abandoned ferret, and varying numbers of orphaned black bear — animals you're likely not to see up-close anywhere else.

The centre hosts a boggling 30 to 40 injured eagles a year. For eagles on track for release, there's a barn-sized building where they exercise, flying back and forth, while visitors watch from windows. Nearly half the animals who show up at the centre are released. Great fanfare accompanies the release of a big bird, as depicted in the one-hour film, *Wellness to Wilderness*, at the learning centre.

There's a nice open area in back of the 3.2-ha/8-ac centre with the quaint name Magical Field of Stones. There is also a Native Plant Wildlife Garden where people can bring picnics and hang out. That's where the releases happen, watched by a mob of summer visitors. Guy throws the bird into the air and flap flap it's gone. It's very moving. But don't get your hopes up. There's only one public release a year, and 2017's was in conjunction with the Brant Festival, in April.

The centre has labyrinthine walkways and a tunnel, so that you don't know what you will encounter next. You can tour the artificial habitats of a few of the more than 450 animals who have become permanent residents. Well-designed plaques detail each animal's habitat, life cycle and diet and the circumstances of its being at the recovery centre. I just love owls, and they were way more animated than I expected.

There's a sadness to their injuries — or in the case of a Peregrine falcon, born in captivity, trained as a work bird for use at airports and golf courses, but suffered from stress-related seizures, and could not work. Or Brian the eagle, who was provided with a specially-made beak and lived at the centre for more than ten years. Is it right to care for animals who would not survive in the wild? It seems to me a nobler calling than, say, your average zoo or aquarium.

It all started in 1984 with the rescue by Robin Campbell of a great horned owl caught in barbed wire in Buckley Bay. Founders Robin and Sylvia Campbell established The North Island Wildlife Recovery Association, and in 1986, opened this facility. Word got around and soon they were fielding inquiries about their injured subjects from all over the island and even other provinces. The event that put the centre on the map was the rescue of nearly 30 bald eagles that had dined on a euthanized cow and ingested near-fatal doses of barbiturates. The centre was eventually able to release 25 of the poisoned birds.

Besides a board of directors and a staff of six, the recovery centre has a corps of volunteers, local citizens who are passionate about their mission, including local veterinarian Malcolm McAdie, who for more than a decade has donated his work. The centre also prepares orphaned bear cubs for release into the wild, their mothers having been shot by hunters, hit by vehicles or euthanized by Conservation officers.

"The society has spent more than $400,000 of public money," writes Sylvia Campbell in a 2015 newspaper article, "to build a treatment centre and three bear enclosures for infant bears, junior bears and bears being prepared for release. Bears may stay at the centre for up to 18 months depending on the scarcity or abundance of food sources upon release." The controversial practice has the support of zoologists.

Not surprising that fund-raising is an integral part of the non-profit society's work, and their charitable status enables them to attract support through its "adoption" program by which the public can sustain the life of an animal. There's also an active educational program of school visits and class field trips to the wildlife recovery centre. They spread the word about the dangers of adopting wildlife as pets, not to mention the harms done to wildlife by discarded plastic bags, drink rings, lead shot and many other incidental detriti of the human ecosystem.

Details

- North Island Wildlife Recovery Centre, 1240 Leffler Rd, Errington; 250-248-8534; niwra.org; open March-December; to report a wildlife emergency: 250-927-6025.

The vast shallows of the Parksville-Qualicum shoreline are an important wildlife area. Every March, they attract thousands of Black Brants migrating north from their winter grounds in California and Mexico. The Pacific herring spawn attracts clouds of geese, gulls and other seabirds, raptors and sea mammals. Brants — little sea geese — feed, rest, socialize and fly on. Humans do the same after flocking to view the spectacle during the **Brant Wildlife Festival**. There is a month-long spring celebration in Qualicum Beach, the Brant Festival stages tours and excursions, talks, a photography competition, wildlife woodcarving competitions, special events for kids and other feathery, furry pursuits. The festival recently celebrated its 27th anniversary.

The initial spark for the Brant Festival came in a period of rapid growth in this well-heeled community of about 9,000, more than a third of whom are over 65 years old. Areas in greatest demand as human habitat are near the water. People are attracted to the spacious views of Georgia Strait.

As in the Gulf Islands and elsewhere, development often means wildlife habitat lost. It's an arduous and expensive task to buy bits and pieces of the landscape to keep them functioning as habitat. The Nature Trust of BC took the lead in assembling lands in what became the Parksville-Qualicum Beach Wildlife Management Area (WMA). The Trust has been involved in buying salmon spawning habitat on the nearby Englishman River since 1978, and in the 1980s, began buying bits of the river's estuary totaling 77 ha/190 ac. The Parksville-Qualicum Beach WMA knits together many small parcels assembled since the 1980s from the Little Qualicum River estuary to Madrona Point — 17 km/10.6 mi of shore, mainly intertidal areas. Total area of the WMA in 2017: 1,024 ha/2,530 ac.

Viewing platforms along Qualicum Bay have displays with more information about agencies and groups involved with the preservation of local wildlife habitat.

Citizen action was also responsible for creating the **Qualicum Beach Heritage Forest**, a 20-ha/50-ac block of old-growth forest near the Island highway, with charming trails.

A short excursion to the 28-ha/70-ac **Milner Gardens** is highly recommended. The Qualicum Beach estate of Alberta oil landlord Ray Milner and Veronica Milner includes 4 ha/10 ac of sumptuous gardens overlooking Georgia Strait and a remnant old-growth Douglas fir forest. Tea is served in the lovely house.

Details

- Brant Wildlife Festival: brantfestival.bc.ca.
- The Nature Trust of British Columbia: naturetrust.bc.ca.
- Qualicum Beach Heritage Forest brochure:
  https://qualicumbeach.civicweb.net/document/4012.
- Milner Gardens and Woodland, 2179 Island Highway West, Qualicum
  Beach; 250-752-6153; https://www2.viu.ca/MilnerGardens/; open daily
  from April-Sept.

 54   **Old Country Market, Coombs**

Coombs is a rural community inland of Parksville, based on logging, but with relic orchards planted by the Salvation Army in the early 1900s. Its chief claim to fame is the Old Country Market, where goats graze on the grass roof.

Owner Larry Geekie is a third-generation Coombster. He tells how when they built the produce store, his father-in-law put sod on the roof to remind him of Norway. The goats were an idea cooked up over a jug of wine in the run-up to the Coombs Fall Fair. A friend volunteered some pet goats. "I had to drive them home at the end of the day," Larry recalls. The rest is history. People come from all around to see the goats (in season). Their phenomenal popularity was totally unforeseen. "It just happened."

Thanks to the goats, the market has grown "creatively," Geekie says, with many "organic" additions. (The building inspector caught up with them and put an end to that.) There's a local smoked salmon shop and deli, a bakery, a restaurant, a *trattoria*, and a *taqueria*. There is also a specialty grocery that stocks interesting European imports, an ice cream shop, a gift shop, a garden accessory shop, a shop that sells Chinese antiques, a surf shop, and of course the original grocery, which buys both imported and local vegetables. (It may be organic but is not certified.)

This wholesome family-run business has nothing to do with the commercial slum just down the road, although that, too, is all about the economic power of goats on the roof. *Graze them, and it will come.*

Details

- The Old Country Market in Coombs is 9 km/5.6 mi W of Parksville,
  7 km/4.3 mi W of Highway 19, on the Old Alberni Road (Highway 4A);
  Hours, directions: oldcountrymarket.com.

Free Spirit Spheres 55

A place to stay so unusual there's probably nothing like it in the world, Free Spirit Spheres puts you up in the trees in a cozy environment reminiscent of, say, a cabin on a sailboat. Two spheres are 3.2 m/10.5 ft in diameter, and the third is 2.8 m/9 ft. People come from near and far to sleep in a sphere.

Poring over the guest book in ours, Melody by name, I find notes by people from California, Kentucky, Belgium, China — this in December and January. A common theme is romance. Another is healing: "I had a profound healing dream … My husband who died when our daughter was five came to visit me …" . People also come for the proximity of nature, love of fine craftsmanship, attention to detail and the hospitality. There is quite a lot of New Age consciousness, expressed in runes and references to Hobbits. To some, it's the imaginative participation in the world of childhood, the wind rocking you to sleep as in the nursery rhyme. Some say the spherical space is conducive to meditation and repose.

Free Spirit Spheres is a must-do because it is unique. That there are many forms of elevated lodgings, but only one that puts you in a sphere, the travel book *Bed in a Tree* attests. There is a loose association of treehouse builders to which our host belongs. He attends its meetings south of the border. None of his colleagues make habitats remotely like his.

Inventor Tom Chudleigh took some time while constructing his eighth sphere to outline his vision and retrace the history of his unusual enterprise. A marine engineer by trade, Tom veered off into this line of work after being inspired by Jacques Cousteau, who explored the deeps in a bathysphere. Tom experimented with a smaller model (Eve) and made the first larger sphere (Eryn) with a shell of Sitka spruce strips before settling down to the signature molded fiberglass model. One of his spheres hangs on an estate at Cap d'Antibes on the French Riviera.

The present location, a second-growth forest on 2 ha/5 ac of rented land in Qualicum Beach, is transitional. Tom and partner Rosey's dream is to hang his spheres in an older, owned forest. Trouble is, they have to compete with logging companies to bid for such land, a million-dollar proposition on southern Vancouver Island. Plus, they have to jump through multiple hoops to get the permits that will allow them to expand beyond three units. They have considered moving to a site on the BC Central Coast.

Staying in a sphere requires you to follow instructions when, for example, opening and closing the delicate round windows, and, in Melody, when collapsing a little table and lowering the Murphy bed. Getting used to the limited space requires both planning and improvisation. You need to don footwear and a head-lamp (both supplied) before visiting the outdoor loo in the night.

Amenities include a French-press coffee maker as part of a do-it-yourself breakfast arrangement. (The hosts provide a nice basket of goodies on arrival.) There's a shower room for each sphere in the combo bath-and-cook-house. Embellishing the grounds is a large pond. The pathways are festooned with whimsically painted stones.

The word for Free Spirit Spheres is glamping, glamorous camping. It's no place for claustrophobes. Spheres are not wheelchair-accessible. Nor are they kid-friendly, and before moving in, you face a blizzard of rules, instructions and paperwork. They're not cheap, but your fee reflects the going rate for meticulous craftsmanship, vision and originality.

Should Tom and Rosey's spherical dream come true any time soon, the website will announce their new locale.

Details

- Free Spirit Spheres, 420 Horne Lake Rd, Qualicum Beach; 250-757-9445; freespiritspheres.com.
- Reading: *Bed in a Tree and Other Amazing Hotels from around the World*, by Bettina Kowalewski (DK Eyewitness Travel, 2009). Free Spirit Spheres has pride of place in the book.

56   Horne Lake Caves

The Horne Lake Caves, 25 km/15.5 mi west of Qualicum Beach, are the only place on the island (one of two in BC) where guided tours of caves are offered in a provincial park.

Vancouver Island has more than 1,500 known caves. The concentration of caving destinations is unique in Canada and the stuff of legend among cavers worldwide.

Three principal caves are protected in Horne Lake Caves Park, with a buffer zone totaling 158 ha/390 ac.

The Riverbend Cave, 276 m/942 ft long and 67 m/220 ft deep, is gated but accessible May-Sept via 90-minute guided tours by the park operators. These are billed as family tours, but not suitable for young children. The three-hour adventure is offered year-round, and there are Extreme tours that involve rappelling. It's a fascinating world of swirling earthtones and marble-like surfaces, with stalactites hanging tight and mounded stalagmites.

Two smaller caves without gates are open year round. (Access to one of the caves has been restricted due to a blocked trail.) There, you're on your own. The openings are negotiable by any reasonably fit individual.

I noted that the air below was always fresh.

The most rudimentary rules include these: cave in groups of 3-6; bring at least two flashlights; wear helmets and old clothing; dress warmly; take nothing but pictures and avoid leaving traces of your visit.

Details

- Horne Lake Caves Provincial Park: The parking lot is 14 km/9 mi W of Highway 19 on Horne Lake Rd; then a walk to the caves. Access map: env.gov.bc.ca.
- Horne Lake Caves & Outdoor Centre, 3905 Horne Lake Caves Rd, Qualicum Beach; 250-248-7829; hornelake.com. In winter, the operator's office is at the Horne Lake Campground, 13 km/8 mi W of Highway 19. "We are tricky to find … [website provides GPS locators] … If you get lost, call us …"

Cathedral Grove 57

MacMillan Provincial Park protects the most outstanding and easily-accessible old-growth forest on the island. Cathedral Grove is the imposing 15-ha/37-ac forest of giant Douglas fir, western red cedar, western hemlock and grand fir trees that flanks the Port Alberni road (Highway 4) just west of Cameron Lake. Douglas firs and cedars up to 4.5 m/15 ft in diameter and estimated to be 800 years old, are the biggest attractions in the 301-ha/744-ac park.

The Nanaimo-Alberni road was punched through the ancient forest in 1910, while the E&N Railway's Alberni line was being built along the north shore of Cameron Lake, complete with a railway resort, the Chalet, at the east end. Cathedral Grove was beginning to be touted as a tourist destination even then.

Despite petitions and testimonials urging its protection, it was part of the E&N Railway Lands and remained in private hands for decades. The story goes that in Port Alberni, MacMillan got into a shouting match with the relentless tourism lobby. He caved in with the immortal words, "All right, you can have the goddamn grove."

The park has become a hugely popular roadside stopping place, attracting some 300,000 visitors annually. It has so many visitors it's in danger of being loved to death. The foot traffic is compacting the soils.

That's nothing compared to the devastation wrought by flooding and high winds. "Logging of the remainder of the upstream valley has resulted in significant damage to the Cameron River's course and the adjacent forest," retired BC Parks forester Kerry Joy wrote in 2005.

"In 1990, extreme runoff from a tropical storm caused extensive flooding, and high winds resulted in 6 ha/15 ac of blowdown and streambank erosion. In 1996, high winds estimated at 110 kph/68 mph resulted in windfall and broken treetops, causing extensive damage to the grove and surrounding forest."

I have had a near-religious experience in the ancient forest, and not because its towering trunks resemble columns in a gothic cathedral. It's more about becoming aware of the dance of life and death. Fallen giants are an essential part of the nutrient cycle in a self-perpetuating old-growth forest. The problem in Cathedral Grove is that so many have fallen in recent years.

Here's another reason to treasure MacMillan Park. Surveying the island, it's shocking how little old-growth Douglas fir forest has been protected. This is the heartland of the Douglas Fir Empire. It was the economic foundation of thousands of jobs, dozens of communities and many a fortune beside MacMillan's.

For sheer magnificence, Cathedral Grove has no rivals in the zone of Douglas fir forests.

Details

- MacMillan Provincial Park: env.gov.bc.ca.
- A Swedish website with a radical conservationist POV: cathedralgrove.eu.
- Reading: "A Brief History of Cathedral Grove, MacMillan Provincial Park," *Forest History Newsletter*, No. 78, December 2005; https://www.for.gov.bc.ca/hfd/library/Forest_History_Newsletter/78.pdf

58 Hornby Island

Of the multitude of islands between Vancouver Island and the mainland, my favorite is Hornby. It's a bit more remote than others, requiring two short ferry rides to get there, and is consequently less developed. It's flatter than most, so marginally more agricultural than other, seriously rugged Gulf Islands. Hornby seems somehow sunnier than the more southerly Gulf Islands. Hornby Islanders boast of having the warmest water temperature in the Gulf. With gorgeous beaches and cliffside trails and an abundance of natural wonders, Hornby is, I think, the most beautiful Gulf Island, with a wholesome, paradisal quality.

From the ferry dock at Shingle Spit to the end of the road at Ford's Cove is 13 km/8 mi. You have to drive around the landmass at the centre of Hornby, Mt Geoffrey with its splendid L-shaped escarpment. The island's middle is roadless, laced with hiking and biking trails. Much of it is protected in parks.

The road winds along the shore and through cottage country, past farms and artists' studios, past a bakery where you can sit in a heavenly garden and eat fresh blackberry pie, and past a **community hall** whose foyer looks to be fashioned from one huge western red cedar stump. Past the Co-op store and the funkiest shopping mall ever. Past the beaches of **Tribune Bay** and clothing-optional **Little Tribune**. Past an underground house on a cliff and various hand-made free-form houses. Then down a long hill to **Ford's Cove,** where there are docks, a marina, cottages and a campground, a farm behind and abundant blackberry brambles. You pass a cluster of cabins and a washhouse to reach the campground, a nice clean field bordered by a forest of sizeable Douglas firs. In the night, the place is utterly dark and quiet.

Along Hornby's southwest side, facing its mate Denman Island across a little strait, you can walk from Ford's Cove northwest to Shingle Spit along a forest trail strewn with gigantic boulders, some 4 m/13 ft high. That's in **Mt Geoffrey Escarpment Provincial Park**. It covers 187 ha/460 ac, and there's also **Mt Geoffrey Regional Nature Park**, 303 ha/750 ac, and **Mt Geoffrey Bench Park**, a wedge of steep rock near Shingle Spit on the western slopes and a vertiginous climb from tidewater. Both parks are in the Comox Valley Regional District system.

Back to Ford's Cove. The secret gem is the sandstone shelf that extends from Ford's Cove to Heron Rocks. A spectacle unfolds of galleries and fret-works carved by the waves of millennia. "The honeycombed surfaces we see today in the De Courcy [Formation] sandstone," resident geologist Olivia Fletcher writes, "are produced by the weathering of a carbonate-filled network of cracks. The sea washes out the softer sand, leaving the sandstone, lithified with more cement, standing out in relief." A large chiseled and painted pictograph is barely visible in morning light, but stands out vividly when I return in the evening. It depicts a sea monster.

To do justice to Hornby's amazing sandstone shores requires a day in a vessel. Come to think of it, there are no islands around which I'd rather mess in a boat. The premier waterborne destination has to be the splendid peninsular **Helliwell Provincial Park**, with its conglomerate cliffs and 2,803 ha/6,926 ac of protected foreshore so popular with divers. The 69 ha/171 ac of land protected in Helliwell Park has a fabulous 5-km/3-mi looping trail that takes in the grassy peninsula and a beautiful old-growth forest.

Hornby's permanent residents numbered 1,016 in 2016, on a landbase of 30 sq km/12 sq mi. The summer-only crowd swells the population to perhaps 5,000. It gets busy; accommodations book up early. An index of demand: at writing (March 2017) most of the accommodations listed in the excellent website hornbyIsland.com were already booked for July. At one end of the spectrum is **Seabreeze Lodge**, with east-facing waterfront cabins and a great buffet dinner. At the other is **Bradsdadsland**, a large commercial campground. Tribune Bay Provincial Park is spacious (95 ha/235 ac) and handy to the commercial centre and Helliwell Park, but you can't camp there. Whatever you do, don't expect to find a place to stay when you get there.

If at all possible, plan your trip for the ten days of the **Hornby Festival** in early August. Little Hornby brings international talent to two stages: the out-of-doors, at Olsen's Farm, focused on jazz/folk/world music; the other, at the community centre, is pretty high-toned. We attended three such events in 2016, all memorable: the brilliant Ukrainian-born pianist Stanislav Khristenko, the all-woman, all-Canadian Cecilia String Quartet, and the erudite Canadian novelist Lawrence Hill (*The Book of Negros*). Hill capped a one-day writer's festival that we did not attend. The walls of the hall were enlivened with for-sale local art work.

Details

- Hornby Island information, with detailed accommodations pages: hornbyIsland.com.
- Ford's Cove Marina, "cottages, camping, store & pizza:" 250-335-2169; fordscove.com.
- Seabreeze Lodge, 5205 Fowler Rd, Hornby Island; 888-516-2321; seabreezelodge.com.
- Bradsdadsland, 2105 Shingle Spit Rd, Hornby Island; 250-335-0757; bradsdadsland.com. Peak season 2016 rates for tent sites were $44.50-54.50CDN+tax per night, one night payable in advance and nonrefundable; showers extra.
- Provincial parks (Helliwell, Mt Geoffrey Escarpment, Tribune Bay): env.gov.bc.ca.
- Mt Geoffrey Nature Park trail map: comoxvalleyrd.ca.
- Hornby Festival: hornbyfestival.com. Tickets go on sale in April.
- Reading: *Hammerstone: A Biography of Hornby Island*, by Olivia Fletcher (Edmonton: NeWest Press, 2001).

Comox Seafood   59

Fanny Bay is the epicenter of the island's flourishing shellfish industry. The waters of Baynes Sound and Comox Harbour are shallow and relatively warm in the shelter of Denman Island — just right for growing oysters and clams. North of Fanny Bay is Buckley Bay, where the ferry departs for Denman Island, with connections to Hornby Island. Between there and Union Bay, Highway 19A runs along the shore. The views of agricultural Denman Island are captivating. The intervening passage is often busy with the routines of aquaculture. There are places to stop and drink it in.

Stellar Bay Shellfish, in Bowser, markets a Kyusshi oyster, with a distinct "buttery texture, rich & salty with a sweet, mildly fruity finish."

At **Fanny Bay Oysters**, the signature product is the Fanny Bay, a farmed oyster of "pronounced sweetness and saltiness with a refreshing finish." Their Vancouver branch, the Fanny Bay Oyster Bar, recently captured Gold with their smoked oysters in that city's 6th annual Poutine Challenge.

Fanny Bay oysters are served in restaurants and oyster bars the world over. And **Mac's Oysters** has been growing them here since 1947, both on the beach and by aquaculture. "Mac" was Joe McLellan. The fourth generation of the family is involved in the diverse operation. Mac's specialty is the Signature Beach Harvest Oyster, meaty and "deliciously salty."

The speciality at Pentlatch Seafoods, the K'ómoks First Nation's mariculture operation, is beach-grown Komo Gway, a "plump oyster with a dark velvety mantle, medium salt and a nice cucumber finish." The First Nation markets it and a ton of salmon at its **Salish Sea Foods** retail store in Comox.

Every June, the **Comox Valley Shellfish and Seafood Festival** attracts a crowd of chefs from Vancouver. Among those slated for 2017 are Taryn Wa, Savory Chef Foods; Angus An, Maenam; and Chris Whittaker, Forage; joined by local lights Ronald St. Pierre, Locals Restaurant, Courtenay, and Nigel McManus, Blackfin Pub, Comox. The mainliner is the Comox by the Sea Celebration, with all-day cookery, eating and drinking, oyster shucking (annual competition) and something called the Oceanwise Chowder Challenge, which I have not witnessed (sure hope it's not a drinking contest). There are tours of a local hatchery and an oyster farm and plant; wildlife viewing and snorkeling expeditions. Meanwhile for ten days at select dineries, the palate is tickled with fresh sheets daily. A 2016 highlight was the Shellfish Showdown, an eight-dish extravaganza prepared by four chefs, at $124 a plate. There's also a Seafood Expo.

Details

- Stellar Bay Shellfish Ltd, 7400 West Island Highway, Bowser; 250-757-9304; stellarbay.ca.
- Fanny Bay Oysters Seafood Shop, 1–6856 Island Highway S, Fanny Bay; 250-335-1198: fannybayoysters.com. Fanny Bay Oyster Bar & Shellfish Market, 762 Cambie St, Vancouver; 778-379-9510.
- Mac's Oysters Ltd, 7162 S Island Highway, Fanny Bay; 250-335-2129 macsoysters.com.
- Salish Sea Foods store, 820 Shamrock Place, Comox; 250-339-6412; salishseafoods.ca.
- Guide to BC oyster varieties and growers: pacifickiss.ca.
- Comox Valley Shellfish and Seafood Festival: discovercomoxvalley.com.

60 Comox Valley

The Comox Valley is a fertile strip of lowland prairie and Douglas fir forest between the Vancouver Island Mountains and the Strait of Georgia. A farming district and former logging centre, it has a salubrious climate and stupendous surroundings, poised between the alpine reaches of Forbidden Plateau and Mt Washington and the sea washed shores of Denman and Hornby Islands. No wonder people have been flocking to the valley to live, in either the city of **Courtenay**, the district of **Comox**, or the village of **Cumberland**.

The heart of the Comox Valley is lush bottomland and estuary where the Puntledge and Tsolum rivers join and, as the 3-km/1.9-mi-long Courtenay River, empty into Comox Harbour.

The lowland and shallows comprise one of BC's most abundant wildlife areas. It's especially enriched by wintering waterfowl. The waters teem with fish and are famous for shellfish. Waterfront parks provide excellent views of the harbour and its gorgeous surroundings.

From the **Royston Viewing Stand**, 6 km/3.7 mi southeast of Courtenay city centre, Comox town centre lies 3 km/1.9 mi northeast, on the opposite shore. From it protrudes long-necked Goose Spit. The harbour's navigable water is between the Goose's Head and the Comox pier. Texada Island is visible to the east, across Georgia Strait. Beyond are the snowy peaks of the Coast Mountains.

Dyke Road Park, Comox, has viewing platforms overlooking the estuary — a sumptuous spot, with Comox Glacier dominating the western horizon.

European settlement began with ten miners from Nanaimo in 1861. Only one endured — George Mitchell. He started a farm at the mouth of the river and married a First Nations woman. More would-be farmers were dropped into the valley in 1862 aboard a Royal Navy gunboat.

Explorer Robert Brown visited in August 1864 to find "monster potatoes, onions as large as Spanish ones, parsnips, wheat and oats full headed, and sound turnips, splendid butter & milk … During our visit, hay was being cut in the meadows at the river's mouth for the Victoria market."

The district continues to attract new settlers at a brisk rate. The Comox Valley Regional District, (2016 census population 66,527, a gain of 4.7 percent from 2011) is projected to continue to fill in. While that's good news for the economy, it may not necessarily be good for the environment. Random unplanned development is having a huge impact on the valley's ecosystems. A 2007 study found that 60 percent of pristine sensitive ecosystem lands remaining in 1992 were disturbed by 2002, while 97 percent of high-value second-growth forest and seasonally-flooded agricultural fields had become fragmented. A 2014 follow-up report found that only 3.6 percent of the lowland Comox Valley is under some kind of protection. "Such low levels of protection, combined with intense human impact, creates devastating pressure on Comox Valley's natural areas," the report stated.

Details

- Comox Valley Regional District website has details and maps of Royston Viewing Stand and Dyke Rd Park: comoxvalleyrd.ca.
- Other parks worth a visit: Goose Spit, Seal Bay, Nymph Falls.
- Reading: *The Wilderness Profound: Victorian Life on the Gulf of Georgia*, by Richard Somerset Mackie (Victoria: Sono Nis Press, 1995).
- Comox Valley Sensitive Ecosystems Inventory Disturbance Assessment, 2014: cvconservationstrategy.org.

TAKE 5 *Award winning brews*

Vancouver Island craft breweries did well at the 2016 Canadian Brewing Awards in Vancouver:

1. **Gladstone Brewing Company**, Courtenay
   (gladstonebrewing.ca)
   Gladstone Czech Dark Lager — Gold in the European Style Amber to Dark Lager category
   Gladstone Belgian Single — Bronze in Belgian Style Abbey Ale/Pale Ale

2. **Moon Under Water Brewery**, Victoria
   (moonunderwater.ca)
   Creepy Uncle Dunkel — Bronze in European style Amber to Dark Lager
   Potts Pils — Bronze in Kellerbier/Zwickelbier

3. **Red Arrow Brewing Company**, Duncan
   (redarrowbeer.ca)
   Piggy Pale Ale — Bronze in English Style Pale Ale
   Midnight Umber Ale — Bronze in North American Style Amber Lager

4. **Merridale Cidery**, Cobble Hill
   (merridalecider.com; see #28)
   Merri Berri — Silver in Cider with Other Fruit
   Scrumpy — Bronze in Specialty Cider

5. **Hoyne Brewing Company**, Victoria
   (hoynebrewing.ca)
   Dark Matter — Bronze in Brown Ale

In all, British Columbia breweries won 52 of 163 medals at the awards. Sources: canadianbrewingawards.com; *Georgia Straight* magazine (straight.com).

K'ómoks First Nation 61

The **I-Hos Gallery** is an attractive showplace for First Nations art, carving, jewellery, textiles and clothing on the beautifully-situated Comox Harbour land of the K'ómoks First Nation. A powerfully carved and painted figure of the double-headed sea serpent I-Hos is part of the façade facing Comox Rd. Made by Calvin Hunt and associates in 1995, the figure illustrates a cultural hybridity unique on the Islands.

The Comox Valley marks one of the island's important cultural boundaries — between the northernmost *Salish* nations and the southernmost of the so-called *Kwakwaka'wakw* nations. The boundary used to be much further north, around Kelsey Bay. Sometime before European settlement — it may have started before the first European visitors in the last quarter of the 18th century — the valley's natural riches prompted others to encroach. Comox Harbour became the domain of three First Nations.

The Pentlatch First Nation was a powerful Salish people whose winter village was on the lower Puntledge River. They suffered a succession of disasters. They had a ruinous back-and-forth feud with the Nuu-Chah-Nulth people in the Alberni Valley. They were ravaged by European diseases. Their northern neighbours the Comox First Nation — an allied Salish people — encroached on their lands. The Comox nation had five winter villages on Johnstone Strait. They began moving south and settling in the Comox Harbour area. They fought with the Pentlatch, who at length made peace and threw in their lot with their oppressors.

The Comox were forced in turn into making alliances with an oppressor — the Lekwiltok First Nation, a Kwakwaka'wakw people previously living even further north, on the mainland coast. The Lekwiltok migrated south and were a terror everywhere their swift canoes probed. The Lekwiltok took possession of the former northern lands of the Comox and availed themselves of the bounty of Comox Harbour in season. By marriage and colonization, the Lekwiltok absorbed the Comox, at the cost of their Salish Identity. Today, the K'ómoks First Nation has both Kwakwaka'wakw and Salish affiliations.

A catastrophic smallpox epidemic began in the spring of 1862. One half of the Comox people died and seven in ten Kwakwaka'wakw people, coastwide. The Pentlatch people all but disappeared. It was a time of great disorder for First Nations. As in the Cowichan Valley, the colonial government promoted settlement in the wake of the epidemic — without bothering to buy the land from its rightful owners. "It is no easy matter," visitor Robert Brown wrote in 1864, "to answer the question satisfactorily when an intelligent Indian looks up in your face and asks 'Had you no good land of your own that you come and deprive us of ours?'"

The K'ómoks First Nation has undertaken many commercial initiatives in recent years, notably in producing and marketing seafood (see #59), that have made it one of the Islands' resurgent Aboriginal communities.

Details

- I-Hos Gallery, 3310 Comox Rd, Courtenay; 250-339-7702; ihosgallery.com.
- Spirits Of The West Coast Native Art Gallery; 2926 Back Road, Courtenay; 250-338-2120; spiritsofthewestcoast.com.
- K'ómoks First Nation: comoxband.ca.
- The First Nation operates a campground seasonally by the Puntledge River, a short walk to downtown Courtenay.

62   Cumberland

Cumberland is an attractive, slow-paced community that is reinventing itself as a outdoor recreation centre and small-town residential enclave after a long career as a coal-mining town.

The oldest municipality in the Comox Valley (established 1888), Cumberland was a hard-working city of 3,000, not including Asian miners relegated to outlying swamps. At one time, eight mines produced coal, and 18 km/11 mi of railway carried it to tidewater at Union Bay. The whole enterprise, including the town, was a Dunsmuir family project.

Since the last mine shut down in 1966, Cumberland has devolved into a village while the population has actually increased, to 3,600 in the 2016 census, for a 5-year increase of 10.1 percent. The core area of 30 blocks retains a good stock of heritage buildings among more recent constructions. There is a modest commercial zone on Dunsmuir Ave, including the nice, healthy, full-service **Seeds Food Market**. (The nearest supermarket is in Courtenay, 8 km/5 mi away.)

Cumberland has arguably the best hostel on the island — certainly the best named. The **Riding Fool Hostel** occupies a nicely redone 1895 commercial building. Upstairs there's a spacious lounge with a pool table. You can rent bikes from the **Dodge City Cycles** shop on the street and pick up maps of the area's extensive network of mountain bike trails.

Up the way is the **Waverley Hotel** bar, legendary for live music and crowds from Mt Washington. The Waverley Hotel opened in 1894 as a temperance — anti-booze — boarding house. The Wave has been serving drinks since the 1920s.

The nearby **Cumberland Museum and Archives** celebrates the valley's coal-mining heritage. Outstanding exhibits simulate the work in the mines and the life of the town. The museum's excellent website is crammed with photos and narratives of the old days. There's an exposition of the intricate structure of Cumberland's Chinatown, once one of BC's largest.

A forward-looking group, the **Cumberland Community Forest Society**, is fund-raising the purchase of private forestland surrounding the village. So far, they've raised about $1.2 million and bought some 71 ha/175 ac of second-growth forest. It is now a municipal park. The group's target for the Cumberland Community Forest is 263 ha/650 ac.

Details

- Seed Food Market, 2733A Dunsmuir Ave, Cumberland; 250-336-0129; seedsfoodmarket.ca.
- Riding Fool Hostel, 2705 Dunsmuir Ave, Cumberland, 1-888-313-3665; rIslandingfool.com. Dorm $28CDN+tax; private room $60-70; family room $80.
- Dodge City Cycles, 2705 Dunsmuir Ave, Cumberland; 250-336-2200; dodgecitycycles.com.
- Waverley Hotel, 2692 Dunsmuir Ave, Cumberland; 250-336-8322; waverleyhotel.ca.
- Cumberland Museum and Archives, 2680 Dunsmuir Ave, Cumberland, 250-336-2445; cumberlandmuseum.ca.
- Cumberland Community Forest Society: cumberlandforest.com.
- Comox Valley Mountain Biking, online maps and guide to trails: cvmtb.com.

Mount Washington and Forbidden Plateau 63

Mount Washington, the island's premier alpine sport centre, 33 km/21 mi west of Courtenay, is known for snow, and it's also a popular summer destination for hikers. Paradise Meadows, Mt Washington's cross-country ski area, is the gateway to the sublime alpine reaches of Strathcona Provincial Park. The 12.4-sq km/47.9-sq mi Forbidden Plateau area was added to BC's oldest provincial park in 1967. (See also #s 89 and 90.)

Easy trails, including 2 km/1.2 mi that are wheelchair-accessible, wind around little lakes in the exquisite subalpine meadows of Forbidden Plateau, 1,050-1,200 m/3,445-3,937 ft in elevation above sea level. Despite its name, Forbidden Plateau is actually quite ridged and inclined. In this enchanting landscape of rock dotted with subalpine spruce and fir trees, there are 45 campsites in three camping areas to choose from.

The plateau sweeps up to the glacier-girt peak of Mount Albert Edward, elevation 2,094 m/6,870 ft. The ascent onto the treeless alpine slopes is easy work, except for some steep climbing onto the ridge east of Albert Edward; and the flies get bad. The hike, at least six hours one-way from the Paradise Meadows trailhead, is best undertaken over two or more days. The summit is 14.8-16 km/9.2-10 mi from Paradise Meadows, depending on which trail you take.

The Strathcona Park Wilderness Centre at Paradise Meadows provides back-country travelers with current information (summer only).

For skiers, the peak of Mt Washington, 1,588 m/5,112 ft above sea level, overlooks 60 downhill runs and trails — nearly half for advanced skiers/boarders — dropping 505 m/1,657 ft and blanketed by snow that averages more than 10 m/33 ft annually.

The two high-speed lifts stay open for summer mountain bikers, who can choose from 37 km/23 mi of trails.

Details

- Mount Washington Alpine Resort: 888-231-1499; mountwashington.ca.
- Staying on the mountain: the pleasant subalpine village has a peak population of 4,000. Walk/ski-in accommodations can be booked through Central Reservations: 1-888-231-1499. The downhill and cross-country lodges have food service in season. Grocery shopping is limited; liquor outlet, gas station.
- Guidebook: *Hiking Trails 3: Northern Vancouver Island*, 10th edition, 2008.
- Forbidden Plateau trail map: env.gov.bc.ca.
- Strathcona Wilderness Institute operates the centre at Paradise Meadows: 250-650-4304; strathconapark.org.

*Esowista Peninsula and Clayoquot Sound on Vancouver Island's West Coast:
Cox Bay nearest; Chesterman Beach beyond; Catface Peak at top centre.
Boomer Jerritt/Strathcona Photography.*

III. Southwest Vancouver Island

Wet, windswept southwest Vancouver Island presents a rainforest face to the Pacific Ocean along a dramatically varied coast. The southern part, facing Juan de Fuca Strait, has memorable coastal hiking trails. Landward, the southwest island is the domain of forestry, and there you will find rare and precious ancient rainforests, some of them protected in parks but much more, unfortunately, slated for logging — see them while you can. Barkley Sound and its offshoot the Alberni Inlet reach more than half way across the island, breaking the southwest coast in two. The Alberni Valley's first sawmill started operating in the 1860s but soon closed for want of wood. They could cut the giant trees down, but they couldn't move the logs. About 40,000 people live in the quarter now, more than half in Port Alberni, a major forestry centre, and in the colourful west coast towns Tofino, Ulcuelet, Bamfield and Port Renfrew. They are jumping-off points for the wild island. On the north side of this quarter are gigantic Long Beach, twin-peaked Meares Island and Clayoquot Sound of the enchanting passages — wilderness travel destinations known the world over.

64   The West Coast Road

Beyond Sooke (#25) the narrow West Coast Road (Highway 14) curls around little coves with pebble beaches. There are more spruce and hemlock trees and fewer Douglas fir. The tang of the open ocean becomes stronger.

Between Sooke and Port Renfrew, a distance of 71 km/44 mi, we plunge into forestry country, a land of many trees and few people. The shoulders of the mountains begin to slope into the sea. Spectacular views unfold.

To drive the West Coast Road is to experience the island's wild-ish side, where you are heading toward the opening of Juan de Fuca Strait onto the open ocean.

Stops along the way:

The **Tugwell Creek Honey Farm & Meadery**, just past Otter Pt Rd, where mead is made from fermented wildflower honey gathered in the vicinity.

French Beach, 19 km/12 mi west of Sooke, has an excellent provincial campground. Gravelly shallows, just offshore, is a good place to see Gray whales in spring.

Point No Point Resort, Km 22/Mi 14, has 25 well-appointed cabins ranged along the beach. Meals are served in a charming tea house that commands sweeping views of the coast. It was built by Evelyn Packham, the original proprietor. Miss Packham used to serve tea. Dine there and you gain access to the scenic point, with its curious log bridge. Stay at the resort, and you can book a spa treatment in your own room.

Jordan River, Km 29/Mi 18, is a logging centre and the site of a 170-mw hydroelectric generating station built in 1911. A few residents, a café, a burger shack and a gas station kept the little hamlet alive, but in recent years the risk of earthquake-induced flooding from an old dam has left the place a virtual ghost town. Only the **Cold Shoulder Café** remains open. There's good winter surfing off the mouth of the Jordan River. The views across the Strait of Juan de Fuca are spectacular.

China Beach, Km 35/Mi 22, is the eastern terminus of the **Juan de Fuca Marine Trail**, which winds along the coast 47 km/29 mi to Botanical Beach. The trail is accessible (with parking lots) at Sombrio Beach (29 km/18 mi from China Beach) and Parkinson Creek (37 km/23 mi). China Beach has a beautiful campground and a day-use area.

Sombrio Beach is a famous surfing area. Until recently, the beach was the residence of a legendary community of hippie squatters. The parking lot is in second growth that was, in recent memory, a magnificent forest of old-growth Sitka spruce.

See also #65, Botanical Beach and #66, Big Trees of San Juan Valley.

Details

- Tugwell Creek Honey Farm & Meadery, 8750 West Coast Rd, Sooke; 250-642-1956; tugwellcreekfarm.com.
- French Beach Provincial Park: env.gov.bc.ca.
- Point No Point Resort, 10829 West Coast Road, Shirley; 250-646-2020; pointnopointresort.com.
- Cold Shoulder Café, 11950 West Coast Rd, Jordan River; 250-646-2181; on Facebook.
- Juan De Fuca Marine Trail: env.gov.bc.ca. Stretches of beach hiking that require knowledge of tides and an eye-out for orange balls that mark trails.

Botanical Beach

Botanical Beach, on the open coast near Port Renfrew, is an area famous for tidepools. These shapely rock pools were etched into flat sandstone that is located between high and low tides — covered at high tide but exposed at low. Tidepools are microcosms of ocean life, of dazzling variety, brimful of pale green anemones, little darting fish and crustaceans hiding in eelgrass.

In all, more than 100 species of invertebrates and 231 species of plants have been counted in the tidepools of Botanical Beach. It's worth a special trip (a two-hour drive from Victoria) to peer into these cauldrons of ocean life. Just be sure to time your visit to coincide with an ebbing tide, 1.2 m/3.9 ft or lower. And mind you don't stick your hand in the pools — contamination could be lethal to some tidepool denizens.

Sea urchins play an important role in tidepool formation. Geologist Chris Yorath writes: "The extraordinary erosive power of sea urchins, which have populated the oceans for 450 million years, has yet to be appreciated by geologists." Many pools are exquisitely shaped, with smooth vertical sides, often honeycombed with purple sea urchins, each in its own circular recess, slowly eroding the rock with its five teeth, enlarging the pool.

During one visit to Botanical Beach, I watched a small fish jump out of a tidepool and flip-flop across the flat sandstone, pursued by a tiny octopus. Guess it couldn't stand the thought of waiting for the next tide. The octopus barely glanced at the ring of visitors who were gaping at it.

The place was discovered in 1900 by Josephine Tilden, a biologist who had recently earned her Master of Science degree at the University of Minnesota and was the first woman professor in science there. A native of Iowa, Tilden located Botanical Beach by canoe. She invested her own capital to help establish the Minnesota Seaside Station, the first marine biology research facility on the northwest coast.

A profile on the university's website sketches the scene at Botanical Beach:

> Up to 30 professors and students journeyed to the station every summer to study geology, algology, zoology, taxonomy, and lichenology. World-renowned scientists participated in the lecture series. Letters from student Alice Misz to her mother during the summer of 1906 make it clear that her six-week stay at the station was the most unforgettable experience of her life.

The station closed in 1907 — the university declined to continue supporting it.

Josephine Tilden (1869-1957) never took a doctorate, but she became a renowned authority on algae. *The Algae and Their Life Relations: Fundamentals of Phycology* (1935) is still in print.

Protected in a provincial park since 1989, with 331 ha/818 ac of upland and 120 ha/297 ac of foreshore, Botanical Beach is now part of Juan de Fuca Provincial Park. It's the western terminus of the highly scenic but still very rough Juan de Fuca Marine Trail. Much of Botanical Beach itself is rough walking across broken terrain.

The network of trails around Botanical Beach includes a circuit by way of a short, scenic trail west to Botany Bay, where the geological history of the region is written in the rocks.

Details

- Botanical Beach parking lot is 3 km/1.9 mi S of Port Renfrew, then an easy walk through young forest less than 1 km/0.6 mi.
- Juan de Fuca Provincial Park: env.gov.bc.ca.

66 Big Trees of the San Juan Valley

The largest Douglas fir tree in the world and the largest Sitka spruce tree in Canada can be seen in a day trip to the San Juan Valley near Port Renfrew. Little visited because of the turbulent terrain and isolation of the San Juan Valley, the Red Creek Fir and the San Juan Spruce are not difficult to find, and they are on the same route. But the approach is rugged; spare tires, jacks and tire inflation kits are a must.

These giants beggar description. Their massive trunks are draped with ferns and epiphytes. The first branches are higher than most trees. One has monster forks and strange deformities. Their size and undoubted great age inspire awe.

The **Red Creek Fir** is 73.8 m/242 ft high and 13.28 m/43.57 ft in circumference. Its crown spreads 22.8 m/74.8 ft. Its total volume is estimated at 349 cu m/12,235 cu ft. It's not just the largest known Douglas fir — it's the largest known tree in the entire family of *Pinaceae*, which includes pines, spruces, true firs, hemlocks and larches as well as Douglas fir.

The **San Juan Spruce**, in a Forest Service campground, is 60.5 m/198.5 ft high, has a circumference of 11.65 m/38.25 ft, with a crown that spreads 23 m/75 ft. Its total volume is estimated to be 333 cu m/11,760 cu ft, making it the second largest known Sitka spruce and the third largest Pinacea. (The tree has been taken off the Big Tree Registry owing to what I am told is probably a "loss of mass." The problem may be with the registry, which recently migrated to the UBC Forestry website.)

Such record holders are the remnant of a population of superbig trees that once inhabited the Pacific coast. There's evidence that Douglas fir trees grew as tall as 125 m/410 ft on the island — likely through a combination of super genes, superproductive microsites and tenacity.

A special breed of adventurer prowls the back country looking for giant trees. The Ancient Forest Alliance (AFA) is carrying on the work of A.C. Carder and Randy Stoltmann, publishing photos of Vancouver Island's amazing giant trees and stumps on the internet. The Red Creek Fir and the San Juan Spruce, like most giant trees, languish unknown and unvisited, utterly unprotected, on public land, in active logging zones.

The AFA has championed the logging-threatened **Avatar Grove** in the nearby Gordon River valley. Their publicity and trail-building resulted in an explosion of interest worldwide in "Canada's gnarliest tree" and the big trees of the San Juan Valley. The group is trying to halt logging of endangered old-growth on the island and promote sustainable logging of second-growth forests instead.

Port Renfrew, a fishing village and logging centre on scenic Port San Juan, is enjoying a minor renaissance as the Tall Tree Capital of Canada. The centre of town is the government wharf, often busy with West Coast trail hikers leaving for or returning from the trailhead on Gordon River. Visitors from Victoria can continue on mostly paved roads to the Cowichan Valley and make a circuit.

Details

- Ancient Forest Alliance: directions to the San Juan Spruce and Red Creek Fir, Avatar Grove, other big trees and old-growth forests, plus stunning photo galleries of big trees and big stumps: ancientforestalliance.org.
- *The Vancouver Island Backroads Mapbook* (8th edition, 2017) is helpful for finding these areas.
- Register of Big Trees in British Columbia: bigtrees.forestry.ubc.ca.

West Coast Trail   67

The West Coast Trail is 75 km/47 mi of up and down — down yet another endless ladder and up another — across, over, under, around, through — slithering through openings that snag your pack and leave you wriggling like a turtle. In return, you get seascapes that give you a feeling of being present at the Creation. You feel fresh and new beside Mother Pacific. Her breathing wakes you up in the larger sense. The crashing surf and vivid sea smells are your constant companions, whether you're on the forest trail or walking the beach or the sandstone shelf. Equally in-your-nose are the rank smells of earth — of a fallen log turning to soil, remnant annual rings peeking out of a mound of bright red humus.

Along the shore of much of the southern half stretches a remarkable sandstone shelf, certainly one of the most amazing landforms I've ever seen. It's the most notable landscape of the Trail, a must-see with warnings. At times, hundreds of metres wide, flat as a pancake, the shelf occupies the intertidal zone. It's exposed at low tide, covered at high. Timing is of the essence. With a map and current tide tables, you can calculate when it's okay to walk the shelf, where to get down off the trail and, more important, when and where to get back up.

There are many scenic highlights along the Trail — Tsusiat Falls, the cliffs north of Nitinat Narrows, the old-growth forest between Nitinat and Clo-ose, the pebble beaches near Carmanah Point, the lighthouses. To the list I would add several hair-raising passages: wading across the mouth of Walbran Creek; negotiating the surge channel and waterfall at Adrenaline Creek.

I recommend first-timers start at Pachena Bay, at the northwest (Bamfield) end. You get the easy part at the beginning and the long climb over the height-of-land at the end. I've done it both ways. Some people, beginning at Port Renfrew, avoid the big climb by hiring a boat to take them to Thrasher Cove, where there's a really long ladder climb, and even Owen Point, which shortens the trip by a day and puts you right on the shelf.

The trail has been improved with boardwalks, bridges and cable car crossings that have tamed some of the more rugged bits. Still, you don't trifle with the Trail. You mustn't mind being wet. It might rain for six days and six nights, even in summer. Plan accordingly. Be strategic. Take lots of socks. But go. Allow at least six days. Research the campsites.

If you travel from west to east you will, with luck, somewhere east of Pachena Pt be able to pick out Cape Flattery, the northwest corner of the Olympic Peninsula marking the entrance to Juan de Fuca Strait. The discovery and rediscovery of Juan de Fuca Strait is one of the region's foundational stories.

The Strait of Juan de Fuca had huge currency in the legends of European discovery. A Greek shipman, working for Spain on the Northwest Coast of America in 1592, was supposed to have discovered the fabled *Strait of Anien* leading to an inland waterway. He claimed to have returned to the Atlantic Ocean by a large river. The Spanish name of the Greek mariner was Juan de Fuca. Was de Fuca's strait the fabled Northwest Passage? North European interests in Asia trade and colonies had to travel by the southern hemisphere passages around Cape Horn and Cape of Good Hope. How much would they save taking a northern hemisphere shortcut? For 200 years, the entrance to Juan de Fuca eluded the searching of European explorers. Captain Cook was looking for it in 1778 and missed it. It was (re)discovered in 1787, by Charles Barkley, an English sea otter trader working for the Austrian Crown. His wife Frances later described what happened: "From Barkley Sound the Imperial Eagle again proceeded to the eastward, and to the great astonishment of Captain Barkley and his officers, a large opening presented itself, extending miles to the eastward with no land in sight in that direction. The entrance appeared to be about four leagues width and remained about that width as far as the eye could see. Captain Barkley at once recognized it as the long lost strait of Juan de Fuca." They didn't continue into the strait but crossed the opening. Captains John Meares (England) and Robert Gray (USA) are supposed to have peered in before the strait began to be explored systematically by Spanish Naval parties in 1790-92. Captain George Vancouver, RN, took up the search for the Northwest Passage in a four-year exploration from 1792-95, of every part of the coast, from Washington to Alaska, that might have a large, navigable waterway eastward. Nothing turned up.

The story of the West Coast Trail begins with the wreck of the SS *Valencia*, east of Pachena Pt, which shocked the nation in 1906. See #71.

Details

- The West Coast Trail is part of the Pacific Rim Park Reserve of Canada and is open May-Sept. Parks Canada (pc.gc.ca) requires all users to purchase passes and take an orientation. Access is restricted to a daily quota. During high season, visitors can reserve a start time (fee) or show up and wait for openings. The points of access are Pachena Bay, near Bamfield, Gordon River, near Port Renfrew, and Nitinat Village. First Nations operators provide crossings at Gordon River and Nitinat Narrows and water taxi service between Nitinat Village and the trail. A shuttle service from Victoria and Nanaimo drops and picks up hikers. A leisurely scenic approach is via the coaster MV *Frances Barkley* between Port Alberni and Bamfield.
- The Dididaht First Nation operates a Visitors' Centre and motel at Nitinat Village (seasonal) and a water taxi service; 250-745-3999; westcoasttrail.com.

 Nitinat

Nitinat Lake is famous for the westerly winds that rise every morning like clockwork from April to September. The winds, strong and steady, make Nitinat a top North American destination among superathletic windsurfers and kiteboarders.

From afar, you see the taut sails cutting back and forth across the lake. Less than 2 km/1.25 mi wide, the lake is 23 km/14 mi long from the outlet of the Nitinat River to the mouth of **Nitinat Narrows**. Nitinat Lake is a finger of ocean — the tides fairly rip through the 40-m/131-ft wide narrows.

For most of us who don't do high-energy windsurfing, Nitinat is the portal to the West Coast Trail (#67) and Carmanah-Walbran Provincial Park (#69).

This is the traditional domain of the **Ditidaht First Nation**. A visitor centre at the north end of Nitinat Lake has a café, store, gas station and small motel. There's a campground, popular in summer, on the lake. The Ditidaht people are also boat operators for West Coast Trail hikers crossing Nitinat Narrows.

For those inclined to poke around, a visit to the **Cheewhat Lake Cedar** is a must. It's a 20- to 40-minute hike off the Rosander Main, the logging road that leads to the Carmanah Valley. The trail is rough and poorly marked. The reward is to stand next to the largest known tree in Canada — a western red cedar 18.34 m/60.17 ft in circumference and 55.5 m/182.1 ft tall, with a 15.6 m/51.2 ft spread and an estimated volume of 449 cu m/15,856 cu ft. Estimates of the age of the vast, still-growing conifer range up to 2,500 years.

A place that's good to know about, but don't feel you have to go there, is the **Nitinat Triangle**, a rugged area of small lakes and old-growth forest on the west side of Nitinat Lake. Protected in the 1970s, when the area was added to Pacific Rim National Park, the triangle is renowned among wilderness trekkers. A combination of paddling and grueling portages puts one at the head of beautiful Tsusiat Falls, above the West Coast Trail. The hardcore rope their vessels and supplies down to the trail, launch into the chuck from the sandstone shelf (highly dangerous) and paddle through Nitinat Narrows (ditto). The more sensible rope their stuff down and then wait for a Ditidaht water taxi to transport them through the Narrows. The circuit is 38 km/24 mi and requires three to five days.

Details

- Nitinat Lake is usually approached from the east side via Youbou or Port Alberni, on logging roads. A scenic route from Victoria follows the West Coast Road to Port Renfrew, the Harris Creek Road to Cowichan Lake and the South Shore Rd to the Nitinat Main. Either way, logging road travel is involved.
- Ditidaht First Nation, 664 Malachan Indian Reserve, Nitinat Lake; visitors' centre 250-745-3999, motel 250-745-3844; visitors' website westcoasttrail.com; First Nations website ditidaht.ca.
- Cheewhat Lake Cedar: Roadside parking at N 48° 41.562, W 124° 44.154; site at N 48° 41.7, W 124° 44.376. The tree is within the boundary of Pacific Rim Park, but the road isn't.

Carmanah Walbran Provincial Park | 69

The old-growth forest in Carmanah-Walbran, south of Lake Cowichan and west of Port Renfrew, is a world of perpetual shade broken by shafts of light, of profound silences punctuated by birdsong … the creaking of ancient wood … the plash of water on creek rock. The provincial park, established between 1990 and 1995, protects 16.37 sq km/6.32 sq mi of west-coast rainforest in the adjacent valleys of Carmanah, Walbran, Logan and Cullite creeks. There are three small campgrounds in the park.

Access to Carmanah is via Cowichan and Nitinat lakes and the Rosander Main, through areas of active logging. Be prepared to meet — and know how to avoid — logging trucks. The trailhead is about four hours from Victoria.

First-time visitors head for the Three Sisters, a 2.5-km/1.6-mi hike upriver, and the Randy Stoltmann Commemorative Grove, 2.6 km downstream. Stoltmann, a tireless advocate for ancient forests, brought Carmanah into the public eye in 1985, when it was under imminent threat of logging. It took a public outcry to tip the balance toward preservation of the entire Carmanah valley. Park advocates succeeded in adding the lower half of the Walbran Valley to the park in 1995. Logging proceeds at a fearsome pace in the upper Walbran. Regrettably, slashed BC Parks budgets have left the trails in a soggy state, and difficult going. More worrying, huge cedars at the edges of the park have been poached.

The Carmanah Giant, at 96 m/315 ft, the tallest known tree in Canada and believed the third tallest Sitka spruce anywhere, is growing in a ravine near the bottom of the lower Carmanah Trail, which is officially closed.

Approaches to the larger and equally interesting Walbran Valley requires a left fork after the Caycuse Bridge. Best access is via McClure

TAKE 5 *Star Weiss's Sacred Places*

Victoria author Star Weiss, a native of New York, has lived up and down Vancouver Island for more than 30 years.

"I am fascinated by the power of place on the west coast, and by the locations British Columbians choose as havens. Here are five sacred places from my book, *Havens in a Hectic World: Finding Sacred Places* (Touchwood Editions, 2008; see *starweiss.ca*)."

1. Yuquot
Ancient home of the Mowachaht people on Nootka Island. One of the most spiritual places in BC — mystical, historical. Accessible via the *Uchuck III* from Gold River.

2. Congregation Emanu-El, Victoria
Oldest surviving synagogue on the west coast, now a National Historic Site, restored to its former beauty; tours can be arranged.

3. Providence Farm, Duncan
A place of compassion and inclusiveness, sacred to the Quw'utsun people, now well-known for its horticultural therapy program. Sits on a beautiful 400 acres — a magical setting.

4. Mt. Albert Edward, Forbidden Plateau
This is my church, halfway to heaven, a place where I feel close to the divine — accessible via the Paradise Meadows trail at Mt. Washington.

5. Carmanah-Walbran Provincial Park
A mystical spot where, as Leonard Cohen wrote, "God is alive, magic is afoot." It is the forest primeval. You'll feel like a tree-elf standing among the ancient giants. Worth the daunting trip to get there.

Main and Glad Lake Main. Logging companies have been working in the 7.5-sq km/2.9-sq mi Upper Walbran for years, and you will find many a cedar stump 5 m/16 ft in diameter. But some of the Upper Walbran is still clothed in old-growth forest, which the Ancient Forest Alliance is trying to save (see #66).

The bridge on Walbran Creek, near the park boundary, makes a fine destination for car camping and day trips. The Upper Walbran has some good trails, some with boardwalks, stairs, bridges and also gorgeous riverside campsites.

Not far from the bridge is Castle Grove, one of the best remaining old-growth red cedar forests on the island. Nearby swimming holes include Walbran Falls, with tiered waterfalls and deep pools, a 15-minute walk upriver.

BC Parks' map warns that the Lower Walbran is *potentially unsafe* and *discourages access*. I've hiked far down the Walbran creek bed from the bridge. It's a miracle of geologic diversity and great beauty.

Details

- Carmanah Walbran Provincial Park: env.gov.bc.ca; mas map, directions to Carmanah.
- Walbran Creek bridge: GPS lat 48.650887, long -124.593415.

70   Bamfield and Barkley Sound

Bamfield is a quaint fishing village with arms on either side of little Bamfield Inlet, near Barkley Sound. Access to the west side of Bamfield is by water. A boardwalk runs between the houses and the tide. Front doors open off the boardwalk.

Bamfield is blessed with remarkable surroundings. Across the little peninsula of Bamfield West is exquisite **Brady's Beach**. Along the same coast is *Kiix?in* (pronounced "kee-hin"), ancient fortified village of the Huu-ay-aht First Nations, "the only known First Nations village of the more than 100 villages on the southern British Columbia coast, that still features significant, standing traditional architecture" — now a National Historic Site of Canada.

On the eastern slope of Banfield Inlet is the **Bamfield Marine Sciences Centre**, a renowned university-level centre of field research and training that offers tours to summer visitors. The tanks of local seal-ife are eye-popping. The site was long occupied by the Bamfield Cable Station, connected by a single 4000-km/2,485-mi-long underwater telegraph cable with Fanning Island, Fiji. It was one lap in the round-the world telecommunications system known as the All Red Route — so named because it was routed entirely through British possessions. At the cable station, the barely perceptible clicks of faraway telegraph machines would be amplified, picked up by batteries of headphoned clerks and relayed to Port Alberni.

Bamfield is still relatively isolated, with logging road access from Cowichan Lake and Port Alberni. There's a half-day cruise from Port Alberni aboard the packet freighter *Francis Barkley*. The approach by sea

TAKE 5 *Bruce Whittington's Excellent Birding Adventures*

Naturalist, writer and photographer Bruce Whittington is author of three books, most recently What's That Island? — a Guide to the 90-minute BC Ferry Crossing between Tsawwassen and Swartz Bay *(Stray Feathers Press, 2010; strayfeathers.ca). He lives in Ladysmith and leads interpretive cruises to such special places as Haida Gwaii.*

1. Herring spawn
Early in spring the herring spawn along the east coast of the island. The water takes on a milky colour. The spectacle attracts many species of wildlife, including numbers of sea lions and thousands upon thousands of seabirds that feed on the herring and their roe. But it's hard to know where the herring will appear. One way is to follow the herring fishery. The fishboats get short openings on short notice. You have to ask around.

2. Raptor migration
One of my favorite birding spots is a rocky promontory in East Sooke Park I call Hawk Lookout. I like to sit up on the rocks on a nice September day and watch the Turkey Vultures stage their annual migration across the Strait of Juan de Fuca, joined by as many as a dozen other species of raptors.

3. Active Pass
On the Swartz Bay-Tsawwassen ferry route through the Gulf Islands, this Important Bird Area (IBA) is especially interesting during migration times, when you will see thousands of Bonaparte Gulls and Pacific Loons that stop to refuel for the next leg of their travels.

4. Pelagic birding
On these boating excursions from west coast ports — Port Renfrew, Bamfield, Ucluelet or Tofino — you travel 50 km or more offshore. You're in a wilderness where you see Black-footed Albatrosses and several species of shearwaters, birds that travel huge distances without ever setting foot on land except to breed.

5. Saanich Peninsula
Wintering birds, including waterfowl and the raptors that feed on them, gather in the Martindale Valley, along with the vagrant species that set birders' hearts aflutter. The Victoria Christmas Day Bird Count consistently records more than 100 species in the valley, including a lot of individual rare birds and some spectacular native species — Snowy Owls and Gyrfalcons — you don't often see.

is highly recommended. Make sure to get the right day. The boat sails to Bamfield on Tuesdays, Thursdays and Saturdays year round (4½ hours one way) and in the summer, Sundays, with a turn through the Broken Group on the outbound (5½ hours). On other days, the freighter goes to Ucluelet.

The cruise down 40-km/25-mi-long Alberni Inlet — longest of many fjords on the island — is scenic enough, but save your batteries for the gorgeous vistas of Barkley Sound. The most open of the island's five *sounds*, Barkley Sound is 24 km/15 mi wide and indented as much as 25 km/15.5 mi, not including Alberni Inlet. *Sound* is a misnomer — they are not *passages* but whole complexes of *inlets*.

Kayakers bound for the Broken Group do not cross the open water from Bamfield unless they are storm-hardened Eskimo-rollers. The highly scenic Deer Group of Islands is much nearer, and there's a put-in near the Centennial Park campground on Port Desire, Bamfield East. Many campsites are perilously close to high tide, but on the other hand, the Deer Group has relatively few visitors to its sea caves and sparkling white beaches. (More on access to the Broken Group in #74.)

Charming sea-drenched Bamfield is near the western terminus of the famed West Coast Trail (#67).

Details

- Huu-ay-aht First Nation: huuayaht.org.
- *Kiix?in* Village and Fortress National Historic Site of Canada: historicplaces.ca.
- Lady Rose Marine Services, 5425 Argyle St (Harbour Quay), Port Alberni; 250-723-8313 (year 'round during office hours) 1-800-663-7192 (Apr-Sept): ladyrosemarine.com.
- Bamfield Marine Sciences Centre: bms.bc.ca.

Bamfield Coast Guard Station and Cape Beale Lighthouse — 71

The province's oldest lifeboat station has occupied the picturesque grassy grounds and white heritage buildings of the Canadian Coast Guard base in Bamfield West since 1908. It had the world's first purpose-built power lifeboat.

Part of the vital work of the Bamfield Coast Guard is looking out for the safety of the waterborne visitors to Barkley Sound and hikers on the West Coast Trail.

The lifesaving station was established after the wreck of the SS *Valencia* in 1906. The same catastrophe sparked construction of the Pachena Point lighthouse and the West Coast Lifesaving Trail.

The coast of Vancouver Island on either side of Barkley Sound is known as the Graveyard of the Pacific. The craggy shores south of Bamfield form one side of the funnel that is the Strait of Juan de Fuca. The strait is a major shipping channel to ports at Vancouver, Point Roberts, Seattle and Tacoma and dozens of smaller ports around the so-called Salish Sea. The coast is pounded by the frigid Pacific and lashed by howling winter winds. It's one of the wildest stretches anywhere. Beneath lie dozens of ships' hulls. More than a few travelers have found a watery grave there.

Many an approaching ship was driven onto the rocks during storms. If you were bearing north along the Washington coast, and you missed the Cape Flattery Light — marking the entrance to Juan de Fuca Strait — you might continue north until the dreaded cry went up: "Breakers ahead!" The captain of the doomed *Valencia* was heard to reply, "My God, where are we?"

The Cape Beale Lighthouse was built at the southern entrance of Barkley Sound in 1874 to guide Alberni Valley traffic. The lightkeepers saved lives, as when in 1906 Minnie Patterson slogged 10 km through swamps in the teeth of a howling December storm to summon the survey vessel *Quadra* from Bamfield. It was able to rescue all aboard a ship that had swamped near the Cape.

The Carmanah Point Lighthouse was built in 1891 to help ships find the entrance of Juan de Fuca Strait. In January 1906, the SS *Valencia* was carrying nearly 180 passengers and crew from San Francisco to Seattle when it missed the entrance of the strait and ran onto a reef near Pachena Point. The captain disengaged it, then ran it on the rocks again to avoid sinking.

As the storm raged, huge waves ripped people off the decks. Lifeboats spilled the occupants into the ocean. Some made it to shore, only to be plucked off the rocks. Those who struggled up the cliffs encountered impenetrable thickets of salal.

Survivors found the Cape Beale Lighthouse and summoned rescuers who flocked to the ship by land and sea, only to discover they could do nothing but watch. They saw women lashed to masts with their children to avoid being swept away, calling for help until succumbing to hypothermia. Only 37 survived — all adult males.

Rarely has Canadian public opinion changed political wills as quickly as when the news of the *Valencia* disaster hit the wires.

Today, a fleet of 14 vessels, two hovercraft, 16 search and rescue lifeboats and five helicopters patrols the Graveyard of the Pacific. The Bamfield station has a staff of four and two lifesaving boats.

The rescue coordination centre in Victoria responds to more than 2,100 maritime search-and-rescue calls annually, of which about one-fifth are in distress. Their responses save an estimated 1,400 lives a year.

Details:

■ Graveyard of the Pacific: Saving the Wrecks website: virtualmuseum.ca.

- Minnie Patterson, Cape Beale Lighthouse keeper who saved the crew of the *Coloma*: lighthousefriends.com.

72 — Alberni Steam Train to McLean Mill

Port Alberni is a forestry centre and deep-sea port at the head of Alberni Inlet. The inlet is a *fjord*, long (45 km/28 mi) and narrow with steep sides rising to low mountains. It opens out onto Barkley Sound — which makes "Port" a Pacific port, even though it's closer to the Salish Sea. (As the crow flies, Port Alberni is about 22 km/14 mi from the inland sea, less than half the distance, 58 km/36 mi, from the open Pacific.) Port Alberni boasts of getting the hottest summertime temperatures on the island.

In summer months, the town's big attraction is a medley of machinery from bygone days, a steam train that carries you out to the site of a steam sawmill that really works. To some, that's akin to watching paint dry, but others thrill to this connection with the past, the steam-powered machinery that disappeared like morning dew when the petroleum-powered internal combustion engine took over the world of power machines.

The Alberni Pacific Railway's 1929 Baldwin steam logging locomotive pulls open cars from the CPR railway station four days a week on a 9-km/6-mi, 35-minute excursion through town and out to the McLean Mill. This is one of very few working steam sawmills, where (in the words of a TripAdvisor review, "workers (not actors) bring logs to a loading-point, load restored logging-trucks, haul the logs to a mill-pond (where they are dumped into the water), then bring them up onto the mill floor where the logs are milled into commercial lumber."

The mill operated as a family-run business from 1925 to 1965, and is today a National Historic Site on 13 ha/32 ac, with bunkhouses, worker houses and other mill facilities in pretty much their original states. Volunteers drawn mostly from the logging community operate the saws, whose engines date from 1870 and 1890, and demonstrate other steam logging operations. There's a high-lead rig attached to a spar tree and operated by a steam donkey engine. A guided tour goes with the price of admission. One's only complaint would be that two hours is not enough time to absorb everything before the train reverses back into town.

Back in town, several other public attractions near the railway station display the valley's industrial heritage. Harbour Quay, across from the railway station, is a pleasant mélange of shops, a boat ways, and a clock tower you can climb to take in the splendid views of the canal and valley. The town is economically reduced from its heyday, but it retains a paper mill, a sawmill and a deep-sea port.

The Alberni Valley Museum, about 3 km/2 mi from the railway station, is well worth a visit for the quality of the exhibits, the range of the collection and the interpretive skills of the staff. It's located in a well-appointed community centre with a pool and public library.

Details

- Alberni Pacific Railway, 3100 Kingsway Ave, Port Alberni; toll free 855-866-1376; albernisteamtrain.com; open beginning of June to early Sept.
- McLean Mill, 5633 Smith Rd, Port Alberni; 855-866-1376; Facebook page; open year round; parking, gift shop, café.
- McLean Mill National Historic Site: historicplaces.ca.
- Alberni Valley Museum, 4255 Wallace St, Port Alberni; 250-720-2863; portalberni.ca.
- Industrial Heritage Centre, 3250 9th Ave, Port Alberni; 250-723-4285; alberniheritage.com.
- Maritime Discovery Centre, 2750 Harbour Rd, Port Alberni; 250-723-6164; alberniheritage.com.

Della Falls 73

Della Falls is a grand spectacle on the remote southern edge of Strathcona Park, where Drinkwater Creek tumbles off a towering rampart of rock. Della Falls drops, cascades over rocks, then drops again. The falls and cascades total 444 m/1,456 ft, making Della Falls the tallest waterfall in Canada — officially. The relative lengths of the segments have been triangulated as about 4:1:2. That was its state when I stood at base of the falls. During heavy rains, observers report, Della Falls becomes one long arc.

There are several ways to approach Della Falls, all on foot. From the north, it's possible to drop into the subalpine valley via extremely rugged trails from Bedwell Lake or Cream Lake.

The only access from below is by way of the moderately challenging trail up Drinkwater Creek. Getting to the trailhead can be a challenge in itself. It's at the west end of Great Central Lake. The lake is only traversable by boat, about a 35-km/22-mi trip. If you are self-propelled, it's important to know that the lake can be inhospitable. Never mind finding a campsite — there's virtually no place to land. Winds can blow up in the afternoon and make a hell of paddling. There is an alternative — a water taxi service.

Even with the motor assist, a trip to Della Falls requires at least one night of camping. There are campsites, of varying dampness, along

149

the trail. If you're paddling, allow three to five nights. It's a seven hour hike to the base of the falls. The altitude gain is about 500 m/1,640 ft, mostly in the last third. There are three crossings. According to the Trails BC website, "the first 10 km is essentially a rail grade interrupted by creek washouts and water damage causing many detours and slippery rocks while crossing creeks. There is frequent water damage on the trail."

For a view of the falls from above, plan to climb an extra three hours up to Love Lake. The switchback trail gains 800 m/2.625 ft in altitude and is best undertaken by experienced hikers without full packs. There are several lookouts en route to charming Love Lake.

Della Falls — getting there is more than half the fun.

Is Della Falls really the highest waterfall in Canada? There are many higher unmeasured falls on northern Vancouver Island. Kiwi Falls in Schoen Lake Provincial Park is estimated to be 475 m/1,560 ft . There are reports of falls more than 700 m/2,297 ft on BC's mainland coast.

Details

- Great Central Lake RV Resort & Marina, 11000 Central Lake Rd, Port Alberni; 250-723-2657; greatcentrallake.ca.
- Della Falls Water Taxi: alberni.ca.
- Guidebook: *Hiking Trails 3: Northern Vancouver Island* (10th edition, 2008). Detailed coverage and maps of trails around Della Falls.
- Trails BC: trailsbc.ca.
- World Waterfall Database: worldwaterfalldatabase.com.

74 Ucluelet

The oceanside village of Ucluelet — pronounced *You CLUE lit* and often *You CUE lit*, but even more often shortened to Ukee — straddles a rocky peninsula just west of the entrance of Barkley Sound and 8 km/5 mi south of Highway 4. Not that long ago Ucluelet was a lunchbucket town, a rough-edged service and residential centre for the logging industry. To get there, you drove through a moonscape. Politically, it was Tofino's opposite.

The loggers have moved on, the lunar (some would say lunatic) landscape has greened up, and the unTofino has become a destination in its own right. Ukee's most notable feature is the highly scenic broken outer coast, now wonderfully sightseeable by the addition of the Wild Pacific Trail (#75).

The waterfronts on both sides of the peninsula are so close and accessible, there's nothing to compare with that elsewhere on the lowland strip known as Esowista Peninsula, between Ukee and Tofino. Ucluelet is also on the map as the gateway to marine wildlife viewing, including several species of whales, in settings of staggering beauty. Otherwise, Ukee suffers in comparison with its twin. Having become something of a bedroom community for Tofino — rents in Ukee are more reasonable — it doesn't have a vibrant shopping district, and it gets pretty sleepy during the day. Ukee does have the stimulating **Ucluelet Aquarium**, showcasing the wonders of the deep. Next door on the inlet is the eye-catching Whiskey Landing, a spectacular confection of wood and stone that would stand out anywhere, with splendid jutting gables and massive standing poles dominating the façade. It operated as a luxury hotel until recently closed and sold. What does that mean?

We recently stayed at **Namasté B&B** on the Ucluelet Inlet waterfront, and Linda, our host, pointed out that Emily Carr visited Ucluelet as a young woman, as narrated in *Klee Wyck*, the artist's first published work (1941), a set of brief memoirs of Carr's early encounters with First Nations. The lead memoir, of the same name, relates how the Ucluelet people gave her the name — *Klee Wyck, laughing one*. Linda said her beach was where Carr sketched the village. That rang a bell, and sure enough, there's Carr's 1899 pencil sketch of the village of Etedsu in my book, *Victoria a History in Photographs*. It has the same perspective and proportions that I saw from Linda's beach. Linda is an Ucluelet hand from Hippie times who returned and took up this modest commercial enterprise. The upstairs suite looks out over the inlet and across to the village, with moundy green mountains in the distance. I asked Linda how she came to name the place Namasté. It was an act of devotion to the upward way of Yoga and mindfulness. "When I named the place," Linda added as an afterthought, "I hadn't noticed this." She pointed to a figure etched in the wood panelling adjacent to the table where we sat. It was of praying hands beside a woman's face, smiling in a way that was very familiar. I was just forming the thought, "That looks like Godfrey's work," when Linda said, "It was made by a famous artist, Godfrey Stephens, long before my time here."

We had take-out seafood that was sensational from the **Ravenlady Oyster Forte** food truck on the main drag. The fish croquettes, yum. We went to Black Rock Resort and I ordered the prawn tacos ($13). The tacos were of the hard commercial variety, good Old El Paso, the prawns whole, breaded, tasting of a spell in a box in the freezer.

Ucluelet is the terminus of the packet freighter *Francis Barkley* from Port Alberni (see #70), one of its many links with Barkley Sound. The nearby **Broken Group of Islands** is part of Pacific Rim Park. Myriad tiny islets and reefs line the channels. You can be dropped off in your kayak, and camping is excellent on the seven designated islands in the Broken Group, but know that the tiny archipelago gets busy by mid-summer, and above-tide sites block up. Be sure to book transport for your craft well in advance. Ucluelet is not such a good place to launch kayaks for a crossing. The open water can become dangerous without warning. One place to launch for the Broken Group is Toquaht Bay, on the highway side of the sound. A campground, marina and store are operated by the Toquaht First Nation. Or you can take the *Francis Barkley* to Sechart Lodge, stay there, rent kayaks. Many choose the group excursion route, guided by a seasoned wilderness kayaker.

Ucluelet's wildlife touring and whale watching businesses have grown enormously, and the leading tour outfits are highly rated, both power cruises and kayak touring. Among many attractions are spring and fall migrations of gray whales and humpback whales between southern and northern waters. Sport fishing for salmon and halibut is another mainstay of local enterprise.

Details

- Yuułuʔiłʔatḥ (Ucluelet) First Nation, 700 Wya Road, Hitacu; 1-877-726-7342; ufn.ca.
- Namasté B&B, 1201 Eber Rd, Ucluelet; reservations through booking.com. Cash only.
- Ravenlady Oyster Forte food truck, 1801 Bay St, Ucluelet; 403-472-1944; ravenlady.ca.
- Ucluelet Aquarium, 180 Main St, Ucluelet; 250-726-2782; uclueletaquarium.org.
- Broken Group Islands camping information on the Pacific Rim National Park Reserve of Canada site: pc.gc.ca .
- MV *Frances Barkley*, Sechart Lodge: 250-723-8313; ladyrosemarine.com. Sechart Lodge is open year-round on the American plan. The *Frances Barkley* visits Ucluelet Mondays, Wednesdays and Fridays, June to mid-September.
- Toquaht Bay Campground: reservations 250-726-8349; toquartbay.com.
- Archipelago Wildlife Cruises, Whiskey Landing Marina, 1634 Cedar St, Ucluelet; 250-726-8289; archipelagocruises.com.
- Majestic Ocean Kayaking, 1167 Helen Rd, Ucluelet; 1-800-889-7644, 250-726-2868; oceankayaking.com.
- Pacific Rim Whale Festival (2 weeks every March): pacificrimwhalefestival.com.

The Wild Pacific Trail provides the best oceanfront hiking on the island, bar none. The competition is stiff because Vancouver Island has a bunch of outstanding coastal trails: the West Coast Trail, the Juan de Fuca Marine Trail, East Sooke Park, the Wild Side Trail on Flores Island, the Nootka Island trail and the North Coast Trail. The Ucluelet trail is a remarkable civic achievement — the most accessible, with the easiest walking, on well-drained gravel paths, yet challenging for the way Mother Pacific gets in your face. Which is the case, especially in winter, when the storms roll in and huge swells pound the jagged rocks in unfiltered natural splendor.

The several sections of the 12-km/7.5-mi Wild Pacific Trail really do deliver. A logical place to begin is the 2.6-km/1.6-mi Lighthouse Loop at the end of the peninsula. The loop is easier than the other sections, with no stairs, and fabulous views of the rocks and coves on the southwest side. But for the loose gravel and some steep, short hills, I'm tempted to say it's wheelchair-accessible. My second choice is the 3.5 km/2.2 mi east of the ancient cedar grove — same gravel walk, with a few stairs, and an amazing number of side trails to scenic lookouts, some of them truly jaw-dropping.

The Wild Pacific Trail originated with resident bivalve farmer Oyster Jim Martin, who was able to negotiate with the landowners of Ucluelet's outside coast, chiefly forestry giant Weyerhaeuser Corp, and marshall huge amounts of labour, beginning in 1999. The work is ongoing: 2016 trail-building added ten more viewpoints on the Lighthouse Loop. Also in 2016, Oyster Jim's work, together with Wild Pacific Trail Society president and fund-raiser Barbara Schramm's, were honoured with BC Community Achievement Awards.

Details

- Wild Pacific Trail: wildpacifictrail.com. Recommended: the 22-minute video on the history of Oyster Jim's trail.
- BC Community Achievement Awards: bcachievement.com.

76   Long Beach

Long Beach is the heart of Pacific Rim National Park Reserve. It was established in the 1970s to protect sections of the island's spectacular west coast.

Pacific Rim Park encloses 290 sq km/112 sq mi of land and 220 sq km/85 sq mi of foreshore in three sections. The Long Beach section includes

SOUTHWEST VANCOUVER ISLAND

30 km/19 mi of varied coast and nearby old-growth forest between Ucluelet and Tofino on Esowista Peninsula. The other sections are the Broken Group of Islands in Barkley Sound and the West Coast Trail.

Long Beach was a legend for decades before Highway 4 was completed from Port Alberni, and streams of people started to travel the winding road to camp in the west coast wilderness. When Parks Canada moved in, a community of squatters pulled up stakes, but many stuck around, making a go of it on a bit of land or in nearby Tofino. Some are there today.

Long Beach is the centre of a 16-km/10-mi continuum of sand that is wider than most beaches are long. The scale of it defies description. The roar of the pounding surf is a constant. It rumbles under your feet. The spray resolves into rainbow mists. Depending on the season, there's a scene of wet suited surfers. They grab their boards and vanish into the distances. Some visitors attribute spiritual qualities to Long Beach after experiencing its vast openness.

You come to this spectacle through a curtain of ancient Sitka spruce trees. Their lichen-trailing branches harbour ravens and eagles. Sitka spruce grows well here, even when the roots are lapping in salt water. The standing dead shed their scaly bark to reveal the massive cylinders of the trunks, scored by spiraling fissures.

There are 12 km/7 mi of boardwalk and trails through the nearby forests and bogs, with guided tours in season. A great place to start would be the **Schooner Cove Trail** to the west end of Long Beach. The trail is entirely boardwalked, including three sets of stairs to cross creek beds — 336 steps in all, so the 2-km/1.2-mi round trip offers a good little workout. In the forest are some really big Western red cedars and Sitka spruce, one giant with its top sheared off, new leaders still growing.

Details

- Pacific Rim National Park Reserve of Canada: pc.gc.ca. Day-use fees apply. To camp at Green Point, you'd better reserve during the summer months.
- Trails: tofinhiking.com.
- Schooner Cove trail: parking lot 200 m/600 ft west of the Esowista village turnoff.
- Kwisitis Visitor Centre, 485 Wick Rd, 4.8 km/3 mi west of 3-way intersection. Feast House restaurant: 250-726-2628.
- Pacific Surf Co, 441 Campbell St, Tofino; 888-777-9961/250-725-2155; pacificsurfschool.com. Rentals, instruction, transportation.

Clayoquot Sound is the stretch of west coast Vancouver Island between Esowista and Hesquiaht peninsulas. The whole complex of islands, inlets and drainages is about 100 km/62 mi across. It measures in all 3,500 sq km/1,351 sq mi, and about two-thirds of that is land. But those are just names and numbers. You simply have to be there to appreciate the piercing beauty and wild energy of Clayoquot Sound. It's a place where sensory stimuli crowd in on you — the exhalations of its mudflats, its fine mists, a passing pod of whales, the eagle's keening cry. There's a lot to take in. Clayoquot is vast, varied, profound.

It should be stated from the getgo that Clayoquot Sound is the unceded domain of Nuu-Chah-Nulth First Nations. The Tla-o-qui-aht First Nation occupies the southern parts of Clayoquot and part of Esowista Peninsula. Their principal village is Opitsat on Meares Island. The middle portions of the sound are the domain of the Ahousaht First Nation; Marktosis, on Flores Island, is their principal village. The Hesquiaht First Nation occupies the northern reaches of Clayoquot, and their village is Hesquiat, on the peninsula of the same name.

An early English immigrant named Fred Tibbs bought a little island near Tofino — it's the middle of the three islands nearest the 4th St docks. He called it Dreamisle. Others named it Tibbs' Island. Today it's known as Arnet Island. Tibbs logged the whole island, leaving just one giant spruce. He topped it at 30 m/100 ft, limbed it, and nailed rungs to the trunk. For safety, he added a framework of lumber bottom to top, and capped it with a 3x3-m/10x10-ft platform. Early photos suggest that it looked pretty ghastly, although it was doubtless viewed at the time as a civilizing touch. A bit of a hermit, Fred would sit there listening to gramophone records on a wind-up machine or playing his cornet. Tibbs clearly didn't get Clayoquot. Still, I'd like to have ten minutes on that platform, just to look around.

Meares Island dominates the landscape with its two sugarloaf peaks, Mt Colnett, 5 km/3 mi E, and Lone Cone, 6 km/4 mi N. (See #78.) The third prominent landmark is Catface Mountain, 13 km/8 mi NW of Tofino. The three mountains are remarkably alike in shape and alignment. Between the peaks and the apron of lowland in front of them, geographers draw a line to mark the boundary between the Estevan Lowland and the Vancouver Island Fiordlands. Outside the line are landscapes exposed to the ocean, hugely composed of sand. Esowista Peninsula and Vargas Island are very sandy. They are underlain by relatively recent rock formations.

On the inland side of the line, and strikingly parallel, are nine inlets and lakes that flow into Clayoquot. The longest inlets, Herbert and

Bedwell, originate 30 km/18.6 mi from the outside coast. They are true fjords, sculpted by ice, with side walls extending deep into water at the heads. The inland boundary of Clayoquot is defined by the watersheds that drain into the nine inlets and lakes.

From Tofino, you can look between Meares's peaks into Bedwell Inlet towards snowy Mariner Mountain, 36 km/22 mi distant, but still within Clayoquot's boundaries. What a view, looking into the heart of Vancouver Island from tidewater.

Rearing up in the middle of all this is the Catface Range, isolating the north and south ends of Clayoquot and posing a serious obstacle to paddlers. To the north are Sulphur Passage and Hayden Passage, gateways to western Clayoquot Sound. The Megin River, the largest primeval watershed remaining on the island, flows into Shelter Inlet, one of four on that side of Catface.

Hot Springs Cove, in Maquinna Provincial Park, west of Sydney Inlet, is the most popular destination on the western reaches of Clayoquot, 35 km/22 mi by air from Tofino, by boat 27 nautical mi. **Cougar Annie's Garden** (#83) is in nearby Boat Basin.

A must-do for visitors is to take a wildlife tour on the water around Clayoquot. Some take you scanning beaches for black bear and other large carnivores. Others make for the whale grounds a bit offshore. You have a multitude of tour outfits to choose from. The best offer experiences that are as good as it gets. I would account a smashing success a recent (March 2017) excursion to view giant Gray whales between Lennard and Cleland islands with Howie, a First Nations guide for more than 20 years who works with The Whale Centre in Tofino. Howie has an uncanny ability to steer the Boston whaler to the giant mammals, who can swim underwater for 10 minutes and then barely break the waves. We spent more than an hour following three Grays. Back of Meares Island, Howie showed us a sea otter. Rounding Meares on the way back to Tofino, we asked about the recently completed trail up Lone Cone. Howie told us he helped his grandfather and uncles from Opitsat build the trail.

Details

- Tour operators, dozens listed: tourismtofino.com.
- Tofino Hiatus, a hiker's website: tofinohiatus.com.
- The Whale Centre, 411 Campbell St, Tofino; 250-725-2132, 1-888-474-2288; tofinowhalecentre.com
- Jamie's Whaling Station and Adventure Centres, 606 Campbell St, Tofino; 800-667-9913; jamies.com; and in Ucluelet: 877-726-7444.
- Black Bear Kayaking, 390 Main St, Tofino; 250-725-3342; blackbearkayak.com.
- Tofino Sea Kayaking Company, 320 Main St, Tofino; 1-800-863-4664; tofinoseakayaking.com.

- Clayoquot Ventures Tofino Fishing, 561 Campbell St, Tofino; 888-534-7422; tofinofishing.com.
- Readings: *Tofino and Clayoquot Sound: A History* by Margaret Horsfield (Harbour Publishing, 2014).
  Settling Clayoquot by Bob Bossin (Sound Heritage 1981). Oral history, including the story of Fred Tibbs.

78 Kennedy River Bridge

Clayoquot Sound caught the world's attention in the summer of 1993, when some 12,000 people made their way to the Peace Camp in the forestry wasteland Black Hole. They came to put their bodies in the way of the logging trucks at the bottleneck Kennedy River Bridge, point of entry to the area where loggers were working.

The first trucks would appear at about five am. Those who were willing to be arrested blocked the truckers' access to the bridge and refused to move. All were pledged to practice non-violence. Media attention was already focused on the island's red-hot, anti-clearcut logging dispute. At the Kennedy River Bridge, it went viral. The protest was also a magnet for logging advocates.

The company obtained court injunctions prohibiting obstruction. A protester's second arrest — when the person was in knowing violation of the injunction — drew criminal contempt charges. The RCMP would confront the defiant and cart another limp body away. On one tumultuous day, August 9, more than 1,000 people gathered, and more than 300 were arrested. It took seven hours to clear the bridge.

In the months that followed, 857 people were tried and convicted in several courts. The sentences included fines as high as $3,000 and as much as six months in prison. All the convicted got criminal records.

Why did they do it?

Clayoquot's 2,400 sq km/926 sq mi of land comprises about eight percent of Vancouver Island, but it has six of the island's seventeen remaining intact watersheds larger than 50 sq km/19 sq mi. It has the largest area of old-growth forest left on Vancouver Island, and some of the best, most intact, ancient temperate rainforest remaining anywhere.

Clayoquot Sound has been clearcut logged since the 1960s. Steep slopes facing the ocean were particularly prone to *mass wasting* after roading and logging. The long plumes of avalanches become starkly visible as the surroundings green up. Logging increased dramatically in the 1980s. In 1988, the equivalent of 29,000 truckloads of logs were hauled out of Clayoquot.

Local citizens tried every avenue to get a hearing. Industry and government followed the line of *Talk and Log*. They would invite the public to sit on *teams* and help *plan* the future of the sound, while the trees just fell faster. In March 1993, the provincial government of the day, the left-leaning NDP, put forward a plan that opened 85 percent of the productive forests of Clayoquot Sound to logging. Tofino-based Friends of Clayoquot Sound organized the blockade.

"Civil disobedience," Ontarian Sheldon Lipsey, one of the convicted, told the court, "is a refusal to comply with laws that are perceived as unjust, in this case, laws that protect a private company's financial interests in cutting down trees but fail to protect the public's interest in preserving this country's natural heritage, as well as land to which the First Nations have never given up title."

One result was that the BC government promised to reform logging to where it would stand up to world scrutiny. A blue-ribbon scientific panel recommended adoption of a valley-by-valley approach to logging and protection of all pristine watersheds. Mapped on Clayoquot Sound's myriad watersheds, the scientific panel's restrictions allowed logging in just 230 sq km/89 sq mi — less than one-tenth.

First Nations firms now own the industrial logging rights on Crown land in Clayoquot Sound. They were logging much less than in the 80s. The rate is now determined by the area. But the companies are logging in pristine watersheds. Iisaak Forest Resources has rights to log 870 sq km/ 336 sq mi in Clayoquot and Mamook-Coulsen, 490 sq km/189 sq mi. Other companies have logging rights on Crown land. Private forests in Clayoquot are logged with little regulation of rate or method.

"Most people believe that Clayoquot Sound is saved," said Valerie Langer of Friends of Clayoquot Sound a decade ago. "It is not."

Notwithstanding all that, the people of Clayoquot Sound, of both First Nations and external descent, have hitched their wagons to an economic mix more oriented to helping people experience the natural splendor of the island's temperate rainforest.

Details

- Directions to the Kennedy River bridge: from Highway 4, 1.6 km/1 mi NNE of the intersection of the Tofino-Ucluelet road, turn NW on the poorly-marked West Main logging road; the bridge is 11.2 km/7.2 mi from the turnoff.
- Tla-o-qui-aht Tribal Parks: the Kennedy River Bridge is the point of access to the area the Tla-o-qui-aht First Nation has designated Ha'uukmin Tribal Park, with a protection zone, *qwa siin hap (leave as is for now)*, around the pristine upper Kennedy and Clayoquot river valleys and part of Clayoquot Arm: wildernesscommittee.org.
- BC Government summaries of 1993 Clayoquot land use decision and initiatives after: for.gov.bc.ca/dsi/Clayoquot/clayoquot_sound.htm.
- Clayoquot Sound scientific panel report: for.gov.bc.ca/tasb/slrp/lrmp/ nanaimo/clayoquot_sound/archive/reports/clay1.pdf

- *Talk and Log: Wilderness Politics in British Columbia* by Jeremy Wilson (Vancouver: UBC Press, 1998).
- Friends of Clayoquot Sound: focs.ca; Reliable perspectives on local resource issues.

The Wickaninnish Inn   79

The Wickaninnish Inn is a trifecta of luxe lodgings in a magnificent setting — the open North Pacific coast at Chesterman Beach — with food and drink to match the islands' best. The one-of-a-kind resort in Tofino is a member of the Relais & Châteaux worldwide association of 540 hotels and restaurants and has been a member since 1997, its second year. During a weekend at The Wickaninnish Inn, I talked with a Victoria-based gourmand, an upper-echelon guy who has stayed at the inn a half dozen times before. We later messaged. He pronounced it "just superb; a match for any oceanside resort in the world; fabulous views and Relais et Châteaux standards that are no mean feat to achieve since 1997."

A local family enterprise, the inn has 75 rooms and suites in buildings named The Pointe and The Beach. Our west-facing room in The Pointe overlooked a little cove about 20 m/66 ft away. When the tide is in, the briny green swell hits the rocks in great white sprays. The bathroom has a shuttered inside window facing the room and the view beyond. How quirky is that? The appointments in our room included the very best Turkish sheets and towels, carved wooden aircon vents, and an inlaid wooden tissue cover.

The Beach is more set-back. (Trees screen the views from some rooms.) There, above a little second lobby, I found the cozy library overlooking the beach through a two-storey bank of windows. Below, opening onto the beach, is the Driftwood café-bar. The patio, nestled in the beachside grasses, is just magical. A carving shed is right nearby. Chesterman Beach is spacious, but not staggeringly huge like its neighbor Long Beach.

The ambience of The Wick's interior spaces announces in hushed tones a place that embraces proximity to nature, commitment to stewardship, linkage with First Nations, local vision and the spiritual dimension. A place where everything matters. The art work displayed at every turn. The full-size octopus carved of a creamy hand-inviting granitic rock. The old Douglas fir wood you see everywhere. Long thick slabs of orangey wood, beautifully grained, with nail marks visible, used to make a bathroom door or a dresser top. Given that Douglas fir doesn't grow well on the Wet Coast, and given it's a place that espouses the local, isn't that a little strange? Not at all. It was recovered from a demolition sale at St Ann's Academy in Victoria. (In my mantra of recycling, re-use is the highest good.) Every piece of wood seems to hold a story. The many hand-adzed posts, frames and panels are the signature of master wood-butcher Henry Nolla, the genius of the wood who, the story goes, was their neighbour. Nolla worked with the family for twenty years. His portrait hangs in the carving shed on the beach. The shed was latterly his shop.

TAKE 5 *The Islands' Best Restaurants outside Victoria*

1. Pilgrimme

2806 Montague Rd, Galiano Id, 250-539-5392; pilgrimme.ca.

2016 *Vancouver Magazine* (vanmag.com) Best Vancouver Island Restaurants awards: #1.

2016 Gold Medal Plates (goldmedalplates.com) BC awards: #1.

2015 *EnRoute* Magazine (enroute.aircanada.com) Best New Restaurants in Canada: #3. From the review: "The 25-seat dining room is intimate and calm, with a big twist of driftwood mounted on one wall. Leanne Lalonde ... met her partner, Winnipeg-born chef Jesse McCleery, at an eco-tourist lodge in B.C.'s Great Bear Rainforest. They eventually decamped to Galiano, a Gulf Island halfway between Vancouver and Victoria ..."

Alexandra Gill, *Globe and Mail* restaurant critic, review of March 11, 2017: "It is still a work in progress and will likely only get better. In the meantime, there really isn't any other chef in the province who has given himself over so completely to the Pacific Northwest. His menu is an adventurous microcosm of the region. And for passionate foodies, it is certainly worth the trip."

2017 Canada's Best Restaurants (canadas100best.com): #84.

2. Wolf in the Fog

150 Fourth Street, Tofino; 250-725-9653; wolfinthefog.com.

2016 *Vancouver Magazine* Best Vancouver Island Restaurants: #2. From the 2015 review (awarded #1): "Chef Nick Nutting's 'lusty, generous, and creative cooking' ... burger and fries ... Szechuan Surf & Turf share plate ... seasoned braised short rib and grilled octopus. ... whimsical mismatched china. ... Oysters wrapped in crispy potato with corn puree and hints of truffle ... beef tartare with North African spices and crunchy peanuts ... seared Albacore served with guanciale, espelette pepper, and orange. ... Sharing plates of squid, spot prawns, mussels, and pan-seared rock cod ... punch bowls for two to six people."

2014 *EnRoute* Magazine Best New Restaurants in Canada: #1.

2017 Canada's Best Restaurants: #41. From the review: "Gnarly gooseneck barnacles are poached in garlic butter. Fresh salmon—only fresh, never frozen—is basted with brown butter and stuffed with brown rice, bacon and tart evergreen huckleberries."

3. The Pointe at Wickaninnish Inn

Osprey Lane at Chesterman Beach, Tofino; 250-725-3100. wickinn.com.

At dinner, in the dramatic semicircular Pointe Restaurant, we chose the tasting menu, as did my correspondent, who reported: "I annotated the menu as usual; mostly small seafood dishes; cold poached scallops; foie gras in a very cold éclair (attractive); warm albacore tuna was not exciting; truffled Arctic char was hot and gorgeous; also enjoyed the Alpindon crusted Pork shoulder." Maitre-d' Paul Hitchey was a marvel of

2016 *Vancouver Magazine* Best Vancouver Island Restaurants: #3. The 2015 review (awarded #2): "The gold standard for waterfront fine dining in Canada. A gorgeous cedar room tastefully appointed with art provides lofty views above Chesterman Beach and the crashing waves of Tofino. Accomplished land- and sea-based fare includes albacore escabeche with fennel, basil, and honey water and pig tail with soused cherries and licorice crumble. The wine list represents the shores of B.C., Baja, and beyond, plus there's a formidable scotch list."

4. SoBo

311 Neil St, Tofino; 250-725-2341; sobo.ca.

2016 *Vancouver Magazine* Best Vancouver Island Restaurants: Honorable Mention. The 2015 review: "In 2007, chef-owner Lisa Ahier traded a tiny purple catering truck for this earth-toned storefront bedecked with driftwood tables and slate floors. For sophisticated bohemians [SoBo], the seasonal menu has retained the Killer Fish Tacos, for which SoBo has received national acclaim, and added tempting items like frozen fish chowder for takeout."

2015 Exceptional Eats! Award (eatmagazine.ca): Best Restaurant in BC.

The SoBo Cookbook: Recipes from the Tofino Restaurant at the End of the Canadian Road by Lisa Ahier and Andrew Morrison (Appetite by Random House, 2014).

5. Hudson's on First

163 First St, Duncan; 250-597-0066; hudsonsonfirst.ca.

2015 *Vancouver Magazine* Best Vancouver Island Restaurants: Honorable Mention. The review: "A restored heritage house is where British chef and Top Chef Canada alum Dan Hudson has arrived. Dive into the jewel-like rabbit terrine served with house-made picallili and toasted brioche, or lusciously rich and tender pork belly with housemade sauerkraut, glazed organic fingerlings, and braising liquor. Service is gracious and informed. Sunday brunch provides casual, affordable fun-think eggs with toast soldiers or full English breakfast."

Also buzzworthy:

Unsworth

2915 Cameron-Taggart Rd, Mill Bay; 250-929-2292; unsworthvineyards.com.

2015 *Vancouver Magazine* Best Vancouver Island Restaurants: #3.

attention at the dinner table.

Paul's detailed expositions of each dish's ingredients was echoed in Alexander McNaughton's guided forage tour on the beach and in the forest on Saturday morning. The Wick is enveloped by an old-growth forest of Sitka spruce, western hemlock and western red cedar. Alexander is a supplier of foraged goods to restaurants; likewise, tuna fish caught off these very shores, strictly by hook. Or, if it's Spring and you want some fog chanterelles, he's your man. His discourse was at a high level, but Latin names did not faze the dozen or so attendees. Alexander pulls meaning out of the lowliest objects of our disregard and has a nice recipe in which to use each — or in the case of the seawrack that clings to rocks in the intertidal, the sepia one you can pop, the Japanese make the pulpy insides of the bladders into a slurry that is put into hot baths as an anti-inflammatory. Alexander's No. 1 Must-see on the island? Marble Meadows in Strathcona Park, near his native Comox Valley.

In the spa, Paula had a custom facial. It was, bar none, the best she ever had. I went for a Sunday morning yoga class. I was the only student, which suited me fine. (Body image thing.) There's a little cabin on the rocks where two may get side-by-side massage treatments. The doors are flung open to capture the therapeutic omniphonic surf.

What else to say? We were seriously impressed by the animation, sincerity and unfailing courtesy of the staff.

A peak experience for sure.

Details

- The Wickaninnish Inn, 500 Osprey Lane, Tofino; 1-800-333-4604; wickinn.com.
- Relais & Château: "For more than 60 years, Relais & Châteaux has been a unique benchmark of excellence in the field of hospitality and fine dining," states the downloadable guide to joining the association. "It is not a chain, but an Association of exceptional properties in more than 64 countries." How Relais & Châteaux evaluates members' compliance with its standards: "Within the framework of a regular quality audit of the services provided by the members, all member properties of the Association are inspected at least once every three years. A quarterly review of guest comment forms and the processing of guest correspondence are additional quality tracking tools. Failure to comply with the quality criteria as established by these different tools and procedures can result in a decision by the Board of Directors to exclude a member."
- Other members of Relais & Châteaux within the purview of this book: **Clayoquot Wilderness Resort**, Bedwell Sound: wildretreat.com. **Hastings House**, Salt Spring Island: hastingshouse.com. **Sonora Resort**, Sonora Island: sonoraresort.com.

80 Tofino

Approaching Tofino on twisty Highway 4, you get glimpses of the long beaches on one side and the mountains on the other. If you are a first-time visitor and the day is clear, by the time you reach the middle of town you will be utterly gobsmacked. Tofino is possibly the most spectacularly-located town in Canada.

The little fishing village has changed quite a bit since becoming a household name. First it attracted visitors from the long beaches, then Clayoquot got on the environmental radar. It has become a gateway to wilderness recreation and a surfing centre, as well as the site of the most urbane wilderness resorts and a slow food epicenter (see the Take 5: The Island's Best Restaurants). It is also an upscale cottage enclave and an epicentre of green economic thinkers and doers.

Sociability is part of Tofino's appeal. An annual tide of visitors crests in summer. Wild youth, whole families in Bermuda shorts, groups of kay-akers joggling around in spray skirts, all prowling Tofino's few streets, sucking on lattés and smoothies, queuing at the one supermarket and one laundromat and rubbing shoulders with the locals — First Nations people from nearby villages, the descendants of pioneers, the fisherfolk, the ageing hippies, the weekenders who never left.

It's no paradise. I arrive at my morning hangout, one of the picnic tables near the kayak put-in, beside the 1st St (Government) wharf. The table is a good place to watch the theatre of arrivals and departures at the dock. Dozens of empty bottles and cans litter the site from some buddies' night of carousing. I've noticed a certain amount of public drinking here. Tuff City is a party town.

Tofino has a wholesome side — a sober dedication to social change — that is inspiring. The bank and gas stations are about the only chains. The village council told McDonald's restaurant to take a hike. This is a community with vision.

The nearest point of access to the outer coast is at Tonquin Park. The 12-ha/30-ac civic park is a 10-minute walk from the centre of Tofino. A boardwalk leads to a sandy beach, broken by outcrops of polished blue rock, facing lively Duffin Passage and green Wikaninnish Island. Just off-shore, the American fur trader *Tonquin* is supposed to have gone down in 1811 after being swarmed by First Nations and blown up by a sole surviv-ing crewman. An anchor believed the *Tonquin*'s was brought up in 2003.

Much more popular beaches are McKenzie and Chesterman, 3.5-5 km/2.2-3 mi south of town. A paved sidewalk separates the self-propelled from crazy highway traffic. En route, in Outside Break, a funky little shopping centre that caters to the surfing crowd, you will find arguably the best hamburger in town, at **Wildside Grill**, the best taco, at **Tacofino Cantina**, and the best coffee, at the newly refurbished **Tofitian Internet Café**.

Details

- Tonquin Park: Left on First St, R on Arnet St, left on Tonquin Park Rd, to end; limited parking.
- Godfrey Stephens's monumental 6.4-m/21-ft-tall carved and painted *Weeping Forest Woman* (1984) stands in the Village Green, Campbell St between 2nd and 3rd Sts.
- Outside Break, 1180 Pacific Rim Highway, Tofino.

Meares Island Tribal Park — 81

The two lobes of Meares Island overlook Tofino on either side of muddy Lemmens Inlet. The visual centerpiece of Clayoquot Sound, 8.4 sq km/32.4 sq mi in area, Meares has two peaks, Mt Colnett, elevation 792 m/2,598 ft to the east, and Lone Cone, 742 m/2,434 ft high to the north. Lone Cone offers the best vantage point for taking the whole area. But the island is best known for its ancient forest walk.

A short boat ride from Tofino across Browning Channel and a walk on the boardwalk brings you to the ancient western red cedars. With their dead tops and multiple leaders, the big trees are grotesquely beautiful. While they're not all that tall, they have vast trunks — the largest cedar on the island measures 18 m/59 ft in circumference.

These trees are believed to be 1,000 years old or more. They are part of a mixed-species, multigenerational rainforest that is self-perpetuating. Seedlings of spruce, hemlock and cedar take root in the rotting wood of their fallen ancestors, growing in woven shade. You are enfolded by an organism whose strand-entwining roots reach back thousands of years.

Meares owes its pristine character to a blockade that prevented a logging company from gaining entry in 1984. The hereditary chief of the Tla-o-qui-aht First Nation declared Meares Island a tribal park and opened it to visitors, including loggers, without their saws. Both parties applied for court injunctions to prohibit the other from the island. First Nations' legal action won the day. Logging was prohibited on Meares pending resolution of First Nations land claims. That's where it stands 25 years later.

I took the invitation to heart. In Lemmens Inlet there are wonderful places to camp. You can watch the eagles play tag, while you wait for the tide to float your boat.

The hike up Lone Cone starts near Kakawis, the former Catholic Indian Residential School that is on the traditional land of the Ahousaht First Nation. It's a steep and strenuous climb, and an all-day excursion.

Details

■ Meares Island Tribal Park and the much larger Haa'uukmin Tribal Park that includes it: tribalparks.ca.

■ A Meares Island big tree and Lone Cone trail water taxi is operated by Ocean Outfitters, 368 Main St, Tofino; 250-725-2866; oceanoutfitters.bc.ca.

82 Cultural Adventures

The sea-otter trader *Lady Washington* appeared in Clayoquot Sound in July 2005. It was last seen there in the 1790s. You couldn't miss the two-masted sloop's three tiers of gleaming white puffy sails gliding along in front of Vargas Island. The 90-ton replica was out of Grays Harbor, Washington, visiting on a mission of reconciliation. A former master of the *Washington*, Captain Robert Gray, was a bit of a hothead, it seems. A descendant came to apologize to First Nations people for his bad behaviour when in the vicinity. A private ceremony was followed by public celebrations. There was an outdoor feast at Wickaninnish Island, on the ocean side of Tofino. It was a poignant meeting of communities.

The setting was a meadowy prairie just above an amazing hump of sand that stretches through to the ocean side of Wickaninnish, and at high tide separates it from Echachis, a smaller island long used by First Nations. People off the boat in period garb mingled with the local citizens. Teams of local residents bustled about serving dinner. Contributing the haunches of beef and other food was William Twombly, a social worker from Corvallis, Oregon. He treats troubled youth and sometimes charters the *Lady Washington* for training cruises that challenge kids to crew the vessel in risk-taking and team-building activities and to set and furl the sails, among many tasks.

Twombly was atoning for the catastrophic actions of Robert Gray in Clayoquot Sound in 1791. The arrival in Clayoquot Sound of the *Columbia Rediviva* was noted by John Boit, 5th mate:

> [August] 29 [1791]. N. Latt. 49° 5′ W. Long. 126° 0′. At noon, the entrance of Clioquot (or Coxes harbour) bore NE 4 leagues. Standing in for the harbour, and towards evening anchored in our former station. Vast many of the Natives along side, and seemed glad to see us again. Found riding here the Brig *Lady Washington*, of Boston, John Kendrick, master. He had made up his voyage and was bound for Canton. He appeared happy in meeting with his old friends.
>
> N. Latt 49° 9′ W. Long. 125° Captain Kendrick informed us that he had had a skirmish with the Natives at Barrells sound (in Queen Charlotte Isles) and was obliged to kill upwards of 50 of them before they would desist from the attack.

On Meares Island, up the east side of Lemmens Inlet, is little Adventure Cove where Gray and company wintered that year. A painting on glass shows his famous ship *Columbia* with Lone Cone's distinctive silhouette in the background. You won't find a trace of Fort Defiance. Thick mosses cover all. I've camped there, in pouring rain. The First Nations village of Opitsaht is on the south shore of the island's western lobe. Captain Gray was certain — where others were not — the inhabitants were planning to attack his fort. Having noted the village was empty, Gray sent a force over to burn it. John Boit wrote in his log:

> This village was about half a mile in diameter, and contained upwards of 200 Houses, generally well built for Indians; every door that you entered was in resemblance to a human and Beast's head, the passage being through the mouth. Besides which there was much more carved work about the dwellings some of which was by no means inelegant. This fine village, the work of Ages, was in a short time totally destroy'd.

The feast was co-hosted by Joe Martin and family, who have a home on Echachis. Joe is a master Tla-o-qui-aht boat carver. The assembled crowded into a big teepee for some speeches. Joe Martin sang a Nuu-Chah-Nulth song. The ancient summer village of the Tla-o-qui-aht was at Echachis. It was where the larger nation gathered for halibut fishing and whaling. I got a sense of how it might be empowering to welcome visitors to your place with generations of ancestors at your side.

T'ashii Paddle School conducts tours in a canoe made by Joe Martin and led by T'simka Martin. You can paddle to Echachis, or paddle to Meares Island and walk the ancient rainforest trail. You can also take a stand-up paddleboard (SUP) course with T'simka's partner Emre, or hire him as an SUP guide.

Details
- T'ashii Paddle School, Tofino; 855-883-3787/250-266-3787; tofinopaddle.com.

Cougar Annie's Garden 83

In Clayoquot's many roadless reaches, Boat Basin, in the lee of Hesquiat Peninsula, is one of the remotest. It's 55 km/34 mi northwest of Tofino — not the most likely place for a show garden, a 2-ha/5-ac plot hacked out of thick undergrowth amid forests of cedar, spruce and hemlock, ringed by mountain slopes. Cougar Annie's Garden is the largest known pioneer garden on the island's west coast. Its many pathways provide glimpses of a once-flourishing homestead, the buildings slowly returning to nature. The garden captures the spirit of those who settled in Clayoquot Sound — both early and late. Fact is, this is the garden's second go-round. Indeed, it is an epic tale of wilderness living that is still being told.

The Rae-Arthur family arrived in 1915, and Ada Annie started the ceaseless work of land clearing while raising their eleven children. Her husband Willie was not cut out for pioneering. He was more of a house-husband. The older of the eight surviving children helped to pull stumps. Cougar Annie became a well-known figure around Clayoquot Sound, with her four husbands — serially — and her mail-order seed and plant business, which evolved into the Boat Basin post office. A well-spoken, cultured person, Ada Annie famously defended her turf with aggressive use of firearms. To make ends meet, she hunted cougar for bounty. A later acquaintance remembered "a tiny old lady with hands like a logger."

Ada Annie did manage to get a couple of husbands interested in gardening. She was an endearing character, with an energy that attracted others. In later years, her home became the retirement project of a Vancouver stockbroker. Peter Buckland bought the place and allowed her to stay there into her 90s. He set to work maintaining and restoring the garden and orchard. He endowed the non-profit Boat Basin Foundation to keep Cougar Annie's Garden going and promote awareness of rainforest ecosystems.

If you go back to the beginning, with the help of Margaret Horsfield's substantial biography *Cougar Annie's Garden*, and look at the Vancouver wedding picture of Ada Annie Jordan and Willie Rae-Arthur, you can see great clarity in the eyes of the young woman. Someone recollected she had the eyes of a seer. Maybe the garden came from that visionary state. After all, here it is, nearly a century later, flourishing again.

Details

- Boat Basin Foundation: boatbasin.org.
- Guided day visits to Cougar Annie's Garden, Fri/Sun seasonally, 4 hours by floatplane from Tofino, $225 pp (2016). "Neither the garden nor the Temperate Rainforest Field Study Centre is a tourist destination. People who visit are in good physical condition, highly motivated, and have a keen interest in the natural and cultural histories of the West Coast." Drop-ins are okay; there's a $30 fee.
- Reading: *Cougar Annie's Garden*, by Margaret Horsfield (Salal Books, 2000).

MV Uchuck III *in Yuquot (Friendly Cove). Boomer Jerritt/Strathcona Photography.*

IV. Northern Vancouver Island, the Discovery Islands and Broughton Archipelago

The northern reaches of Vancouver Island include the wonderfully scenic mountains in Strathcona Park, the island-strewn waters of the northeast coast, the deep channels and passages of the west coast, and tiny islands off the northern tip, where millions of seabirds breed. This varied region is full of wonders — the Orca whales of Broughton Archipelago and the giant trees of Nimpkish Island and White River. Campbell River, "salmon fishing capital of the world," is the gateway to a region with about 60,000 residents. Their numbers include two remarkable environmentalists, decades apart in time, pledged to protect our wild salmon.

 | **Campbell River**

Campbell River is the gateway to northern Vancouver Island and the Discovery Islands. The post-industrial city of 35,000 sits by the southern entrance of Discovery Passage and the north end of Georgia Strait. The waterway is a funnel for traffic between Georgia Strait ports and the north island, north coast and north Pacific Ocean.

Campbell River is also a funnel for overland traffic. The daunting relief of the Beaufort Range squeezes roadways onto a narrow lowland strip. If you're bound to, or from, Strathcona Park or Nootka Sound on Highway 28 or the North Island on Highway 19, you'll go through Campbell River.

From the south, the scenic way to approach Campbell River is by way of the **Oceanside** highway, 19A. Route 19, the so-called Inland Highway, speeds motorists to the city through dull upland. Highway 19 is a two-laner north of Campbell River.

On the southern fringe of downtown Campbell River is the historic district. There you will find the splendid **Discovery Fishing Pier**. The view across the 2-km/1.2-mi passage is worth an excursion by itself. It's a good place to take in Campbell River's maritime life, armed perhaps with an ice cream cone from the take-out on the pier.

You'll spot fishing boats — nowadays mostly for sport rather than commerce — tugs with barges, whale- or bear-watching Zodiacs, pods of kayakers. The occasional freighter or container carrier from the north

Pacific slides down the passage. You may see a multitude of Alaska-bound monster yachts and a few cruise ships.

Near the pier is the impressive **Maritime Heritage Centre**. It houses the fishing boat depicted on Canada's $5 dollar bill from 1972 to 1986. The seiner belonged to Harry Assu, late chief of the We Wai Kai First Nation of Cape Mudge on nearby Quadra Island.

For more than 100 years, Campbell River has been celebrated as a salmon sportfishing centre with — as Assu put it in his readable memoir, *Assu of Cape Mudge* — five species of Pacific Salmon readily available year-round. Chances are you'll find some fishers trying their luck on the pier. You can rent the gear and buy a license on the spot.

A two-block stretch north of the centre is known as **Historic Pier Street**. This is where the original Campbell River steamship wharf stood, across the street from the Willows Hotel, the town's first building (1904). Loggers bound to and from remote logging camps put up there.

Informative markers throughout the downtown area recapitulate the heritage of this blue-collar town.

The excellent **Museum at Campbell River** is a short walk south of the Maritime Heritage Centre. Among its exhibits is the recreated Willows Hotel entrance and lobby. A theatre shows, among others, a short film about the local author and pioneer conservationist Roderick Haig-Brown. The museum website has fascinating portfolios of historical photos.

Campbell River is near the northern margin of the great Douglas fir forest. In 1906, the International Timber Company started railway logging 12,000 ha/2,965 ac of forestland between the Oyster and Campbell rivers. Trackage and a log dump occupied much of downtown Campbell River. High-lead logging was the rule, and the workers were housed in camps. Their danger-filled work was captured in Haig-Brown's novel *Timber*. Campbell River was their Saturday-night party town.

An era that began with Campbell River's first sawmill (1922) came to a shocking end in 2010 when the nearby Duncan Bay pulp and paper complex, including the city's last sawmill, closed for good. After more than 700 mill workers lost work, though, the area's population increased modestly and has continued to do so. The 2016 census count was up 5.1 percent over 2011 at 35,138. The area, including nearby Quadra Island, has a large and growing community of artists and crafters. Poised at nature's doorstep, Campbell River's attraction as a place to live includes relatively cheap property, while its fame as a salmon fishing centre is helping the town become a major base for adventure recreation. Wildlife is the big draw — whales, sea lions and other marine mammals, bears of several kinds — viewed up-close from tour boats or kayaks.

From the pier, you barely get a glimpse of the region's fabulous wildlife habitat — the near-wilderness of the Discovery Islands, their intricate waterways and the dramatic fjord-carved mainland coast beyond.

Details

- Maritime Heritage Centre, 621 Island Highway, Campbell River; 250-286-3161; maritimeheritagecentre.ca.
- Museum at Campbell River, 470 Island Highway, 250-287-3103: crmuseum.ca.
- Readings: *Assu of Cape Mudge: Recollections of a Coastal Indian Chief*, by Harry Assu (Vancouver: UBC Press, 1989).
  Timber: A Novel of Pacific Northwest Loggers, by Roderick Haig-Brown (1942, reprinted Oregon State University Press, 1993).

Haig-Brown House | 85

The Haig-Brown family are Vancouver Island royalty. Writer and naturalist Roderick Haig-Brown (1908-1976) put the island on the map with a stream of books about nature and conservation. He wrote with direct knowledge and keen emotion about the many little rivers of the north island. He knew them well from having logged, guided, hunted and especially, fished since first arriving here at age 19.

In 1934, the expat British adventurer married the intellectual Seattle-born Ann Elmore (1908-1990). By prenuptial agreement, Ann always typed up Rod's longhand drafts. They settled down on an 8-ha/20-ac farm beside the Campbell River, raised a family and created quite a legacy.

Haig-Brown House is now a riverfront bed-and-breakfast inn during summer months. It has an ambience that is at once literary, environmental and historical.

The Haig-Browns' charming gardens and shady riverfront, the fields and second-growth forest are intact, although reduced in size. The setting is so quiet you can hear the river through an open window.

A few who arrive at Haig-Brown House are on pilgrimage. They grew up reading *Starbuck Valley Winter* or *Saltwater Summer*, adventure books for young readers. A *River Never Sleeps* or *Measure of the Year*, may have awakened their love of nature. Some visitors are moved when they sit in the study and handle books in the author's library. The study and three bedrooms are substantially unchanged.

Occasionally, guests are on a sentimental journey. They found safe harbour here during a difficult time. Haig-Brown, a lay magistrate, was the Provincial Court judge for much of the north island and adjacent mainland coast. Over three decades, he heard 200 to 300 cases a year, everything from DUI to petty theft to assault. The shadow of hardship fell across many a misdemeanour. Rather than handing down sentences that made difficult situations worse, he often gave an offender some work and a place to stay.

Some who stayed at the Haig-Browns' were battered women. Ann

Haig-Brown took a special interest in victims of domestic violence. Her care was recognized at the 1988 opening of the Ann Elmore Transition House.

Rod Haig-Brown published 25 books (some co-authored) in his lifetime. He built a durable reputation as an authority on fly fishing. Before Haig-Brown, few had written about fishing for steelhead, the feisty sea-going rainbow trout. Once there were native steelhead populations in 200 streams on Vancouver Island. To catch a 2.3-kg/5-lb steelhead with a dry fly was the epitome of joy for Haig-Brown.

One of Canada's first conservationists, Haig-Brown bore witness to the destruction of countless little rivers and their runs of salmon and trout — directly, by clearcut logging and damming, and indirectly by pollution from mine tailings.

Articles poured out of his pen, drawing attention to the impoverishment of the commons by the industrial juggernaut. He equated the protection of Earth's productivity with our very survival and often gave vent to a deep pessimism. A philosophic mind was able to draw inclusiveness from this peril:

"It is in searching out the land, learning to live in it, learning to use it, that we have been shaped and tempered," he wrote in *Maclean's* magazine in 1973. "We have made many mistakes, some willful, some founded in ignorance, and we have not always shaped ourselves well. But I love the best of our intentions, hopes and desires, and I love the soul of Canada, the striving for unity and justice that exists in some degree in all of us."

Details

- Haig-Brown Heritage House, 2250 Campbell River Rd (Highway 28), Campbell River, 250-286-6646; haig-brown.bc.ca.
- Manager/host Sandra Chow's blog of visitors: haig-brownhouse.blogspot.com.
- Haig-Brown Kingfisher Creek Society restored the flow through the Haig-Brown property of a much-culverted salmon-bearing creek: greenwaystrust.ca.
- Reading: *Deep Currents: Roderick and Ann Haig-Brown*, by Valerie Haig-Brown (Orca Books, 1997).

86 | Elk Falls and the John Hart Dam

Elemental Elk Falls is an 8-km/5-mi drive from downtown Campbell River. There's also a nice hike in along the banks of the River Campbell. Near the falls, a network of trails wind through fragments of old-growth forest. A suspension bridge provides outstanding views of the 25-m/82-ft high falls from just downriver. At 60 m/196 ft, it's the highest pedestrian bridge on the island, and a small part of an ambitious project to reroute water from the John Hart Dam into an underground power plant.

Elk Falls Provincial Park was established in 1940 to protect more than 10.6 sq km/4.1 sq mi of mostly second-growth forest around the magnificent falls. The ink was barely dry when the river was harnessed for hydroelectric power. The John Hart Dam, completed in 1947 just upriver from Elk Falls, backed up the river for 8 km/5 mi, creating John Hart Lake. Some of the water was diverted from the river into three 1.9-km/1.2-mi-long wooden penstocks. Gravity accelerates the water flowing into turbines at the John Hart Generating Station, and out comes 126 megawatts of electricity.

Nearby Elk Falls is at the top of an adjacent canyon that flattens out below the power plant. Visitors used to approach the falls from a parking lot off Brewster Lake Rd. Since BC Hydro kicked off the John Hart Replacement project in 2014, there's a new parking lot, closer to the falls. A decent interpretive centre for the project has been installed at the parking lot. It's worth a visit just to watch the films depicting the human history of the dam. Now, you cross over the penstocks on a wee bridge, and pick up a new trail to the canyon, where the Rotary Club of Campbell River put up the 64-m/210-ft-long **Elk Falls suspension bridge**, fundraising the $750,000 cost. A wheelchair-accessible path leads to a lookout directly across from the falls and thrillingly close.

Continue further into the park to find the **Old Growth Loop Trail** through a beautiful remnant old-growth forest of Douglas fir and western red cedar. On the **Riverside Loop Trail**, there are lookouts near smaller waterfalls en route to the Elk Falls and the sheer rock canyon below. The trail has steep sections and unprotected dropoffs.

Elk Falls poses an impassible barrier to migrating fish, and runs are confined to the 5-km/3-mi-long lower Campbell. The **Canyon View Trail** is a 4-km/2.5-mi loop along both banks of the river. The western terminus is a footbridge near the generating station. Its eastern terminus is a logging bridge 400 m/1,312 ft east of the Quinsam River bridge. The Canyon View river walk has lookouts for observing runs of salmon and seagoing trout in season. You may spot some river kayakers as well as abundant wildlife. Near the footbridge at the generating station, the Canyon View Trail hooks in with the 2.4-km/1.5-mi **Millennium Trail**, which follows the impressive canyon upstream to link with the Elk Falls trails.

The provincial campground along the Quinsam Estuary is a short walk from the Canyon View Trail. Haig-Brown House (#85) is a summer-months B&B right on the Campbell River.

The estuary of the Campbell River is a highly scenic area approachable via Spit Rd, north of Highway 19A. Dick Murphy Park is dramatically situated at the end of the spit, with great views of the estuary's extensive wetlands and abundant waterfowl.

Details
- Elk Falls Provincial Park: env.gov.bc.ca.
- John Hart Dam: bchydro.com.

Quadra Island

A 10-minute ferry ride across Discovery Passage from Campbell River lands you in briny Quathiaski Cove on Quadra Island. The picturesque cove is a maritime service centre, with fishing boats bobbing at the docks. A cannery was once the local mainstay. The largest of the Discovery Islands — considerably larger than any of the Gulf Islands — Quadra measures up at 310 sq km/120 sq mi and has about 2,700 residents. Its more settled southern peninsula supports a number of smallhold farms — even a winery — and every Saturday in season at the Quathiaski

TAKE 5 *Godfrey Stephens' Anchorages in Paradise*

Bohemian world traveller, psychedelic artist and carver Godfrey Stephens has been a boatman in these waters since the 1960s. His recent creation was a 44-ft steel-hulled sailboat Mungo ChingTing. *"Mungo Martin was chief of the Kwakiutl, a great carver and mentor. ChingTing means 'dragon fly' in Chinese. With its red junk-rigged sails, that's what the boat looks like."* See Wood Storms, Wild Canvas: The Art of Godfrey Stephens, *by Gurdeep Stephens (Victoria: D&I Enterprises, 2014).*

1. Sea Otter Cove, west of San Josef Bay, Cape Scott Park
You can walk west over the headland to a wild windswept beach on Lowrie Bay.

2. Columbia Cove/Peddler's Cove on the South side of Brooks Peninsula Park
You walk southwest to an outside beach. Watch out for cougars!

3. The head of Mathilda Inlet, near Ahousaht, on Flores Island
Has warm springs. This is where Gordon Gibson, the "Bull of the Woods" (to quote the title of his autobiography) constructed a concrete tank. A trail south leads to Whitesand Beach, where there are vistas of Clayoquot Sound.

4. Sandy Island Marine Park, north end of Denman Island
This is a very nice open area. Henry Bay, looking west toward Union Bay, provides shelter from the winds.

5. God's Pocket Marine Park, a group of islands on Queen Charlotte Strait
One of them has sheltered anchorage and a dock where I once sought refuge — a memorable place.

shopping centre, a farm market.

Southern Quadra is relatively flat and bike-friendly, at least compared with the gravel logging roads of the rugged north end. A number of interesting destinations are just a short hop from the ferry.

Rebecca Spit is a 2-km-long finger of sand enclosed in a 177-ha/437-ac day-use park that offers many trails through forest and field to outside beaches with engaging views eastward to Cortes Island. A nice campground on nearby Drew Harbour is run by the We Wai Kai nation. It's surrounded by nature — but good luck getting one of the 44 waterfront campsites after the beginning of the season. We have picked oysters off the outside beach and cooked them for dinner there.

The hamlet of **Heriot Bay** is a sportfishing centre with a marina, grocery store and the venerable Heriot Bay Inn, which traces its origins to the 1890s. There's a restaurant and pub here and the adjacent waterfront is gorgeous, just a great place to sit and watch the boats come and go.

Tsa-Kwa-Luten Lodge occupies a wonderful location at the opening of Discovery Passage. The First Nations-themed establishment sits on an eminence above an expanse of rocky beach, with various accommodations, including waterfront cottages with kitchenettes.

In the nearby We Wai Kai First Nation village of Yaculta (Cape Mudge) is the **Nuyumabales Cultural Centre**. The museum displays an important collection of Potlatch treasures and regalia, confiscated by the government of Canada in the 1920s and returned from three museums in 1979.

Cape Mudge Lighthouse, near the lodge, is the islands' only manned lighthouse that is accessible by road and open to visitors. Built in 1898, it's staffed by the Canadian Coast Guard.

Quadra Island is acquiring fame for its artists' colony, especially for unique pottery. There's a studio tour and arts festival every June.

Heriot Bay is the terminus of the Cortes Island ferry. Outbound boaters should consider making a stop on Cortes. The Gorge Harbour Marina Resort has a lodge, cottage and campground on spacious grounds, and the Floathouse Restaurant serves very decent seafood dinners.

Details

- BC Ferries: bcferries.com; frequent service between Quadra Id and Campbell River, Cortes Island.
- Rebecca Spit Marine Provincial Park: env.gov.bc.ca.
- We Wai Kai Campground, Heriot Bay Rd, Quadra Island, 250-285-3111; wewaikai.com.
- Heriot Bay Inn, 250-285-3322; heriotbayinn.com.
- Tsa-Kwa-Luten Lodge, 1 Lighthouse Rd, Quadra Island; 1-800-665-7745/250-285-2042; capemudgeresort.bc.ca.
- Nuyumbalees Cultural Centre, 34 WeWay Road, Cape Mudge Village; 250-285-3733; museumatcapemudge.com.

- Quadra Island artist directory, guide to studio tours: quadraislandarts.com.
- Trails on Quadra Island, overview and map: quadraisland.ca.

 Strathcona Park Lodge

Strathcona Park Lodge is an outdoor adventure centre on Upper Campbell Lake. It introduces people to the wonders of wilderness travel — climbing the myriad of peaks in Strathcona Park, kayaking on the east or west coast, hiking on sea-lashed Nootka Island. The Lodge provides the equipment, the transport, the guides, and meals.

Its enthusiastic staff — many trained in the centre's outdoor leadership program — also train novices in wilderness travel, mostly in the benign surroundings of the Lodge, along the lakeshore and amid nearby rocky outcrops.

Guests stay in rustic cabins or suites and can either bring their own supplies or dine at the Lodge. You can sign up for all-inclusive multi-day packages. You might learn how to exit an ocean kayak in shallow water in the morning … practice rappelling down a 10-m/33-ft-high bluff in the afternoon and join a guided nature walk around the bog in the evening. It's less a lodge than a year-round camp. For families on a budget with young children, I'd say it's unbeatable.

The Lodge was the vision of Myrna and Jim Boulding. Their outdoor education program was based on a deep belief in the value of the wilderness experience. Their son Jamie Boulding and his partner Christine Clarke are now the co-directors. Both have won awards for outdoor education.

The Lodge is close to the alpine wonders of central Strathcona Park, but not actually in the park. It's less than an hour to either the west coast near Nootka Sound or Johnstone Strait to the east. The setting is quite scenic — on a lake about 20 km/12 mi long and 1.5 km/1 mi wide, surrounded by low mountains, with dramatic views westward into the heart of the range. Pristine wilderness it is not; Upper Campbell Lake is the reservoir of the Strathcona Dam. The lake's much-enlarged shores are a study in altered landscapes.

Details

- Strathcona Park Lodge & Outdoor Education Centre, 41040 Gold River Rd (Highway 28), 42 km west of Campbell River: 250-286-3122; strathconaparklodge.com.

Strathcona Provincial Park

Strathcona was BC's first provincial park, created in 1911 by an act of the BC Parliament to protect the alpine splendour of central Vancouver Island — its myriad jagged peaks, its exquisite subalpine valleys and plateaux dotted with turquoise lakes, its giant ramparts of granite on the approaches. Enclosing 2,458 sq km/949 sq mi, about eight percent of the island, the park is laced with trails, some distinguished from the surrounding rock only by tiny inukshuks, piles of stones. At the centre of the park are three no-vehicle, no-fire wilderness conservancies, totaling about half its total area, and meant to stay truly wild.

For drivers, there are two approaches to the park (not including Paradise Meadows to Forbidden Plateau, #63, in a geographically-distinct part of Strathcona). The main road in is along Buttle Lake, south of Highway 28. There are nice campgrounds around the park portal at the foot of the 22-km/14-mi-long lake. One trailhead is across the lake, beginning a steep climb of 4-6 hours to the exquisite **Marble Meadows**. Another trail climbs from a trailhead on the east side of Buttle Lake onto **Flower Ridge**. Yet another trail begins in the vicinity of the now-closed Myra Falls mine past the south end of the lake, to **Phillips Ridge**; and several others.

Highway 28 runs through Strathcona Park en route to Gold River, and the head of the **Elk River Trail** is there. A good day's hike brings you to the vicinity of Landslide Lake and its astonishing mountain backdrop, truly an elemental landscape.

Hike-ins on the south side of Strathcona include the **Della Falls Trail** (#73) and the **Bedwell Centennial Trail**, which uniquely begins at tidewater in Clayoquot Sound (on private land), and over 34 km/21 mi provides a spectrum of altitude change. The Friends of Strathcona Park took on the task of restoring the trail in 2010 to reopen in time for the park's centennial.

All of these trails are challenging, and there may be snow on the ground late in spring and early in fall.

At the park's southwest corner, in Clayoquot Sound, is its most recent addition (1995), the pristine, intact Megin River-Talbot Creek. At 273.9 sq km/115.8 sq mi, it's the largest remaining undisturbed watershed on the island. Wilderness camping is allowed. Access is by way of Shelter Inlet.

The framers of Strathcona Park were guided by a Banff-like vision of a mountain wilderness set aside for public enjoyment, with railway access and hotels. Extractive industries were excluded.

Do parks really protect land? In the case of Strathcona, the reality doesn't come close to matching the rhetoric. From the get-go, the

NORTHERN VANCOUVER ISLAND AND ADJACENT ISLANDS

Strathcona Park Act was amended (1913) to allow damming of water. Another amendment in 1918 allowed mineral exploration. Claims were being staked anyway. After World War II, hydroelectric dams brought development into the park. The Campbell River drains Buttle, Upper and Lower Campbell lakes. Soon the rich bottomland around the Campbell lakes became reservoirs.

In 1952, the hydro authority proposed building the Strathcona Dam and raising the water level of Buttle Lake. Edged with ancient forests, Buttle was called the most beautiful lake in the province. Because part of the lake is in Strathcona Park, there were public hearings. Roderick Haig-Brown waged a one-man campaign against the project. The dam went ahead, with its height reduced, and Buttle became a reservoir, its shoreline rising and falling seasonally with the demand for electricity.

Meanwhile, the boundaries of the park have been much altered. Strathcona has been used as a land bank to acquire parkland elsewhere. It started with Pacific Rim National Park. Logging companies were given bits around the edges of Strathcona Park to compensate for timber rights cancelled when Pacific Rim Park was created. These land swaps were back-room deals.

The last straw came in 1988. A government-backed proposal would have drained beautiful Cream Lake and created a second mine in the park (the Myra Falls mine operated there beginning in the 1960s). Local citizens formed the Friends of Strathcona Park. They staged a peaceful blockade that saw 64 otherwise law-abiding people arrested. The BC government changed its tune, and a master plan has been in place since 1993. The master plan allows only minimal human impacts in Strathcona, and a public advisory group was set up to review park-use proposals. The Friends continue to act as an independent watchdog.

Details

- Strathcona Provincial Park: env.gov.bc.ca. Travel advisories posted regularly.
- *Beyond Nootka: A Historical Perspective of Vancouver Island Mountains*, a compilation of mountaineering stories and other memoirs by Lindsay Elms: beyondnootka.com.
- Friends of Strathcona Park: friendsofstrathcona.org. Regular postings of reliable news about the realities of protection.
- Strathcona Wilderness Institute Society operates summer information centres at Buttle Lake and Paradise Meadows and conduct nature talks, walks and hikes: strathconapark.org.
- "'The Park ... Is a Mess': Development and Degradation in British Columbia's First Provincial Park" by Arn Keeling and Graeme Wynn, in *BC Studies*, no. 170, Summer 2011, pp 119-50: ojs.library.ubc.ca.

The heart of Vancouver Island is a vast block of granite rising to whole clusters of craggy peaks. In the middle of this grandeur stands **The Golden Hinde**, the island's highest point, 2,200 m/7,218 ft above sea level. The first known ascent was in 1914. The Hinde was conquered by yours truly in 1988. It's not that difficult — there is a bit of scrambling, but no rock climbing. The reward for my ascent was a windy overview of the entire central island from one very pointed peak. The view takes in most of Strathcona Park. We made it a day trip from our camp at Burman Lake.

One of Strathcona's three nature conservancies encloses the area west of Buttle Lake. No motorized vehicles are allowed and no fly-ins. There aren't even trails, just the occasional stone marker. No fires are allowed, although campers can bring gas stoves. Considering the rugged terrain, central Strathcona is remarkably accessible. The trick is to travel on the granite ridges. Several interconnected hiking routes cross the park at middle elevations. Getting up and down can be challenging.

A hiking expedition to Golden Hinde could be completed in three days —a day from the Myra Falls mine to Burman Lake, a day for the ascent and a day to return. If you have arranged to hike across the area and be picked up, allow three days to hike through the Elk River Valley to or from Burman Lake. It's wise to allow an extra day for the unexpected.

North of Burman Lake we found ourselves in deep snow — in September. We came to the edge of the granite ridge. Thick fog prevented us from seeing into the valley that was our destination. Did I mention there are no trails? Hypothermia reared its ugly head. Luckily, a party of rangers materialized in the mist, heading out on their last hike of the season. One of them stood on the edge of the ridge and was able, by hearing alone, to distinguish two invisible creeks flowing in opposite directions far below. We found our route down by aiming between the two. Further north, a procession of impossibly scenic alpine vistas unfolds — cloud-capped mountains above, jewel-like lakes in sculpted valleys below. Approaching Elk River Pass, you skirt the dramatically stark Landslide Lake.

It's all worth it for the exhilaration of getting above treeline at the very centre of the island. Travel in that elevated country requires psychological preparation, self-sufficiency and orienting skills. A good map, guidebook and compass are essential. Hazards are many — one of our party slipped on wet heather covering a boulder and just about required a medevac. It's a good plan to travel in parties of four, in case of serious injury.

Of alternative routes in to Burman Lake, one that requires a boat begins on the west side of Buttle Lake and proceeds up the Marble

Meadows trail. Another begins at the BC Parks parking lot just past the Myra Falls mine and follows the Philips Ridge Trail.

Details

■ *Guidebook: Hiking Trails 3: Northern Vancouver Island*, 10th edition, 2008. Has good maps.

Gold River Caves 91

Gold River is one tenacious west coast community. It ranges up a long hill, a well-serviced suburb of ranchers on spacious view lots. Gold River was a planned community, built in the 1960s to house the families of loggers and workers in the pulp mill on nearby Muchalat Inlet. The village, 90 km/56 mi west of Campbell River on Highway 28, is an isolated centre in a sea of mountains. But it was rich in amenities and services. It had an aquatic centre, an arena, a golf course, parks and baseball diamonds.

A newsprint mill was added in the 1980s but soon shut down, followed by the troubled pulp mill in 1999. Four-fifth of Gold River's tax base vanished. Its population fell from an historic high of 2,225 in 1981 to 1,212 in the 2016 census. The village's budget shrank to bare-bones maintenance. The only grocery store closed in December 2016.

Gold River's renown as a sport fishing centre generates modest revenues seasonally. It's also a service centre for Nootka Sound and the base of the passenger freighter MV *Uchuck III*. The town is a staging centre for recreation in Nootka Sound and Strathcona Park. Gold River's search for green economic growth includes a scheme that would use the pulp mill plant to generate power by burning garbage, but that came to nothing.

Another asset is the amazing number of caves that occur in the vicinity. Gold River calls itself the Caving Capital of Canada. About four percent of Vancouver Island is covered in limestone formations known as karst. Rainwater forms the weak, solvent carbonic acid as it falls and percolates through the soils. Where karst occurs near the surface, the acid works on the limestone, dissolving the rock and establishing underground drainages. Where, on the other hand, a stream finds a sink point and flows through karst, it dissolves the limestone and forms caves.

When you look east from Gold River, you see the white of limestone. That's the surface karst of White Ridge, whose summit the average hiker can reach from Highway 28 in five arduous hours. White Ridge is protected in a 1,343-ha/3,319-ac provincial park.

The deepest known cave on the island (and sixth deepest in Canada) is the 408-m/1,339-ft-deep **Thanksgiving Cave**. The longest known caves on the island (Canada's fourth longest) is the **Weymer Creek** system with nearly 13 km/8 mi of mapped passages. Both are near Gold

River in rough backcountry — don't even think of going there unless you're an experienced, well-prepared caver.

Much more accessible to casual visitors are the **Upana Caves**, a system more than 450 m/1,476 ft long with 15 entrances, 17 km/11 mi west of Gold River. The Upana River flows in and out of the caves, and there are some gorgeous views into canyons where it flows over karst and forms waterfalls. A self-guided tour, for which there is a map, takes about an hour.

Details

- Village of Gold River: goldriver.ca. Map, information about the Upana Caves.
- Vancouver Island Cave Exploration Group: cancaver.ca.
- White Ridge, Weymer Creek provincial parks: env.gov.bc.ca.

 Yuquot (Friendly Cove)

The tiny outpost of Yuquot (Friendly Cove) on Nootka Island is the site of an ancient First Nations whaling base and summer village. It's also the place of the Europeans' first landing on the Northwest Coast — Captain James Cook, HMS *Resolution* and *Discovery*, 1778. The passenger freighter MV *Uchuck III* calls in at Yuquot. During the summer, you can make the scenic 40-km/25-mi Saturday trip from Gold River, stroll around, and return the same day. If you want to stay, *Uchuck III* will call back during its regular two-day circuit of Nootka and Kyuquot sounds, servicing logging camps, fish farms, Tahsis, Zeballos, Esperanza and other isolated communities. You can also get dropped off or picked up by chartering a water taxi or float plane in Gold River.

Deeper immersion in West Coast wilderness and culture is recommended. You can go out on Saturday and stay a few nights in a beachfront rustic cabin on Nootka Island, as paying guests of the Mowachaht/Muchalaht First Nation. There are six cabins. You bring your own bedding, lighting and food. I strongly recommend a few nights in the cabin facing out to sea. (The other five face a boggy lake back of the shore.) We were treated with multiple displays of humpback whale tails. There's also a wilderness campground. The hosts were beyond friendly, giving us fresh baked goods and showing us around the community centre and museum, once a church.

A bolder approach is to load your kayak aboard the *Uchuck* and be put in the water in your craft. Most head for the wilderness wonderland of **Santa Gertrudis-Boca del Infierno Park** (440 ha/1,087 ac) and **Bligh Island Marine Park** (4,455 ha/11,009 ac). Advanced skills are required for Nootka Sound's fast waters, considerable swell and strong westerly winds (at any season). You can also take a backpack and hike the rough 35-km/22-mi trail across the outer coast of Nootka Island. Beautiful! Be prepared for some bushwhacking.

Europeans called the old village *Nootka*. It became a base of exploration, the centre of a flourishing fur trade and the site of several brief settlements. On the maps of the day, Nootka was the only place between Spanish California and Russian Alaska.

From the contact emerged a picture of First Nations society unrivalled for human interest. A wealth of eyewitness reports was published by journal-keepers on visiting vessels. The most famous of these is likely *The Adventures and Suffering of John Jewitt*.

A native of England, Jewitt shipped aboard the American trader *Boston* as an armourer at age 19. Americans had gained control of the sea otter trade. Yankee entrepreneurs carried the highly-prized pelts between First Nations suppliers and the Chinese market. They plied this coast until, within a few decades, the animal was extirpated.

The *Boston* arrived in Nootka Sound in March 1803 and traded with the Mowachaht chief Maquinna. Friendly relations led to the gift of a rifle to the chief — followed by harsh words over what Maquinna called a *peshak* (bad) lock on the rifle. The captain, Jewitt related, "called the king a liar, adding other opprobrious terms, and taking the gun from him, tossed it indignantly into the cabin, and calling me to him, said, 'John, this fellow has broken this beautiful fowling-piece, see if you can mend it.'"

Jewitt, a blacksmith, and the ship's sailmaker were the only ones spared in the massacre that revenged the insult. It was not the worst Maquinna had suffered at the hands of lowlife shipmen, by far. Four of his chiefs had been assassinated by Captain Martinez and "upwards of 20" men killed by Captain Hanna, including several chiefs. Maquinna was lucky to have escaped with his life.

The two were enslaved. Jewitt spent the better part of three years in Nootka Sound. His journal was an unused accounts book from the ship. Jewitt made ink "by boiling the juice of the blackberry with a mixture of finely powdered charcoal, and filtering it through a cloth."

Yuquot was a village of 20 houses. The biggest, chief Maquinna's, measured 45 m/148 ft by 12 m/39 ft. Every September, the entire village was dismantled, except for the massive log house-frames, "to pass the autumn and winter at Tashees and Cooptee." Tashees (Tahsis), the winter village, lay "about thirty miles up the Sound, in a deep bay." The cedar-plank walls and roofs were removed from the houses and carried away. "To a European, such a removal exhibits a scene quite novel and strange: canoes piled up with boards and boxes, and filled with men, women, and children, of all ranks and sizes, making the air resound with their cries and songs."

Maquinna and his family opened their hearts to Jewitt. The Englishman was a favourite of Maquinna's, especially after making him a steel whaling harpoon. The way the family drew him into their confidences is deeply moving.

Jewitt's narrative captures the intimate details of Nuu-Chah-Nulth life. The ranking men, for example, while fearsome warriors and fearless whalers, spent hours painting their faces. They applied sparkles and powdered their hair with white down. The women did not share the men's taste for make-up.

The captives escaped to the first American ship that called in after the massacre. Jewitt's devilish ruse is one for the movies. He managed to retrieve the *Boston*'s plundered goods as well — all without loss of life or face.

Little remains of old Yuquot. Enduring buildings include a lighthouse (built 1911) and a cultural centre in a former church (built 1956).

Details

- *Uchuck III*, Nootka Sound Service, end of Highway 28, Gold River: 1-877-824-8253 or 250-283-2515; getwest.ca. The weekly summer schedule changes from time to time.

- Mowachaht/Muchalaht First Nation: yuquot.ca. Accommodations at Yuquot: 250-850-5239.

- Reading: *The Adventures and Suffering of John R. Jewitt*, 1824 Scottish edition in Open Library: openlibrary.org.

Spring Island 93

I can think of no more beautiful place than Spring Island. It's just off the northwest coast, between Kyuquot Sound (pronounced *kye YOO ct*) and the Brooks Peninsula. Less than 2 km/1.2 mi across, Spring Island is dramatically varied — its leeward side is a broad bay that empties at low tide, revealing a profusion of sea life, while the windward side is a surf-washed prow of rock facing the open Pacific.

A grassy meadow on the north side of Spring Island furnishes the base camp of **West Coast Expeditions**, a top-flight kayak tour operation with an interesting history. Rupert Wong's family fled China during the Revolution and settled in Vancouver. His uncle, a commercial fisherman, discovered Spring Island. It evolved into a summer camp for the extended family. Rupert grew up navigating these waters and, after earning a degree in marine biology, started the kayaking outfit. It's now run by long-time associate Dave Pinel.

The open ocean, with its long swells, takes some getting used to. It's no place to trifle with nature. Expeditions, mostly by kayak, but also in a V-bottom aluminum boat, touch many memorable places. The scenic backdrop, about 25 km/16 mi west, is mountainous Brooks Peninsula. During the last glaciation, the Brooks was a rare ice-free area. It is a refugium of plant communities found nowhere else in North America. There are beautiful sand beaches on Brooks' eastern edge. The rest is inaccessible to all but the hardiest. Cape Cook is the roughest passage on the island.

A pristine wilderness area of some 399.36 ha/154.19 sq mi is protected in **Mꟁuqʷin (Muquin)/Brooks Peninsula Provincial Park**. It includes the Nasparti River, an intact drainage of old growth forest and abundant wildlife. The nearby **Bunsby Group** of islands is a kayaker's paradise. The province has protected 658 ha/1,626 ac of it in Big Bunsby Marine Park.

A major attraction for sea-based wildlife viewing is the core habitat of the sea otter, protected in the 346.5 sq km/133.78 sq mi **Checleset Bay Ecological Reserve**. The once-vanished sea otter was reintroduced in 1969 with breeding pairs from Alaska. They have flourished, and their huge appetite for shellfish has generated biologically-rich kelp forests. (Some First Nations people view the sea otter as a competitor and take a dim view of their protected status.) The ecological reserve is the site of considerable scientific research.

In an intact drainage in Kyuquot Sound, a mosaic of ecosytems is protected in **Tahsish-Kwois Provincial Park** (100.92 sq km/138.97 sq mi) and 70-ha/173-ac Tahsish River Ecological Reserve. The valley's estuary and old-growth forest are prime habitat of the rare and endangered Roosevelt elk.

Details

- Ka:'yu:'k't'h'/Che:k:tles7et'h' (Kyuquot/Checleseht) First Nations: 250-332-5259; kyuquotbc.ca. Should be consulted before traveling in traditional territories.
- West Coast Expeditions: westcoastexpeditions.com.
- Muquin/Brooks Peninsula, Big Bunsby Marine, Tahsish-Kwois provincial parks, Checleset Bay and Tahsish River ecological reserves: env.gov.bc.ca.

94　White River Provincial Park

An old-growth Douglas fir forest of a grandeur comparable to Cathedral Grove stands beside a logging road south of the village of Sayward. Protected in 72-ha/178-ac White River Park, this amazing place is easily accessible. Just as amazing is the story of the loggers who put down their saws to save it.

In 1990, Don Zapp and Dave Luoma were felling trees in the White River valley. (A third faller, Dave Morrison, was on light duty.) They lived in Sayward and had worked for MacMillan Bloedel Ltd for 22 and 13 years respectively. They came to a stand of giant Douglas firs and other conifers they knew to be the last old-growth in the valley. These were trees more than 85 m/279 ft in height — still vigorous, with intact tops. Luoma estimates the biggest of the Douglas firs to be 500 or 600 years old, some possibly 800 years old.

The three conferred and decided they just couldn't take down the magnificent trees. They faced possible dismissal and loss of seniority. Morrison, union chair at MB's Kelsey Bay Division, took it on. Fortunately, the company got onside, and in 1995 the provincial government protected the ancient forest.

In 1994, the White River forest attracted the attention of a US film company. A softcore gothic romance, *The Scarlet Letter*, was shot there. Vancouver Island old-growth stood in for the vanished hardwood forest of 17th-century Massachusetts. The crew and cast — Demi Moore, Gary Oldman, Robert Duvall — stayed in Campbell River and choppered in to the site. The film's local legacy is a few nice boardwalks through the park. And the film's cultural legacy? The *New York Times* called it "trashy and nonsensical, " while the *Washington Post* questioned whether 17th-century settlers would have had hot tubs.

Details

- White River Provincial Park is 25 km/16 mi south of Highway 19 on the White River Main, a gravel logging road. From Highway 19, turn S on Hern Rd and at once take the right branch onto Oyer Rd; within about 600 m/1,968 ft, take the left branch onto Salmon River Rd; at 1.0 km/0.6 mi take the right fork onto the White River Main.
- Sayward (2016 census population, 311) is 73 km/45 mi west of Campbell River on Highway 19: sayward.ca.
- While River Provincial Park: env.gov.bc.ca.

Nimpkish Island Ecological Reserve — 95

One of the most impressive forests of Douglas fir trees remaining in Canada grows on an 18-ha/44-ac alluvial flat in the upper Nimpkish River. The huge Douglas firs, so tall relative to their girth, with deeply-fissured bark, are clustered amid a younger forest of mostly western red cedar. The average height of the firs is 66 m/217 ft and their average diameter 1.3 m/4.3 ft. The majority are believed to be 350-400 years old. It's easy to distinguish a number of bigger trees. The biggest rises 94 m/308 ft and the widest measures 2.4 m/7.9 ft in diameter. Those trees are believed older than 600 years.

One of the functions of ecological reserves is to protect remarkable places. The Nimpkish Island forest is considered taller overall than Cathedral Grove, although not as old. Compared to MacMillan Park it's tiny and out of the way. When the object is to preserve a superlative, though, isolation is a plus.

Nimpkish Island was part of the Canadian Forest Products (CanFor) Tree Farm Licence 37. Founder Leopold Bentley intended it to be a gift to his adoptive province. (The Bentley family emigrated from Austria in 1938.) Never happened. Under his successor, Peter Bentley, Canfor changed its tune. Nimpkish Island was held ransom. In 1988, the BC Government coughed up nearly $1 million to compensate the company for lost timber and protect the rare and precious ecosystem.

We expect our protected areas to remain safe forevermore. Nimpkish Island furnishes an object lesson. As surrounding valleys have been logged, much severe flooding has ensued. There are huge gravel deposits around the island. I've been on three trips to Nimpkish Island. It seems that, when the river becomes a torrent, it erodes the banks and all too often the roots of the giant firs. Winter storms bring them down. Riprap embankments have been installed as bulwarks against erosion, but the riverine ecosystem is so dynamic there's no telling how Canada's tallest firs will fare.

Details

- Nimpkish Island Ecological Reserve is 18 km/11 mi SE of Woss Camp on logging roads: env.gov.bc.ca.

96 Broughton Archipelago

Broughton Archipelago is a magnificent near-wilderness in the remote tidal reaches between northeast Vancouver Island and the mainland coast, the renowned and much-visited habitat of Orca whales and other sea mammals.

The archipelago is the dozens of islands (the largest is Gilford, 382 sq km/147 sq mi) and hundreds of islets and rocks that form the eastern boundary of Queen Charlotte Strait and straddle Knight Inlet. Johnstone and Broughton straits form its southern boundary. To the north and east, it becomes a maze of channels, islands and mainland peninsulas, with many pleasant passages and crossings.

Few people live there outside Sointula (2016 population 517) on Malcolm Island and Alert Bay (about 465 residents) on Cormorant Island. There is regular vehicle ferry service from Port McNeill to both islands, or you could aim for Telegraph Cove, where the parking is perhaps more secure and you can rent kayaks and get them transported to your intended destination. Otherwise, you can hire a water taxi or float plane or tour with a group. If your craft is self-propelled, you will note that Broughton has some of the scariest tidal currents anywhere. At some entrances, there are maelstroms that threaten craft both small and large, while other spots develop huge standing waves that can really throw a boat around.

The tiny community of Echo Bay (pop 10) on Gilford Island is en route to some of Broughton's remoter cul-de-sacs. Nearby shores harbour the welcome **Paddlers' Inn**, with its floating lodge and three cabins, two floating. Long time resident Billy Proctor has a small museum crammed with artifacts from the watery work and lifestyle of yore. Broughton was for a while a lively centre of hand logging, where gyppos with steam donkeys on floating A-frames would fell a tree, limb, yard and tug it to the nearest mill. Rowboat fishers harvested waters that teemed with salmon and sold them to floating canneries.

Broughton Archipelago Marine Park is a succession of charming beaches and fascinating rock formations near Queen Charlotte Strait. The 117.5-sq km/45.4-sq mi protected area (including land and water) invites days of exploration. A circuit from Telegraph Cove might track 90 km/56 mi. Not just a place of beauty, the park contributes to the conservation of the much-underrepresented geographic type known as the *Outer Fiordland Ecosection Coastal Western Hemlock, very wet maritime submontane variant.*

The traditional territory of Kwakwaka'wakw-speaking nations, Broughton has an ancient history of settlement and use. There are shell middens everywhere and petroglyphs and pictographs on rocks near sea level. On Village Island is an abandoned village with a musical name, Mamalilaculla.

The ancient proprietor of much of the Broughton Archipelago is the Musgamagw Dzawada'enuxw First Nation. They take a dim view of the open-pen Atlantic salmon feedlots that have proliferated in the region, threatening the health of the wild Pacific salmon runs. In August 2016, they issued an eviction notice to the Cermaq fish farm on Burdwood Islands (owned by the Japanese giant Mitsubishi.)

Details

- Broughton Archipelago Marine Provincial Park: env.gov.bc.ca.
- Paddlers' Inn, Simoon Sound: 250-230-0088; paddlersinn.ca. Catered meals by arrangement.
- Billy's Museum: pierresbay.com.
- Reading: *Heart of the Raincoast: A Life Story*, by Alexandra Morton and Billy Proctor (Horsdal & Schubart, 1998).
- "Musgmagw Dzawada'enuwx First Nation": kingcome.ca.
- "First Nation Serves Evictions Notices to BC Fish Farms" by Andrew Nikiforuk, *The Tyee* (thetyee.ca), August 22, 2016.

Watching Orca Whales   97

The most reliable place to see Orcas — the whale formerly known as *killer*, AKA *blackfish* — is in the Broughton Archipelago. It's frequented by both *resident* pods — fish-eaters — and those of the larger *transient* subspecies of Orca, who roam the high seas and eat sea mammals. The archipelago is considered one of the finest Orca habitats anywhere.

When our family went whale-watching in Broughton, we watched four pods meet in the open water, including a pod of transients, and enjoyed a cutting-edge talk on the matriarchy of Orca pods. Orca males are larger than females — they weigh up to 10 tonnes/tons, have more prominent dorsal fins, are more aggressive, and thus more visible to human observers. Yet, studies of pod behaviour yielded the conclusion that they are typically led by the eldest female. The presenter was a doctoral candidate at the University of California. She left her perch on a rock in the strait to talk to the group and returned there after the talk.

Also in the vicinity is the unique Orca rubbing beach at Robson Bight near the mouth of the Tsitka River, protected since 1982 in **Robson Bight (Michael Bigg) Ecological Reserve**. The name memorializes a pioneering Canadian Orca researcher who worked for many years at the Nanaimo Pacific Biolological Station.

Whale research is ongoing in Broughton. OrcaLab has been the Hanson Island facility of Paul Spong, a student of Orca vocalization, since 1970. Spong is an outspoken advocate of the release of captive whales.

Whale-watching tour operators are based in Port McNeill, Port Hardy, Alert Bay, Sointula, Alder Bay and Telegraph Cove. Most offer wildlife-watching tours as well — to view, for example, grizzly bears foraging on mainland beaches.

It's worth checking tour operators' *modus operandi* before signing up. Do they operate their craft non-intrusively? High-speed tour boats can stampede sea lion and seal colonies. Do they respect the 100-metre legal limit of approach to whales? Some venture closer and — with the best educational intentions — harass and even endanger the animals.

British Columbia's pioneer whale-watching outfit is based in Telegraph Cove. Jim Borrowman moved to Telegraph Cove in the 1970s to work in the sawmill. When the owner retired, Jim bought the 17-metre-long diesel tug *Gikumi*. It was built in 1954 to tug logs to the mill. Soon its ample deck was carrying whale-watchers. When Jim and Mary Borrowman started Stubbs Island Whale Watching in 1980, Orcas were still being shot by fishermen. Their dwindling populations made a remarkable transition to beloved and protected species to veritable icon of nature. Protection of Orcas was hastened by the urging of people who had seen the magnificent mammals in the wild. (The northern resident population, numbering about 200, is listed as threatened under *Canada's Species at Risk Act*.)

Stubbs Island is in new hands, and the Borrowmans have started a new business, Orcella Expeditions, operating multi-day cruises on their beloved *Gikumi*.

Telegraph Cove is worth a visit to experience one of the island's treasures, a tiny former fishing village clinging to the rocky shore with a planked road over the water. The highly scenic boardwalk and adjacent buildings — cabins dating from the 1920s — have been converted to rustic lodgings (seasonal). Do not omit a visit to the **Whale Interpretive Centre** at the end of the boardwalk. When we visited in January 2017, it was being renovated — all for the best.

Details

- Telegraph Cove is 200 km/124 mi north of Campbell River, via Highway 19 and Beaver Cove Rd; follow the signs in; a little logging road travel at the end.
- Stubbs Island Whale Watching, reservations 800-665-3066; stubbs-island.com.
- Orcella Expeditions, Telegraph Cove; 888-928-6722.
- North Island Kayak Trips, Telegraph Cove; 877-949-7707/250-928-3114; kayakbc.ca.
- Whale Interpretive Centre, Telegraph Cove; 250-928-3129; killerwhalecentre.org.
- Telegraph Cove Resort: 800-200-4665/250-928-3131; telegraphcoveresort.com.
- Robson Bight (Michael Bigg) Ecological Reserve: env.gov.bc.ca. Access is restricted.
- OrcaLab: orcalab.org. With an informative blog of observations and encounters in Broughton Archipelago.

 Alert Bay

Alert Bay is the principal village of the Namgis First Nation, a Kwakwaka'wakw people of Broughton Strait. The famous village on Cormorant Island was often photographed when the bay was lined with wooden big houses, their facades painted and monumental poles carved and painted to display the owners' family crests.

None of that remains. Since 1980, the **U'mista Cultural Centre** has been a feature on the Alert Bay waterfront. The handsome museum displays goods confiscated by the government of Canada at a 1921 potlatch and restored to the First Nation latterly. The website has in-depth readings about the so-called Potlatch Collection.

The Islands' Icon: Wild Salmon

What best represents Vancouver Island's many parts and symbolizes the totality? My nominee is **wild Pacific salmon**.

One of the great wonders of nature is the migration of salmon from the freshwater streams of their birth to the ocean and then, after years in the sea, their return to the same stream to spawn and die.

In every part of every island, along thousand of kilometres of coast and far inland, in every little creek and in the mighty rivers, goes the dance of red and silver life. Since time immemorial.

Each population, and there are thousands, of the six oceangoing species of salmon has adapted to a particular ecosystem. To perpetuate their genetic build, they return to the very stretch of gravel where they began life. That's amazing. How do they know to find their way home? The migration of salmon is now thought by some scientists to be guided by their ability to read and remember site-specific geomagnetic configurations.

The population, both successful breeders and un-, then depart this world, leaving behind their carcasses. Every spawned-out salmon carcass contributes nutrients to the forest that cradles every little creek and sustains populations of bear, wolf, cougar and a host of smaller animals, birds, insects. All that rich biomass so far above the ocean, where it lived most of its time. Now enriching the forest. Amazing. The biggest trees are thought to be linked to nutrient deposits bestowed by the river. Salmon give us much besides.

Salmon was the staple of the traditional economies of First Nations on the coast and in the interior. Many richly expressive cultures were based on the abundance of fish.

Fishing was, after mining, coastal BC's foundational industry. Our society is to a degree based on the prosperity generated by the commercial salmon fishery and a host of canneries.

The commercial fishing boat, along with the axe, the rifle and the trap, supported the resourceful, independent lifestyle of generations of families on these islands.

It is now possible to see the end of that priceless legacy. Many runs are disappearing. Many already have. The lights are going out. We have taken the abundance of salmon for granted and overfished many runs. We foster competition among fisheries (commercial, sport, Aboriginal), and they compete with other jurisdictions in many places, while cooperative mechanisms like the International Pacific Salmon Fisheries Commission have limited effects. We have abused and destroyed habitat in a hundred ways. Global warming has warmed the oceans, with incalculable impacts on fish. The latest threat is from open-pen feedlots, which have proliferated around the islands, farming mostly Atlantic salmon.

Alexandra Morton is a marine biologist who with her husband moved to the Broughton Archipelago to study whales. He died in an underwater accident in 1984, and Alexandra raised their two children there. Until recently, the family lived in Echo Bay. After 1987, when fish farms started to appear in Broughton's many inlets and channels — most owned by giant Norwegian companies — Morton started noting declines in salmon runs and suspected impairment of fry by sea lice from neighbouring open pens. Sea lice, tiny leech-like critters, thrive in fish farms. Clouds of them have been observed to spread from the open pens, which are numerous in Broughton. Sea lice attach themselves to salmon fry that are just emerging from the river environment and beginning to swim toward the ocean. One lousy louse can kill a fry. A diligent biologist, Morton attracted collaborators who studied the link and published the findings in *Science* and other reputable journals. She became a dutiful reporter of changes in the local ecosystem of her beloved Broughton Archipelago.

Her work opened a Pandora's box of ridicule and denial. But the research has been amply borne out by science and experience in other places. Fish-farm sea lice are killing salmon by the millions before they ever reach the ocean. Unfortunately, that's only one ingredient of the deleterious soup that slops out of the fish farms and into the surrounding waters. The chemical treatment applied to control sea lice in the pens is highly toxic. There are viruses. There are antibiotics. Wherever fish farms are set up in the paths of migrating salmon, the runs have declined. No fish farms — no declines. Morton urges a ban on pens open to the ocean. The fish farms need to be in tanks. The looming catastrophe is preventable to a degree.

Fish farms have operated largely without regulation in BC, thanks to a protocol that gave the Province the responsibility for protecting the ambient waters. The federal Department of Fisheries and Oceans has the constitutional responsibility to protect wild salmon habitat. In 2009, Morton went to court to compel the Department of Fisheries and Oceans to discharge its responsibility. She won.

In 2010, Morton organized a march from Campbell River to Victoria to protest the preventable decline of the islands' wild salmon. A crowd of 4,000-5,000 showed up at the steps of the Legislature in support — likely the largest environmental protest rally ever staged there. Alexandra Morton has stirred the public conscience. She leads by example, making use of one precious legacy — the democratic right of free speech and protest — to try to protect another.

Details

- Alexandra Morton's blog: alexandramorton.typepad.com.
- Raincoast Research Society: raincoastresearch.org.
- Reading: *A Stain Upon the Sea: West Coast Salmon Farming* by Stephen Hume, Alexandra Morton, et al (Madeira Park, BC: Harbour Publishing, 2004).

NORTHERN VANCOUVER ISLAND AND ADJACENT ISLANDS

Alert Bay is a vivid experience — an in-your-face place.

Once, when up-island, I dropped in on Will Malloff via the 10-km/6-mi ferry trip from Port McNeill to Alert Bay. Will invited me to stay and offered to show me around. A master craftsman and artist in wood, he led me to a carving room in a back corner of the former St Michael's residential school, where an older man sat and talked with a couple of young people. It was Saturday evening. More young people came and went. The talk was light-hearted, but Will had to work to get a conversation going. I might as well have been a piece of furniture. One man was working on a bright yellow mask, made of a bulging semi-sphere of wood — it was perhaps a burl — on which he was painting a stylized face that was startlingly vivid.

I produced some of my books. The older man, whose name was Doug Cranmer, zeroed in on a picture in *Victoria a History in Photographs*. It was entitled *Cheslakee's village on Johnstone's Strait*, an 18th-century engraving from a sketch of the nation's principal village at the mouth of the Nimpkish River. The print was published in *A Voyage of Discovery to the North Pacific Ocean* and *Round the World 1791-1795*, by George Vancouver.

Cranmer pointed to the caption and asked, rhetorically, whether we were really on Johnstone Strait. It was a bit of a booby trap — Captain Vancouver himself named the local waters Broughton Strait after his second in command. The famous mariner died before the book was published. If Vancouver's publisher didn't correct the error, I didn't feel the need to. I'm a bit sensitive on points of geography.

Another scolding followed. Cranmer found a photo of Alert Bay in *Wish You Were Here* to which I had appended the note, "The village of Alert Bay traces its beginnings only to about 1870, when two settlers from the Nimpkish River established a salmon saltery."

This started a discussion about the origins of Alert Bay, which I, of course, took personally. The point was, What did I know about their history and how did I know it? I defended my sources, the best ethnographic and historical and all that. Consensus emerged that there may have been a fish camp on Cormorant Island, but no village. Could have saved my breath.

Doug Cranmer (1927-2006) was a prominent carver and painter of the Namgis First Nation, known the world over for his mastery of both traditional and contemporary idioms. Now that I think about it, his criticism was a gift. He pulled a pointer out of my writing that was valid for any subject. It was telling me to check my sources.

Details

- Port McNeill-Alert Bay ferry: bcferries.com.
- Namgis First Nation land claim on a European website: firstnations.de.
- U'mista Cultural Centre, Alert Bay: umista.ca.

■ Doug Cranmer profile on the website *Ruins in Process: Vancouver Art in the Sixties*: vancouverartinthesixties.com/people/120.

The Hunt Family in Fort Rupert   99

T'sa<u>x</u>is (Fort Rupert) is a major centre of Kwakwaka'wakw culture. The village took form around the Hudson's Bay Company's Fort Rupert. The First Nations community flourished and attracted intense study by anthropologists. For decades, its arts and customs were minutely documented. The village became uniquely well-known. It remains the principal village of the Kwakiutl Indian Band — a crucible of art where visitors are welcome.

The story begins with George Hunt (1854-1933), who was born at Fort Rupert. Hunt's mother was a Tlingit chief's daughter from Alaska. His English father was an HBC trader. Hunt married into the village and fathered eleven children. He is the progenitor of the Hunt family artistic dynasty.

George Hunt was steeped in his adoptive culture and began collecting myths and regalia of the area. By the 1880s, he was working as boatman, guide and interpreter with the Jessup North Pacific Expedition. Hunt spoke both English and Kwak'wala natively and sometimes worked as a court translator in Victoria.

In 1886 Franz Boaz, a young geographer working for a German museum, made the first of many trips to Vancouver Island to study First Nations people. Travelling up-island by steamer, he arrived in Nahwitti hoping to observe potlatch ceremonies. "At first they thought I was a priest, and now, because I had brought nothing, they thought I might be a government agent come to put a stop to the festival." The potlatch, an institution of gifting of central importance in Kwakwaka'wakw society, had recently been banned by the Canadian government. Boas told them he had come only to "see what the people in this land do."

In Victoria in 1888, Boas met George Hunt. Soon Boas's field work attracted funding from American museums to develop interpretations of Kwakiutl culture. The first collaboration of Boas and Hunt was of heroic proportions and caused a sensation. In 1893, at Boas's invitation, George Hunt and 17 Fort Rupert Kwakiutl First Nation people traveled to Chicago. They shipped the timbers of a big house and an array of monumental carvings. Visitors to the six-month World's Columbian Exposition were treated to a recreated Kwakiutl village. (Some of the pieces are still standing in Chicago's Field Museum.)

The following year, Boas visited Fort Rupert and witnessed the first weeks of the Winter Ceremonial, with George Hunt serving as guide and interpreter. Together, they described the rituals and accoutrements of the round of singing, dancing, dramatization and story-telling, feasting, speech-making and potlatching at Fort Rupert. Nothing like it had ever been done.

Boas soon published the trailblazing *Social Organization and Secret Societies of the Kwakiutl Indians* (1897), which he prefaced thus: "The great body of facts presented here were observed and recorded by Mr. George Hunt, who takes deep interest in everything pertaining to the ethnology of the Kwakiutl Indians."

Researcher Judith Berman summarizes the collaboration: "Boas published some 15 books based on their collaborative Kwakwaka'wakw research. Of those, 11 books "consist largely or exclusively of Hunt's Kwak'wala-language texts. While this work was not without flaws, probably no single ethnographic enterprise has documented a Native North American group as completely and from as many different angles."

Today, the Hunt family is still much in evidence in Fort Rupert. Calvin Hunt, proprietor of the **Kwakiutl Art of the Copper Maker Gallery**, is a master pole carver of high achievement. You may have seen his 2012 centennial pole prominently displayed in Duncan (#34). Chief Tony Hunt executed the handsome emblem on the façade of the Fort Rupert bighouse. For the history of the Hudson's Bay Company Fort Rupert, see #100.

Details

- *T'saxis* (Fort Rupert) is 39 km/24 mi west of Port McNeill, 11 km/7 mi east of Port Hardy. From Highway 19, take Byng Rd to Beaver Harbour Rd to Fort Rupert Rd.
- Calvin Hunt, Kwakiutl Art of the Copper Maker Gallery, Fort Rupert: 250-949-8491; calvinhunt.com.
- Kwakiutl Indian Band on German website: firstnations.de/fisheries/kwakwakawakw-kwakiutl.htm.
- Tsaxis Fort Rupert, 38-minute historical slideshow by George MacDonald on youtube.com.

100 The Suquash Mine Fiasco

On the island's wet and windy northeast coast, Highway 19 winds through the Suquash Basin, past the little-known Suquash mine, site of the botched beginning of the colony of Vancouver Island.

In 1836, the Hudson's Bay Company's (HBC) paddle steamer *Beaver* called in at Suquash during its first year on the west coast. Coal had been reported there by a First Nations informant, and shortly the HBC started buying coal from the Kwakiutl First Nation. Steam-powered navy vessels began to visit in 1846. To keep the coal fields out of American hands, a visiting officer took possession for the Crown in 1848.

The HBC obtained a contract to supply coal to the Pacific Mail Steamship Co. The first shipment went out in May 1849. It was quite a leap for the ancient fur-trading company. In the middle of it came the California Gold Rush. The demand for steam coal shot up.

Earlier that year, Queen Victoria signed a grant making the directors of the HBC the "true lords and proprietors" of Vancouver Island and creating the Colony of Vancouver Island. The fine print stipulated that the grant could be revoked if the HBC did not establish a settlement within five years. The clock was ticking.

The HBC pinned its hopes on the Suquash mine. The company could have continued to buy coal but no — they chose to try to attract British miners to a watery wilderness at the ends of the earth, sneak them into the heartland of a warlike indigenous society under the noses of the owners, and get them mining.

Impossible?

Company men arrived in Beaver Harbour in May 1849 to build sturdy Fort Rupert. The HBC continued to pay First Nations for coal, and within a few months, James Douglas reported "most friendly relations with the natives, who, *without being acquainted with our future plans*, are exceedingly useful in getting out coal." (Emphasis added.)

At Suquash, the miners dug 60 feet without finding a seam. When they did start taking out coal, armed First Nations people confronted them and demanded royalties. The fort was in the middle of the ancient village site of *T'saḵis*. Deserted at first, *T'saḵis* soon had several thousand residents. The Kwakiutl were by nature assertive. They observed customs like displaying the heads of their enemies. That gave the settlers pause.

Next spring, the *Norman Morison* arrived with 80 immigrants. Miners and labourers raised a litany of grievances and were, James Douglas complained, "a troublesome useless sett." Soon most were on strike. HBC officials treated it as a mutiny and clapped a few miners in irons. Some settlers had already thrown in the towel. Whole families were slipping away, California-bound.

The cargo ship *England* called in. Three men were aboard who had deserted the *Norman Morison* in Victoria Harbour. When a magistrate came looking for them, they repaired to a nearby island. Soon it was reported they had been murdered. Two bodies were recovered. Kwakiutl informants pointed to people of the Nahwitti First Nation. Into the fray waded the governor of Vancouver Island, Richard Blanshard, to bring the murderers to justice, or, failing that, take revenge. "British blood never dries."

The other view was that British zeal to prosecute the killers might itself provoke an attack. After all, the men were AWOL employees of the Company. An HBC official may have put a price on their heads. The Brits were hugely outnumbered and weakened by internal strife. Whatever the merits of the case — the claim of a bounty on the deserters' heads has been refuted — Blanshard urged a demonstration of British Resolve simply to try to dissuade the indigenous people from attacking the fort.

HMS *Daedalus*, with 20 guns, arrived with Governor Blanshard aboard. A force was dispatched to a Nahwitti village. The village was deserted. Soon it was a smoking ruins. In July 1851, Blanshard sailed north again in search of the murderers. The Marines went to a Nahwitti village. During a brief battle — with a few casualties on both sides and one Nahwitti death — the residents vanished. Their houses and canoes were burned. The Nahwitti leaders negotiated a settlement. Some mutilated bodies were produced, and the case was closed.

Meanwhile, the Suquash coalbeds proved a bust. It took the HBC a year of searching to find the coal seams in Nanaimo Harbour and evacuate the brave coal miners and their families from Fort Rupert. The whole fiasco consumed nearly four years. Apart from that, there was some good chemistry, and Fort Rupert remained open as an HBC fur-trading post, while the First Nations village became a great cultural centre.

The Suquash mine has been worked off and on, mostly off, and not for decades. The miners left considerable industrial machinery behind, and it makes for an interesting tour.

Details

- The Suquash mine is about 17 km/11 mi west of Port McNeill via Highway 19; Rupert Rd to Suquash Main (watch for logging trucks); access to the site is marked with a simple sign about 2.6 km/1.6 mi north of the Suquash Main turnoff.

- **Cluxewe Resort**, about 5 km/3 mi east of Suquash, has cottages, campsites and a café facing the opening of Broughton Strait onto Queen Charlotte Strait: 250-949-0378; cluxeweresort.com.

- *Northern Vancouver Island, the Undiscovered Coast*, local history blog by Brenda McCorquodale: undiscoveredcoast.blogspot.ca

- This history of Suquash/Fort Rupert/T'sakis is based on *Fort Victoria Letters, 1846-1851* (Hudson's Bay Record Society XXXII, 1979), *The Reminiscences of Dr John Sebastian Helmcken* (UBC, 1975) and other primary sources.

Cape Scott Park and the North Coast Trail 101

Cape Scott Provincial Park protects 223 sq km/86 sq mi of Vancouver Island's wild and isolated north end, including 115 km/71 mi of varied coast between San Josef Bay and Shushartie Bay. The extravagantly beautiful Cape Scott area attracted wilderness trekkers long before the park was established in 1973.

Some 90 Danish settlers moved into the Cape Scott area during the 1890s, but the farms produced little and remained isolated from markets.

Many settlers left, and new populations moved in. A long-promised road never materialized, and the area was ultimately abandoned.

The supply centre is **Port Hardy**, a lively town (2016 census pop: 3,643) at the terminus of Highway 19, 500 km/311 mi north of Victoria. The trailhead for Cape Scott Park is on the San Josef River, 64 km/40 mi west of Port Hardy on public and logging roads.

A 2.5-km/1.6-mi trail to **San Josef Bay** has extensions (13 km/8 mi) via Mt Patrick (el 422 m/1,385 ft) to Sea Otter Cove and Lowrie Bay. The San Josef Bay trail is wheelchair-accessible, making it the easiest way to see Vancouver Island's northwest coast. The more difficult extensions lead to good camping areas. The main trail to **Cape Scott** is 23.6 km/14.7 mi, and there's a 2-km/1.2 mi side trail to Nissen Bight.

The challenging **North Coast Trail** extends for 43 km/27 mi between Nissen Bight and Shushartie Bay. Total length of the Cape Scott-North Coast Trail, trailhead to trailhead, is about 58 km/36 mi. There's no overland access to the eastern terminus. You have to approach by water, a 35-km/22-mi trip between Port Hardy and Shushartie Bay.

The trail began with a vision of economic regeneration and the formation of the North Vancouver Island Trails Society. Some Port Hardy residents fundraised $1.2 million, about half of it community support money from the federal government to offset regional economic impacts. It took three years of heroic work by local volunteers to cut the trail, and it opened in 2008. It's great news for wilderness trekkers.

The trail has been compared to the West Coast Trail in the 1970s. It is broken, up-and-down terrain. There are many steeply-pitched gravel beaches on the trail. Allow for 10 km/6 mi of travel a day. It's very remote, and travel requires a high degree of self-reliance. Encounters with black bears, cougars and wolves are common. Dogs are not allowed anywhere in Cape Scott Park.

The north island is just beginning to tap its potential as an outdoor recreation destination. It's ideal for those who enjoy boating, kayaking, recreational fishing, hiking and wildlife viewing in remote landscapes. Scuba divers are attracted by the rich waters in **God's Pocket Marine Provincial Park**.

Details

- Cape Scott, God's Pocket Marine provincial parks, with detailed maps, directions: env.gov.bc.ca.
- North Coast Trail Backpackers Hostel, 101–8635 Granville St, Port Hardy; 866-448-6303/250-949-9441; northcoasttrailbackpackershostel.com.
- Cape Scott Water Taxi and Marine Services, Port Hardy, operates land and water shuttles to trailheads: northcoasttrailshuttle.com.
- The difficulty of the North Coast Trail, article with pages of maps from *Wild Coast* magazine: besthike.com/2012/09/18/don't-hike-the-north-coast-trail.

Sources

Page 11. "To see … "
William Blake, "Auguries of Innocence," written 1803, published 1863.
This version: www.poetryfoundation.org.

Page 16. "They recognize …"
"'They Recognize No Superior Chief:' The Strait of Juan de Fuca in the
1790s" by Wayne Suttles, in *Culturas de la Costa Noroeste de América*,
José Luis Peset, editor. Spain: Turner Libros, 1989, pp. 251-264.

Page 18. "We've not had …"
"Vander Zalm calls anti-HST campaign rebirth of democracy in province
of dictators" by Lindsay Kines and Rob Shaw, *Times-Colonist*, Victoria
(timescolonist.com), April 16, 2010.

Page 20. "Anthony Barrett …"
*Francis Rattenbury and British Columbia: Architecture and Challenge in
the Imperial Age*, by Anthony Barrett and Rhodri Windsor-Liscombe.
Vancouver: University of British Columbia Press, 1983.

Page 31. "In its prime …"
*The Forbidden City within Victoria: Myth, Symbol and Streetscape
of Victoria's Earliest Chinatown*, by David Chuenyan Lai. Victoria:
Orca Book Publishers, 1991, pp 6-7.

Page 34. "It is the single …"
Design Guidelines, Old Town, Victoria, BC (2006) at victoria.ca.
(The quotation is edited for sense and space.)

Page 38. "Search for …"
Hundreds and Thousands: The Journals of Emily Carr. Vancouver:
Douglas & McIntyre, 2006, pp 29-30.

Page 58. "Ex-Mayor …"
In *The Daily Colonist*, Victoria, September 4, 1920. Courtesy
britishcolonist.ca.

Page 83. "The figures …"
Totem Poles by Marius Barbeau. Ottawa: Department of Resources and
Development: National Museum of Canada Bulletin No. 119, Vols. I and II,
1950. Downloadable pdfs available on the Canadian Museum of History
website (historymuseum.ca).

Page 97. "A name …"
"Christening the Salish Sea" by David Karp, *Times-Colonist*, Victoria,
July 16, 2010.

Page 113. "Hearken ..."
The whole affair is recounted in *Gunboat Frontier: British Maritime Authority and Northwest Coast Indians 1846-1890* by Barry M. Gough. Vancouver: University of British Columbia Press, 1984, Chapter 4, The Smouldering Volcano.

Page 125. "The honeycombed ..."
Hammerstone: A Biography of Hornby Island by Olivia Fletcher. Edmonton: NeWest Press, 2001.

Page 128. "monster potatoes ..."
Vancouver Island. Exploration. 1864 by Robert Brown. Printed by authority of the Government by Harris and Company. Victoria, Vancouver Island, 1865. Downloadable at archive.org/details/cihm_28110.

Page 137. "The extraordinary ..."
The Geology of Southern Vancouver Island: A Field Guide by Chris Yorath. Victoria: Orca Book Publishers, 1995, p 138.

Page 140. "From Barkley Sound ..."
"The Cruise of the Imperial Eagle" by Capt [John] Walbran, *Victoria Daily Colonist*, March 3, 1901, p 10.

Page 157. "Talk and Log"
Talk and Log: Wilderness Politics in British Columbia by Jeremy Wilson. Vancouver: UBC Press, 1998.

Acknowledgements

The Wickaninnish Inn extended generous hospitality to my wife and me.

Thanks to Deborah DeLong for kind permission to use the photo of UBC forestry grad students at Cathedral Grove.

Cover photos

Runner on Dallas Road, Victoria, with the Strait of Juan de Fuca and Olympic Mountains beyond. Boomer Jerritt/Strathcona Photography.

Author photo by Paula Grant.